WENDY E. COOK studied art at Cambridge where she met the comedian Peter Cook and later became his wife. Wendy soon gained a reputation as a hostess at their London and New York homes; her guests were as likely to include John Lennon and Paul McCartney as Bernard Levin and Peter Ustinov. When their daughter Daisy became ill with asthma Wendy began a journey of discovery that included complementary treatments and alternative philosophies. She studied many disciplines, including Rudolf Steiner's approach to nutrition and agriculture. Having seen how life-changing nutrition can be, she devoted herself to cooking and teaching in clinics, communities and schools.

The
Biodynamic Food & Cookbook

Real nutrition that doesn't cost the earth

Wendy E. Cook

CLAIRVIEW

Clairview Books

Hillside House, The Square

Forest Row, East Sussex

RH18 5ES

www.clairviewbooks.com

Published by Clairview 2006

A catalogue record for this book is available from the British Library

ISBN 1 905570 01 5

ISBN 978 1 905570 01 0

Book and cover design by Rick Lawrence—samskara@onetel.com

Printed and bound by Cromwell Press, Trowbridge, Wiltshire

Contents

PREFACE

'For every star in the sky there is a flower in the field.'—Paracelsus

When I was approached by Sevak Gulbekian, Clairview's publisher, to write a biodynamic cookery book, my first response was an emphatic 'No!' I could envision months of weighing and measuring, something which I often tend not to do. With years of experience, much of my cooking is done by eye, feel and intuition. I was also aware of a market groaning with cookbooks of every kind and wondered what I could contribute that might be different and valuable. How might a cookbook help in the face of the escalating and alarming world problems, increasing violence, the widening gap between rich and poor, over-consumption, obesity and widespread malnutrition? We can see that food has a central place in how our world operates and we witness increasing numbers of food scares: BSE, foot and mouth disease and, as I write, the contamination of thousands of so-called 'food products' with carcinogenic dye used in shoe-polish. How much is enough? Many of us feel overwhelmed by the mounting catastrophes. Could a cookbook be of any help with these huge problems?

The link to biodynamic agriculture suggested another dimension. Modern industrial-scale agricultural practices have led to so much destruction of our environment. More and more food-related illnesses are coming to light, implicating the overload of toxic chemicals in our food and in our bodies. Farmers sometimes feel disenfranchised, their suicide rate is high and their children often turn their backs on the land. This is serious. It seems that we have short memories. At the beginning of the last World War England had only enough wheat and sugar to last for three weeks; we had been importing much of our food from Britain's colonies. The Germans put an end to that. Parks and school playing fields were dug up to grow food. The difference then was that many people still knew how to grow food and had allotments. That national pastime is fast declining, skills are being lost, so I feel we really need to consider what is happening when more and more of our food—including organically grown food—is imported.

With this in mind biodynamic agriculture might in the future become an increasingly important system. Whilst incorporating the best principles of organic agriculture, it is also directed towards healing damaged soils with its special 'preparations'. In addition, it protects and respects the integrity of any piece of land, attempting to enhance the potential of that land rather than exploit it. It is a system that encourages people who wish to be involved with caring for the land in a profoundly sensible way to have access to community-owned land. To add to this, biodynamic produce is superior in flavour, nutritional status and keeping quality. I know, as I have been using it for the past 35 years. So I am glad to have a further opportunity to draw attention to the importance of biodynamic agriculture as a worldwide movement, involving so many farmers with the kind of commitment and high moral integrity that are getting harder to find. It is intriguing to see the increase in media interest towards biodynamics, following the success of certain French viniculturalists who find its methods produce exceptionally good quality wines.

My book *Foodwise* has been received in a surprisingly enthusiastic way; people have commented on the usefulness of taking a much wider view of the human food story. I began by tracing the links between various specific food substances and evolving human consciousness throughout the millennia, bringing us to the reasons we find what we do on our plates. There are many items that one might question as to whether they really are foods, many of which are addictive (coffee, alcohol and tobacco) or mildly poisonous (the Solanaceae family, potatoes, tomatoes, etc.). How can we see what we need to do in the future if we don't know where we have come from in the past—a very different perspective from the prevailing one, and which I take from Rudolf Steiner, the founder of biodynamic agriculture.

So, in this book there will be some recapitulations of the main themes from *Foodwise*. Different perspectives are urgently needed, for despite all the research and information on diet, most new nutritional theories are still built on old reductionist paradigms and leave some glaring omissions in the way we understand nutrition as a whole. We need to reconnect with what humans had long developed in the past: good instinctual knowledge through a process of observation and self-referral. Access to this natural knowledge has become distorted in the dulling of our palates through unnatural practices in food production and through the addition of substances that the human organism has hitherto never been exposed to.

A very powerful place to begin is the home and kitchen. If you have seen either of the classic food movies *Babette's Feast* and *Like Water for Chocolate*, you will recall just how powerful the act of cooking and sharing food can be. It has certainly had a huge influence on my life. Through many experiences of cooking in schools, colleges, in a medical practice (with a biodynamic garden and restaurant as a therapeutic outreach), clinics and private homes, I have had much opportunity to observe the effect of our eating culture on people of different kinds and ages.

These were some of the considerations that helped to turn my original 'No' to this project into 'Well, maybe'. The 'Yes' came when friend Cathy Ratcliffe, on hearing about the proposed cookbook and my excuses not to do it (many to do with the technical weighing and measuring), said in her quiet, firm way, 'You should have a go at it and I'd like to help you.' Cathy has a domestic science teaching background, is a terrific cook, is meticulous about weighing and measuring, and with husband Gus has a very productive organic kitchen garden. That did it! I invested in a digital weigh-scale. Soon we had a great team in place. Susan Hannis, who was such an asset in the production of *Foodwise*, agreed to come on board again, and I received a gift from a friend that almost covered the costs of the photos. Then, almost by magic, I found myself with a couple of extraordinary photographers: Kate Mount, who has produced most of the pictures, and Selby McCreery.

Later, after deciding to go with the project, I visited the island of Mallorca at Eastertime. (Mallorca has been my home for many years and has been an enormous influence on the way I cook.) During this visit I was lucky to be introduced to Jaume Moranta, a very talented young photographer. Jaume enthusiastically introduced me to family members who shared traditional Mallorcan cooking secrets whilst he took photos, capturing much of the colour, flavour and ambience of kitchens and markets. June

Woodger, biodynamic gardener, climatologist and photographer, has also provided some special-interest pictures. So I have found lots of support and encouragement for this undertaking.

It has been a very full and colourful year and now we have come full circle and full cycle. The wild garlic and nettles are up once again. I have included some wild foods in my recipes because it is useful to know about them. Such plants grow where conditions are most favourable, so they are full of important nutritional vitality (phytochemicals and flavenoids in current 'nutrition-speak'). I'm not recommending a return to hunting and gathering, but these foods are real pointers to seasonality—the subject that is foremost in the aims of this book. For the rest of my ingredients I have used wherever possible biodynamically grown food, buying superior produce from Jo Clark, who teaches horticulture and bread-baking in our local Waldorf school, and from Derek Lapworth, who has a magical piece of land in a valley near here. For the rest I am lucky to have Riverford Organic Farm and shop on my doorstep. (Riverford has the most successful veggie-box scheme in England and is proving to others that good organic husbandry can indeed be viable.)

I brought my own children up on meals that consisted mainly of grains, vegetables, nuts and seeds with some dairy and the usual children's favourites of pizzas and lasagnes. But seeing that there are numerous books full of these kinds of recipes readily available, I thought I should try to engage your interest with dishes that are imaginative and a little different, and show you how you can have stardust as well as sunshine and moonlight on your plates! Seasonality providing the main framework, I have nevertheless taken us on some journeys across the world that do add a few unusual and exotic ingredients and dishes. My many years spent in Mallorca, where the fusion of Spanish, Arabic, French and sometimes Jewish cooking styles introduced me to wonderful combinations of grains, vegetables, spices, nuts and meats, have made that kind of traditional cookery the backbone of my cooking dictionary. (I have organized gatherings around a peace table where we have shared Israeli and Palestinian dishes and food from other traditions. Of the many ways that help us to understand each other, sharing food is very archetypal; the table is such a magnet and around a good one different perspectives may safely be shared.) I have many cookbooks out of which I find perhaps two or three recipes that are favourites. This book will, I hope, bring you many varied dishes and menus and some will become your favourites. Maybe the whole book will become a favourite!

What biodynamic cookery is could be open to interpretation. Apart from choosing biodynamic ingredients and living with the seasons, for me it is a lifetime's study of understanding ingredients on an energetic level and knowing how to combine them in ways that enhance the life-forces within them. In understanding the substances we may begin to know their place in the universe and, correspondingly, our own. If we are to be materialists, let us be really good ones, for matter is *mater* and represents spirit embodied. Some of the recipes require more time than others, but I imagine that having bought this book you are part of the brigade who wish to get away from packaging and ready-made meals and to connect with my patron Hestia, the goddess who presides over fire and hearth, home and community.

It has been a revelation to me, and to many others, to know how to plan a menu where one is not agonizing over proteins, carbohydrates and fats, but instead following the principle of root, leaf, shoot and fruit. It is so much more artistic and satisfying to the soul as well as the body. There may be some apparent anomalies in my practice. I do use wine in some dishes, but have suggested alternatives for those who don't wish to use it (though it might help to know that the alcohol disappears in the cooking). I do use unrefined sugar in numerous desserts, butter rather than margarine, and I often use unbleached white flour in my pastry. I have been through the 70s wholefood cooking era, when everything seemed to look very brown and earthy, and whilst totally endorsing that foods come to us with the appropriate packaging for their digestion, I do feel that there are situations where something a little less than 'whole' can be justified. Rudolf Steiner thoroughly convinced me when he said the most desirable factor of nutrition is that people should *enjoy* their food. People in our culture seem to need lighter food; this is very much connected with lifestyle. But colour and texture are very important, as well as where our nutrition comes from.

I have included some meat and fish dishes because, although vegetarianism is a real force for the good, there are many people who are not there yet. The dishes I have selected on the whole demonstrate the time-honoured peasant tradition of meat being a relatively small proportion of the whole meal. I have included chicken, lamb (because sheep still roam and graze in the open pastures), fish and some seasonal game dishes. Generally I tend not to use much pork or beef.

I am also concerned with correcting the concept that organic or biodynamic food is too expensive. It is true that certain items are more expensive, but used in a 'potentized' way one needs less. You can get 6–8 portions of biodynamic rice for less than £1 and that is a good beginning for any nutritious meal. We might need to prioritize the division of our budget a little differently. Experience will prove my point, I'm sure.

I hope that you will enjoy the results and forgive me for any errors. Sometimes the amounts may work out to be a little more than you expected, for though I have had my friends Cathy and Kit and a few others trying the recipes, I must point out I am not Delia Smith with (I suspect) a whole army of recipe-testers. I am working in quite different conditions, with a thimble for a kitchen. Within these constraints I make my offering and I hope that my love of kitchen activity will rub off on you. Do be experimental, use what you have, improvise, and once you feel confident of the lawfulness that underpins cooking you will go from strength to strength. Culture starts with cooking and the table is the place we learn about our humanity in gratitude for all that has gone into providing us with such bounty. Try never to waste anything; nature never does. Be creative with leftovers!

I look forward to any feedback.

Finally I would like to share a story told by American theologian Huston Smith:

> There was a raging forest fire and many were unsuccessfully trying to put it out. A tiny swallow thought she would also lend her forces. Patiently gathering beakfuls of water, she travelled tirelessly from river to conflagration and her friends joined her. The fire was eventually brought under control and put out.

Well, here I offer my little beakful!

Further Acknowledgements to: Sarah Brook for generous practical help, Eileen Lloyd and Sevak Gulbekian for editing, Valerie Nabarro for use of her kitchen, Kit Buckley for testing recipes and feedback, Hans Steenbergen of Botton Village for photographs of crops, Georgina Pinder for permission to use her almanac for some of the festivals, Dr Ursula Balzer-Graf (and Heinrich Heer) for permission to use images from her laboratory of sensitive crystallization and chromotography, and Warren Lee Cohen for the bread oven session photographed by Duilio A. Martin, and Richard Smith, Richard Thornton-Smith and Tadeu Caldas for help with the chapter on biodynamics. Finally it remains to say what a pleasure it has been to work with Rick Lawrence of Samskara Design, in Dartington.

Left Pic: Jaume and Apolloni.
Right Pic left to right: Cathy, Kit, Wendy, Kate, Selby, Rick, Paris and Ariel.
Bottom Pic: Susan

To all biodynamic gardeners and farmers throughout the world, and to all those who are working to heal the earth.

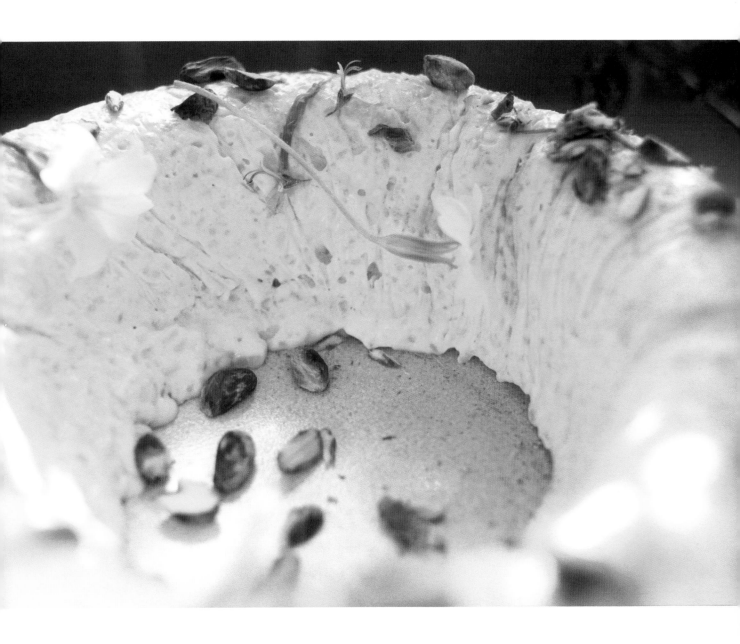

INTRODUCTION

I asked my mother, when she was getting on for 90, what her first memory was. She replied that it was growing an apple tree from a pip that she had managed to germinate. This was no mean feat for a girl who grew up in a Victorian terraced house in the soot-laden streets of Manchester, with perhaps only an aspidistra to hone her latent gardening abilities. Later on it was this extraordinary gift for gardening which softened the harsh impact of food rationing in wartime years for our family. Through my father's work we found ourselves in a rented Edwardian cottage in a small Bedfordshire village, where the saving grace was a large garden with good soil and some fruit trees. So despite the need to agonizingly eke out those precious food and clothing coupons for tiny amounts of butter, sugar, tea, meat and cheese and occasionally very scratchy utilitarian clothes, it felt like we had abundance through the cultivation of this marvellous garden.

It seemed there was always something to be harvested: plums and gooseberries, raspberries, redcurrants, blackcurrants, cooking apples and eating apples of several distinct varieties, and a pear tree whose fruits, carefully wrapped in tissue paper and stored in the attic in a chest of drawers, lasted for a good part of the winter. The pears were augmented by jars of bottled fruit and chutneys that my mother put up each year. Every summer we rejoiced in garden peas, runner beans, marrows, cucumbers, lettuce, fragrant and sweet tomatoes, and as the season developed, cabbages and Brussels sprouts, parsnips, turnips, potatoes and leeks, and from our trees walnuts and hazelnuts—not to mention the dazzling display of sweet-smelling flowers.

We made compost, my father's pride and joy, as he triumphantly followed horses to gather up the fruits of their passing. On went old woollies, kitchen waste, grass-clippings, worn out rag rugs; it all became black gold that was returned to the earth each year. So as a child I lived intimately with the seasons. I was involved with harvesting from an early age and the appearance, flavour and aroma of those fruits and vegetables are indelibly imprinted upon my sensibilities.

Then, any kind of meat or fish had to be eked out with lots of vegetables. It was easier to get the cheap cuts of meat or offal (which I notice are now beginning to come into some up-market restaurants). As a Lancashire woman my mother was proud of her culinary heritage, so we had Lancashire hotpot, oxtail stew, tripe and onions or pigs trotters. On occasion she would carry in a pig's head, later turned into brawn with glistening jelly with bits of onion and celery. Occasionally the neighbours who had chickens would provide us with an old hen in exchange for vegetables, and this would give us a hearty stew for several meals with the addition of pearl barley and lots more vegetables. A few sausages hidden tantalizingly in her famous Yorkshire pudding made toad-in-the-hole a feast. (Apologies here, to our vegetarian friends.) How wonderfully I was steeped in the assets of cooking and gardening.

On top of these gifts my mother made our clothes, knitted our cardigans, painted pictures, played the piano, sang and did a part-time job as well! At that time we had no TV, no car, no telephone and no fridge. We rode our bicycles and used public transport—buses and steam trains. The living room was dominated by the fireplace, an old black-leaded range in which my mother sometimes baked bread, which tasted so different from shop bread. The fireplace was our television set; so many evenings spent staring at the antics of salamanders stimulated my interest in the power and quality of real fire. My father often heated the iron poker in the embers till it was red hot and plunged it into his mug of Guinness, which would then froth and hiss. We loved the drama of it and he seemed to enjoy it too. The ash would fall into the drink—no need for mineral supplements then. There was no central heating either, so cycling, chopping wood, gardening and eating good food all provided warmth and a stronger immune system. (But, my, those bedrooms were freezing sometimes, with ice on the inside of the windowpanes.)

Wild food supplemented what we grew and was an additional treat; field mushrooms with their delicate pink gills fried with home-grown tomatoes were delicious for breakfast. Then there was blackberry and apple pie (my mother's pastry was excellent), crab-apple jelly and the fruits of gleaning from the pea-fields after the pea-pickers had been, all free and as yet uncontaminated by chemicals to any great extent. The wheat fields were spectacularly embroidered with cornflowers, poppies and camomile.

Sweets were rationed until the 50s (so was bread, surprisingly). I've long been trying to understand the present craving for sweet things. Yes, our first food, our mother's milk, is very sweet, but why pure sugar? It causes quite an 'explosion' in the mouth and the bloodstream. The fact that sweets were then in short supply made them even more attractive. My father would slice one Mars bar into razor-thin slices and the same with jelly-babies, arranging them artistically on a plate so we should take them carefully, not to disturb the design.

At the age of six I was sent to a convent-school for a few years (we were not Catholics but it had been recommended), and I have a very vivid memory of the nuns somehow acquiring a consignment of American army supplies: tins of barley sugar, chewing gum and Horlicks tablets. How they came upon such booty—well, the mind boggles! But there were no flies on those nuns; very entrepreneurial they were. They fitted out one of the classrooms with what could only be described as a roulette wheel upon which we could bet our pocket money in break times and win a tin of prized chewing gum and goodies. Here began the seductive power of refined sugar products. The Americans were clearly already hooked and keen to share their addictions.

The next 'foreign' taste adventure was when a precious crate of bananas was delivered to our local grocery store, well after the war had ended. This exotic fruit had been extolled and was the subject of reminiscence for my parents. Each family received two bananas to be shared amongst them—and all eyes were upon me. Well, I just could not understand the fuss; this taste experience did not compare with our raspberries or strawberries. I was genuinely disappointed and so were my parents. It is interesting to observe babies and small children taking in a new food for the first time, watching their expression, sometimes of enjoyment, sometimes immediate repulsion. Out comes the spinach purée or the rice gruel with an expression of 'What is this of the world that I am meant to digest?' The parent patiently spoons it back in. Each food a message from the universe, a piece of encoded information: is it good information, or is it distorted? The child builds up a mosaic of foodstuffs, an internalized world. A good matrix of foods as a child will later give a person better orientation from which to build their palate.

Another factor is the health of the appetite. We in our family had very healthy appetites on the whole, for we were out most of the day when we weren't at school (where we did games or gym three afternoons a week at least). I would be out with my friends on the common, fishing with a bent pin on the river, climbing trees, looking for birds' nests and wild flowers, playing in the farmer's cowsheds. So we didn't have to be cajoled into eating what was placed before us, as I see so many children being these days. No, that was what we had and there were not the endless choices that often bewilder children today.

So this was my basis in food, furthered by an excellent domestic science course at my grammar school (which the boys also did), and the enterprising teacher encouraged us to invite staff members to lunch, taught us how to lay the table, arrange the flowers and to serve, and how to conduct interesting conversation at the same time. Mrs Howe also taught us a version of *koulibiaka*, which has featured in my recipes.

This training became very useful when I was a student at Cambridge living on £4 a week and usually the only one in our digs who could cook. This meant instant popularity with the poorly nourished undergrads of the late 50s. I even remember doing a salad with tiger prawns and passion fruit. How about that on £4 a week? So quite early on in my life I started to enjoy cooking and hosting, and came to appreciate the importance of hospitality in developing culture and a feeling of creativity and well-being. It was at Cambridge that I met my husband-to-be, the celebrated comedian Peter Cook, and we enjoyed a 'salon' atmosphere in the Bohemian setting of an old former pub, owned by two philosophy graduates.

Later we experienced glamorous times in New York where I was astonished to realize that the many invitations to have dinner with people either involved going out to a restaurant or sending out for a take-away. Only twice over two years can I remember being cooked for by our hostess, and that was over 40 years ago! In London, married to Peter, everything seemed to be flourishing; we had wonderful, hilarious, delicious dinner parties that were truly appreciated and even talked about to this day. I became one of the dedicated apostles of Elizabeth David.

Peter and I made quite a heady team. Lucy was born to us first and then Daisy, quick on her heels. I remorsefully admit that I didn't breastfeed Daisy, because of so much propaganda for the convenience (note that word, for much has been lost to 'convenience') of formula milk. I didn't know what I know today, that mother's milk is the most natural and perfectly packaged food for the infant. Daisy suffered first from eczema—I'll never forget the scratching at night—and then from severe asthma attacks. Her father had suffered from asthma as a child and I had had bronchial problems, so this tiny child had to bear a somewhat poor health legacy. We had access to the best medical advice, but the orthodox treatment was adrenaline shots, which seemed violent in their effects, and steroids, which made her tremble. In extreme attacks an oxygen tent was needed. I learnt to orchestrate playtimes with her friends, for above a certain decibel pitch of excitement an attack would often ensue. I became desperate and was convinced that there had to be another way of treating her condition.

During a visit to the Scottish Findhorn community I was told by Paul Hawken how his acute asthma had been helped by a macrobiotic diet, so I returned to London and enrolled on various courses with Michio and Aveline Kushi. We studied what was originally a diet for Zen monks in Japan, and I was fascinated by the wisdom, beauty and purity of this way of cooking, and how cooking was conducted in a very contemplative way. Daisy and her best friend had decided to become vegetarians after our visit to Findhorn, where the community was nourished on the most wonderful and imaginative vegetarian diet, and where Daisy had been free of asthma attacks. The air of course was superior to that of London and there are always many factors in a changing health picture, but within weeks there was such a remarkable change in the health of all of us.

The incidences of cyclical depression that had been part of my health picture evaporated quite magically and Daisy's asthma attacks became much less frequent. We then moved out of London and the girls started to attend Michael Hall Rudolf Steiner School, which has an inbuilt therapeutic approach in its pedagogy. These developments took me away from the glamorous world of showbiz but it set the seal on the rest of my life. I realized that food was not just fuel or a titillating gourmet pursuit, but was medicine of the most primal kind. Since then my path has taken many interesting and enlightening twists. I became involved with questions of agriculture and discovered the superior quality of produce and the healthy-looking animals and poultry all being husbanded by the biodynamic method of agriculture. I studied with Dr Gerhard Schmidt, who had taken up Steiner's work on nutrition, and I tried to make a cohesive picture from the remarkable lessons I had learnt through my practice of macrobiotics.

An incident occurred which made me reconsider many issues surrounding the very strict Japanese practice of macrobiotics, involving no sugar, no dairy produce, large amounts of grains, vegetables, seaweed and aduki beans. I attended a wedding celebration when one of the leading figures in the movement was marrying a French girl. The feast had two distinct types of cuisine: macrobiotic, where the 'cream cheese' cakes were made of tofu, and French, with tempting lemon cream mousses, whole salmon garnished with cucumber and mayonnaise, and crunchy French breads. You may guess what happened: the vast majority of the macrobiotic guests descended on the French food and a good deal of the macrobiotic contribution lay there untouched. This taught me a lesson about fanaticism, which I must say I encountered in the movement and even in myself.

So it was a relief to meet Steiner's ideas, where the bottom line seemed to be 'If you don't enjoy your food it will not do you a tremendous amount of good'. This is really what I had always aimed for in my cooking—that it should be immensely enjoyable. Steiner gave, as a basis for our free choice of appropriate nutrition, insights as to how to view foods in their totality, their relationships to the evolving human being and most of all he gave advice about a totally new approach to agriculture, based on sound husbandry. He pointed out that the earth needs healing and gave pointers for special preparations that can be seen as homoeopathic remedies for the earth.

A synthesis of studies in macrobiotics, Steiner's indications and a brief digest of Ayurvedic wisdom reveals a shared emphasis on the significance of the acid/alkaline basis in our foods and the importance of whole grains in our diet.

In tracing the history and evolution of human nutrition and consciousness in my book *Foodwise,* it became all too clear that our foods have increasingly tended towards the acidic. Our diet has increased the proportion of meat, wine and all types of alcohol, the nightshade family (which includes potatoes, tomatoes, red peppers, chillies, aubergines and tobacco), spicy foods, coffee, tea, cocoa and sugar—all making the blood too acidic. Sourness in the gut can lead to cynicism in our attitudes and behaviour. This is a very serious situation for our health and general well-being.

We are given plenty of advice about what we should be eating and we can watch all those cookery programmes, but how much do we know about the quality of the food we buy and the soil it grows upon? We spend billions on hospitals and drugs, when the starting point should be sound nutrition—enjoyable, socially enhancing and totally reinvigorating—for a society that seems to be losing direction. I will endeavour to develop some of these themes as we progress.

'What biodynamic cookery is could be open to interpretation. Apart from choosing biodynamic ingredients and living with the seasons, for me it is a lifetime's study of understanding ingredients on an energetic level and knowing how to combine them in ways that enhance the life-forces within them.'

Part One: Background

1 THE CULTURE OF FOOD AND COOKING THROUGH THE AGES

'Without a knowledge of history the cook's world remains fragmented.'

Michael Symons, *History of Cooks and Cooking*

What led our ancestors to experiment with eating dangerous and unappetizing-looking things? Can you imagine being the first person to try to eat a lobster or an artichoke (to all intents and purposes a huge thistle)? Did countless people sacrifice their lives to this quest? Was it necessity, hunger or curiosity that fuelled this never-ending exploration of new taste sensations? The hunter-gatherers must have learnt extensive lessons: what was good raw, what needed cooking, at what season to gather the best or in what area, and what happened if you got it wrong. Were they working on intuition, insight, or simply by trial and error? Not all foods are attractive or even interesting in their natural form, and some are positively dangerous. Eventually, as selection and cultivation of the grasses developed and food crops were grown rather than foraged for, so settled agricultural methods superseded the ancient nomadic ways. The biblical story of Cain and Abel is an archetypal image of two groupings, the nomadic—represented by Abel, the shepherd—and Cain, who represented a new way of life, anchored to the soil and agriculture. The slaying of Abel by Cain indicates that this new rootedness superseded the nomadic way, and a certain innocence was sacrificed in this development.

Agriculture changed humanity's relationship with the environment, and consequently our own self-consciousness. A person could elect to grow food not only for their own family but with surplus for their community, thus creating time and enabling people to become craftsmen, poets, architects, dancers and cooks. The ability to grow and store foods such as grains brought security and power and made possible a new kind of diversity. Bountiful harvests brought great displays of hospitality, and gifts of food were offered in gratitude to the gods to ensure continued fertility of the land.

The discovery of fire was another such defining moment, its mastery enabling culture to grow. According to Greek legend Prometheus stole fire from Vulcan, and the price for humanity was to deal with the contents of Pandora's box—a price we have paid dearly for. Mercifully, *Hope* was retained at the bottom of the box. From pebble-lined pits to ovens and hearths, the story of the taming of fire has been held with consummate respect. Some of the earliest evidence of human control over fire was found in the hearths of Peking man, and in the remains of Çatal Hüyük in Anatolia (9000 BC) the hearth was clearly the focus of the living space (*focus* is the Latin for hearth).

The ancient Persians, under the leadership of Zarathustra, took their sacred fires with them when they travelled, a practice continued by the Greeks who, honouring the sacred character of the common hearth, dramatized it with an order that every citizen should take some of his own fire when going abroad to found new colonies. In alchemy the fire is never allowed to go out; it is tended continually. Cooks traditionally kept the fire going

all night by covering the embers with shards, pieces of broken pottery (this is the origin of the word 'curfew' which comes from the French *couvrir*, to cover and *feu*, fire). There is an inn on the top of Dartmoor where the fire has not been allowed to go out for a hundred years.

Hestia was for the Greeks the goddess who presides over the hearth. The principle that all hearths were shared with the gods was known as *hestiatoria*. Hestia has largely been abandoned in our society, where Promethean energy takes up the benign culture of the hearth and subverts the fire energy into guns and bombs. Some of us echo Hestia's lament and wish to see her reinstated. So it is thrilling to see the growth of beehive clay ovens being built in many Steiner schools to teach the children about baking bread in wood-fired ovens, and demonstrate that fire from wood is a real solar event.

From fires to grain and bread

For thousands of years civilizations have been sustained by a diet where nutritional energy was principally provided by grains. For the Egyptians much of the red barley of the Nile was used in beer-making, but a by-product of the process may have been the fermenting beer balm settling into their grain pastes (the original flat breads) and providing them with the first leavened breads. This new bread was a tremendous asset in terms of digestibility, portability and diversity. By the time of the New Kingdom 40 different kinds of breads had been developed, some sweet-flavoured with dates and coriander—others savoury. The importance of bread was recorded in many ways, often as payment for labour.

Cooking became more adventurous. In the household lists of Mesopotamia over a hundred soups and stews appear, flavoured with aniseed, cumin, coriander, mint, juniper, sesame, cardamom and fenugreek. Here we see how the delicate spicing of food became important, together with an understanding of medicinal properties, to be developed even further by the Greeks. The Egyptians placed great value on the alliums—leeks, onions and garlic—as testified by a plaque on one of the pyramids. In addition, 20 different cheeses were mentioned, and sweetness was provided by figs, dates, pomegranates and mulberries. This was a magnificent civilization, as we can see from their artefacts where gold reflected the rays of the god Ra in their headdresses, garments and ornaments.

The Ancient Greeks

For the Greeks, diet spoke for a whole way of living that emphasized balance—in exercise and rest, sleeping and waking, choices of foods, conditions of eliminations. All these elements were regarded as essential pointers to health and beauty. Ritualized consumption of food and drink was part of religious observance, the whole communal activity of eating with fellow citizens included the gods, departed heroes and passing wayfarers. Meat only tended to be consumed following ritual sacrifice. To be employed as a cook in

Greek times required knowledge of a profound spread of subjects, some seemingly unrelated: astrology, architecture, geometry, natural history, military strategy and of course medicine (see Phyllis Pray Bober, *Art, Culture and Cuisine*). They must have been highly rewarded for such expertise. I only hope their employers insisted on some knowledge of the culinary arts as well!

We must not forget that the Greeks—as the forerunners of the questioning, individuated self—developed philosophy, logic and disputation. They were also increasingly taking salt as an external mineral seasoning in their food. Here is a link, which we will discuss later.

Grapes and wine

The vine became cultivated throughout the Mediterranean and its fruit used for wine-making. Originally used only in ritual, wine changes the human being's perception of herself. Amongst other things it creates a kind of communal bonhomie (albeit an artificial, substance-based experience), where more earthly intercourse takes the place of dialogue with the gods and the spiritual, heavenly worlds. Its role therefore can be seen as creating a kind of forgetfulness. This enhanced bonhomie became wildly sought after and in the cults of Dionysus and Bacchus the use of wine increased to the point that these revelries became decadent and orgiastic. Another important ingredient to add to our increasing mosaic of foods was discovered by Alexander the Great: 'the reed that produces honey without any bees'—sugar cane. (For more on sugar see page 26.)

The Romans

Three hundred years later the Roman Empire spread across much of the lands Alexander had conquered, bringing its own culture. Based on strong armies, strong laws and superb engineering, the Romans' rule was firm and efficient. Architecture and sculpture became more gravity-laden, more earthbound. Whereas the Greeks at the apex of their culture had considered that diet should consist of sun-related foods (vegetables, fruits, grains, herbs and curd cheese), the Roman diet became very meat- and wine-oriented. Huge banquets took place that featured 'vomitoriums', so positioned that the diners could vomit up their repast and start all over again.

Salt, pepper and condiments

I must draw your attention to a food item that became so popular with the Romans that it was used in every dish, rather like our ubiquitous tomato ketchup. This sauce, liquamen, was even used in desserts and I have a recipe for Patina of Pears that includes it. Fish (anchovies or mackerel) was the main ingredient, fermented for six months with salt in a ratio of 5:1. Then old wine, shellfish or other things were added creating a cheesy, salty, fishy flavour. This is definitely a Tamasic food, that is, something that has no spark of life left in it. (See discussion of the Ayurvedic system on page 54.)

Salt was increasingly important; so important that their wages or salaries (sal, salt) were reckoned as salt-money. Pepper (a stimulant, as well as an irritant) became almost as valuable as gold. Of course, the Romans used vegetables and fruits and bread, but the central elements of their diet, certainly for the elite, were as described. The culture was warlike and aggressive, with bear-baiting and gladiatorial displays as public entertainments. Much blood was spilt. The Romans, beyond doubt, left us with many important developments and innovations and there are dishes which I value that are descendants of Roman kitchens. Amongst these are the Spanish *paella*, the *cassoulet* of Southern France and the Perigord, the *bouillabaisse* of the Mediterranean and the *tian* of Provence.

The Middle Ages

But now we must rush on through the ages, pausing briefly at the monastic culture of Europe in the Middle Ages. The arts of gardening, cooking, baking and brewing, calligraphy and the illuminating of manuscripts thrived in these stable communities. Prayer, meditation and chanting helped to focus the monks' efforts on a higher reality. Many fine dishes, wines and liqueurs were developed in communities demonstrating sound ecological practices and usually leading to a high degree of self-sufficiency. Such a community would be centred on the church or chapel, surrounded by the living quarters of the monks for sleeping, study and dining. Beyond this stretched the medicinal garden, planted with many varieties of herbs, the vegetable garden, the fruit orchards, the coniger for rabbits, the pond for carp, beehives for honey (also used in the making of mead), fields for grain and surrounding woods for acorn-grubbing pigs. Not only was this a very practical system but it also had a wonderful aesthetic that harmonized with the surrounding landscape. Biodynamic agriculture, when carried out ideally, would echo this kind of harmonious and symbiotic relationship between plants, trees, animals, insects and humans.

Foods from the New World

The Solanaceae

With the rediscovery of the Americas by Christopher Columbus in 1492 came many new foods, amongst them maize and the Solanaceae family, which includes tomatoes, peppers, potatoes, chillies and tobacco. All members of this family of plants carry, to lesser or greater degree, the poison solanin.

You may well ask why we are eating foods that display poisonous traits. It is astonishing to reflect on the degree to which these crops, having been treated with great suspicion for many years by farmers and consumers alike, have now been adopted—even those with an addictive effect, such as tobacco.

The potato and tomato have really supplanted much of the grain eating traditions of Europe and the West. It was agriculturalist and pharmacist Antoine-Auguste Parmentier who turned the tide of French public opinion, which before the French Revolution had trusted nothing but grain. After this, millions of Europeans abandoned

tradition to take up potato nutrition at roughly the same time. Rudolf Steiner had some very interesting things to say about the potato, stating that the introduction of the potato in Europe had a dramatic effect on people's intellectual faculties:

> Potatoes at a certain time began to play a particular role in western development. If you compare the increasing use of the potato with the curve of the development of intelligence, you will find that in comparison with today, people in the pre-potato era grasped things less quickly and readily, but what they grasped they really knew. Their nature was more conservative, profound and reflective. After the introduction of the potato, people became quicker in taking up ideas, but what they take up is not retained and does not sink in very deeply.
>
> The potato makes great demands on the digestion. Very small, almost homoeopathic doses find their way into the brain, but these tiny quantities are very potent, they spur on the forces of abstract intelligence.
>
> (Rudolf Steiner, *Nutrition and Stimulants.*)

Dr Rudolf Hauschka, in his book *Nutrition,* adds: 'We have described how carbohydrate foods are used chiefly to nourish the middle portion of the brain. This is the area that supports creative, artistic and imaginative thinking. If the middle brain is made to serve digestive functions as it has to do after a meal of potatoes, it cannot perform its proper function and the forebrain has to substitute for it.'

The age of rationality, stimulants and the part that they play

Next came a fairly short, but concentrated, period of time where philosophical and scientific ideas gave a completely new interpretation of man's place in the universe. Man was now seen as created purposely to have complete dominion over nature, in a world observed to operate in a mechanical, measurable way. One of the key figures of this revolution was Copernicus who in effect deposed the world from its central position as hub of the universe. The values of the now dethroned human being in this vast and impersonal universe were apparently of no real importance. Other key thinkers of this period were Bacon, Kepler, Galileo, Newton and Descartes. Science started to take over from religion, and art became separated. The basis was thus laid for Darwin's theory of evolution and the idea that seems to drive our western culture: the survival of the fittest.

The new substances (I can hardly call them foods since their nutritional value is questionable) that came into increasing use were coffee, tea and chocolate, all of which probably tasted disgusting in their raw state before sugar was added to make them palatable. As we know from Samuel Pepys's diary, coffee and smoking houses became very popular from the seventeenth century onwards. The substances are all addictive, too, in their varying degrees and have changed human biochemistry and soil biochemistry in their production.

At this point I want to extend our original question: 'What is it that drives the human being on relentlessly, so that we now include poisons and addictive substances in our daily eating habits?' We may add: 'What effects are these substances having on our consciousness?' Firstly, these plant products I have highlighted—wine, sugar, potatoes, tomatoes and tobacco, spices, coffee, tea and chocolate, plus meat, particularly red meat —all have an acidic effect on our blood. The pH of our blood is crucial to our health and mentation; it should be slightly alkaline. When we are 'sour' in our gut we may well become cynical in our disposition. Cynicism seems to be a strong feature in our society. Perhaps we should think about this.

The unconscious and the world of desires

Psychiatrists Jung and Freud uncovered a secret world of the unconscious, throbbing with desires and unfulfilled passions. Manufacturers and advertisers have made much use of this world of desires, especially in relegating us to the role of consumers. Countless products are continually created with much money and energy spent on trying to convince us our lives will be happier if we buy them. It seems obvious to many that this is not the road to happiness or contentment. Contentment comes, for me at least, from being creative.

My favourite places of creativity are the kitchen and the garden. I have never tired of being creative in the kitchen; it has brought me and others endless joy and satisfaction. The kitchen is my alchemical flask wherein magic transformations take place (see more in Chapter 6). I do hope that I may be able to infuse you with some of my enthusiasm for cooking. For me it is a very powerful step in reclaiming our intrinsic power, for the act of growing, cooking and feeding is a seamless story that connects us to our ancestors and is one of the most cultural and generous activities we can engage in.

> 'If the kitchen is the powerhouse of history, then home cooks are important; the hand that stirs the bowl makes the civilization.'

> Michael Symons

2 THE ETHICS OF MODERN FOOD CULTURE

Describing the effects of food on human consciousness in the last chapter, I tried to show how certain widely consumed stimulants and foods (coffee, cocoa and tea, sugar, spices, alcohol, soya and several members of the nightshade family) have been enthusiastically adopted by western culture although they may not be true 'foods'. Many have an addictive effect and affect our inner biochemical environment, and soils have been greatly changed by their cultivation. Further, they are some of the cash crops by which developing countries struggle to survive, and so they have connections to our colonial past. Our addictions have resulted in the West imposing trade rules that frequently lie behind the problems of poverty in the Third World. Should we be buying foods that cause hardship, degradation of soils or depleted seas?

It is time for some reckoning

Oil and petrochemicals

Led by the myth of limitless resources and faith in technology to fix all our problems, we have recklessly and thoughtlessly been driven by our addictions. Oil is one: to fuel the current technological age, an age of luxury and ease, we have become addicted to oil and petroleum products (which play a larger part in food technology than most of us realize). The way we eat now is connected at every stage with the oil industry: fertilizers on the land and pesticides on the crops; mechanical harvesting; transport over long distances; processing; added flavourings, colourings, emulsifiers and stabilizers; packaging and transport again to the shops. The average Sunday lunch (including chicken from Thailand, beans from Zambia and carrots from Spain) travels 26,234 miles to the table. Stop and consider for a moment what might happen when oil runs out.

One of the classical features of addiction is denial, and in this case the denial permits us to sell this lifestyle to the rest of the world. We have become less and less able (or willing?) to make the connection between our lifestyles and increasing world poverty, global warming and chronic health problems. The latter can often be traced to toxic overload as we distance ourselves further and further from nature and the natural environment. Our bodies need good, fresh, uncontaminated food. Releasing ourselves from our addiction to oil and returning to a more sustainable agriculture can only mean more localization.

Coffee

Coffee is another of our addictions, so when you find yourself in the supermarket reaching for a pack of coffee you might think of Aymiro Gedamu. He is an Ethiopian farmer who appeared on the front of *The Independent* on 18 January 2005 under the heading, 'Why this Man holds the Key to Solving World Poverty'. Aymiro is a coffee farmer growing coffee for the West and using donkey power. His sandals are battered and he is probably not yet 40 but looks a lot older. The revelation that provoked this headline was that, together with neighbours, he built some stone walls to stop soils being washed away.

His increased yields have gone from five pack loads to seven. He was given financial help—gift or loan is not clear—and some training. (How revealing of our paternalistic view of the developing world and how revealing of their loss of basic knowledge!) Might he not be more fulfilled if he were growing crops that his family really needs? Do we really need coffee so much that we insist others grow it in place of the crops with which they could feed their families? Whilst we try to placate peasant farmers with the modern equivalent of beads and mirrors—a shiny tractor, a bag of pesticides—we take away the equivalent of gold, their soil. Tim Lang and Erik Millstone, in their book *The Atlas of Food*, comment as follows on this matter of concern:

> Economists insist on the importance of earning foreign currency through export trade, but there is no nutritional logic to the process by which food is transferred from areas where under-consumption is a serious problem to areas where the dominant diet-related problems are over-consumption. Just as Ireland exported food during its Great Famine of the 1840s so Africa exports to Europe today.

Global transportation

Our playground has become the whole world; we expect to holiday wherever we choose, and many of us work abroad. More than 800,000 Australians visited Britain in 2003 and a similar number of Britons visited Australia. Similarly, we are addicted to exotic foods and foods out of season. Let us look at the implications of global food trading:

- Transport generates massive CO_2 emissions, increasing global warming
- Transporting food over large distances increases risk of contamination and reduces its 'energetic' and nutritional content
- Transporting animals creates risks for animal welfare, but also increases the risk of infection
- Farmers in poor countries grow cash crops for export, compromising their ability to feed their own families
- Our own farmers are squeezed by overseas competition.

For every £1 spent on bananas in Tesco, only 1p goes to the plantation growers. An estimated 40p goes to Tesco. Tesco makes a profit of £1 million per week purely from the sale of bananas. In 2003, Tesco's chief executive received a pay package of £2,838,000—some 255 times higher than the average income of a British farmer (£11,000 per annum).

Observer Food Monthly, January 2004

Sugar

Our addiction to sugar began long ago and it is now hard to omit it from our diet as it occurs in most pre-packaged goods. It contributes to sickness, rotten teeth and obesity, makes people lethargic, and creates anxiety for the next dose. Children who have sugary food early on are addicted for life.

Although sugar occurs naturally in ripe fruits, importing fruits from all over the world means that we are eating fruits picked before they ripen on the plant and before the natural sweetness develops (they are often stored in gas to prevent ripening till in the stores). Local fruit, on the other hand, can be allowed to mature in sunlight and fresh air.

The Background—How We Got Here

> The UK has an agricultural area of 17 million hectares. We also have a net import of a further 4.1 million hectares—land in other countries which is used to grow food for consumption in the UK.
>
> Friends of the Earth

Let us try to understand some of the background to the present-day situation. Mankind has used agriculture for around 10,000 years and over that time has been engaged in an unhurried process of observing soils, skies, plants and cosmic rhythms, experimenting, taking risks, experiencing crop failure, famine and abundance, and bringing us to the variety and diversity that we had 100 years ago. Radio and TV presenter John Humphrys has commented, 'If we compressed our time on earth into one 24-hour period, the past 50 years would register as a microsecond. We have done more to disrupt the cycle in that microsecond, that blink of an eye, than in our entire history.' (*The Great Food Gamble.*)

In the sixteenth and seventeenth centuries, the Enclosure Acts drove many people off the land. By the seventeeth century over six million acres of common land had been annexed and enclosed. Later, in the depression of the 1930s, there was a further dramatic fall in agricultural prices, bringing more resentment against the ruling classes. When war was declared in 1939 the folly of the lack of foresight in our food policies was painfully obvious. But people had not forgotten how to grow vegetables; parks and ornamental gardens were dug up for food crops and many women joined the Women's Land Army. The effort was extraordinary and unforgettable. Ironically, after the war, people were said to be generally healthier, but much depended on their access to fresh fruit and vegetables.

In response to the shortages after the war, food was brought in from North America under aid programmes. Conditions were therefore set for the state to intervene to ensure an increase in food supplies and to guarantee incomes for farmers. In England in 1950 there were more than a million families earning their livings from 450,000 mixed farms of varying acreage, but farm wages failed to compare with those offered by industry. At that time government aid to the farming population took the shape of protection

of domestic markets, support of prices, official purchasing at set prices and subsidies to producers. By 1962 the Common Agricultural Policy had set common policies across the European Common Market in cereals, eggs, fruit and vegetables, wine and pork (sugar was omitted).

This new system must have appeared attractive and with the terrible sufferings of the war behind them, people were ready for a new beginning. But how many really understood what kind of Pandora's box was being opened with new developing technologies in farming and food production, or what the eventual outcomes might be? Wetlands were drained, moors and pastureland were ploughed for the cultivation of food. Farmers being paid to produce crops meant that food was piling up in vast quantities. Bigger and more efficient machinery meant that fewer hands were needed and fields had to be larger; hedgerows disappeared at the rate of more than 10,000 miles per year. Apple orchards were grubbed out to reduce the EU's overproduction; our native apples with their abundant varieties couldn't compete with the prices of unblemished Granny Smiths or Golden Delicious from South Africa and New Zealand. The transport involved, with all its attendant environmental costs, was not reckoned and still isn't. How could our farmers reconcile themselves to this?

The growth of food technology

Since the last war food technology has proliferated, ostensibly to take the 'drudgery' out of cooking (or was it to make huge profits by playing on our laziness?), and so-called 'convenience foods' became fashionable. But where have we been led to over the past 50 years? It is normal now for our foods to contain chemical synthesizers, flavour enhancers, colourants, emulsifiers, added minerals and vitamins. Greenstuffs can be treated to appear fresh, by changing the gases surrounding them or by irradiation, when in fact they should have wilted days before.

Special relationships between food manufacturers and politicians have developed. Today great corporations wield enormous power over governments, but their responsibility is chiefly to their shareholders and the stacking up of profits. David Korten reported that 60% of the international food chain is controlled by just ten companies involved in seed, fertilizer, pesticides, processing and distribution (*When Corporations Rule the World*). Jorge Calderon, professor of economics at the University of Mexico, said: 'If multinational companies are successful in creating a truly global agriculture system in which they control prices and movements of commodities, the right of each country to establish its own farming policies will be destroyed.'

Another important trend has been the growth of the fast-food industry. People rarely sit down to a meal around a table, but expect to eat 'on the go', snacking while doing other things, such as watching TV. This confuses the body and directly affects the digestive processes. Fast foods and junk foods are often high in fat, salt and sugar and low in fresh ingredients. There is plenty of evidence how these contribute to the obesity problem (see the film *Supersize Me*, if you can). The passionate campaign in Britain, led by celebrity chef Jamie Oliver, to improve school meals is well overdue, but it has to be accompanied by parents taking the trouble to cook proper meals at home.

> A MORI survey of 8–11 year-olds found that a fifth did not know that cheese comes from milk.
>
> Flair conference report
> (*The Foundation for Local Food Initiatives*)

Industrial-scale farming, intensive production with its fertilizers and pesticides, has been aggressively promoted worldwide but especially in Asia and Latin America. (The Amazon rain forest is disappearing to provide us with burgers and soya.) Such chemicals can have a devastating effect on human health and the environment, poisoning wildlife and contaminating water sources. Intensification of meat production has led to methods that inhibit animals from displaying natural behaviours, keeping them in very confined conditions, causing pain and ill-health. There is more likelihood of transmittable diseases, such as in the Chinese bird flu epidemic. In England, the Foot and Mouth outbreak in 2001 saw the slaughter of ten million cattle, over half of them apparently healthy.

This intensification of meat production is responsible for huge global changes: 75% of agricultural land in the EU is used for growing animal feeds. (It takes 930 kg. of grain to feed one person on a meat diet, whereas it takes 180 kg. to feed a person on a grain-based diet.) In the USA less than 20% of the typical diet comes from cereal products; the high proportion of animal proteins and saturated fats is known to be directly linked to the high rate of coronary heart disease (CHD). Contrast this with the diet of the Nepalese, which consists of 70% cereals; they have no CHD problem. It has been stated that 800 million people in the world do not have enough food to meet their basic nutritional needs.

Although food is redistributed around the globe in forms of trade or aid this does not provide any long-term solution. Food aid is often used by donor countries as a way of influencing the politics in the recipient country. The very threat of withdrawing aid is very destabilizing and using food as a political tool is totally reprehensible. In addition, countries that currently cannot produce sufficient food to keep their people healthy are also the ones facing the most rapid population increase. Food aid leaves people dependent, slaves of the system, and generally adds to the climate change problem by its use of oil-based transportation.

Here in Britain we use approximately 6 million hectares of other people's land to feed ourselves and 1.8 million of those are used to grow feed for British animals. Such a situation is not inevitable: the principles of biodynamic farming ensure that animal feeds are grown on the farm.

We often fall for the lures of the advertisers; products are put across in very powerful images. In 1999, 40 billion dollars were spent on advertising globally; Coca Cola alone spent 1.5 billion dollars. Meanwhile the list of artificial additives—a mere 100 compounds in 1900—totalled 4500 by the year 2000. As I mentioned earlier, recently there has been a huge scare over the red colourant called Sudan 1, the largest scare in British food history. Over 500 products have been listed as containing this cancer-causing colourant, and millions of tonnes of ready-made meals from pizzas to chicken wings, burgers and sauces have been recalled and buried in landfills. In Britain we seem to think that cheap food is one of our most important priorities, yet we are willing to spend billions on diets, nutritional supplements and exercise programmes—all *to avoid living and eating in a healthier way.*

Artificial sweeteners such as aspartame and monosodium glutamate and other flavour enhancers continue to be used by the food industry despite the health problems suspected to be associated with them. These artificial products cause the taste buds to expand and operate by a kind of trickery on our finely organized senses.

One of the most worrying global trends is the development of GM products. Large parts of the world now accept that their use is inevitable and they have penetrated large areas of the food chain. But the public, especially in Europe, are resistant. In GM modification genes are moved from one species to another to carry a desirable trait, whereas conventional breeding methods allow only transfer between members of the same species or very closely connected species. The advantages promised include increased crop yields, increased levels of nutrients, such as vitamins, especially in cereals, and the possibility of getting plants to produce vaccines for us. One of the ways the industry ensures that they get a profit on this technology is to claim patent rights over crops and seeds so they can charge royalties or fees, another is by forcing farmers to buy extra chemicals, and a third is to make their seeds sterile so every season fresh supplies have to be bought. Clearly, it all disadvantages the besieged farmer. Ecologists are very concerned about the escaping of GM seeds, which may introduce unwanted traits and change local ecology in unforeseen ways. There is also the risk that new combinations of genes may have unintended effects on the human body, such as producing toxins. Such is the schizophrenia of our democratic society. Who has the stronger voice, the great global enterprises or the public who have deep suspicions about such developments?

Recently, the Archbishop of Canterbury was quoted in *Resurgence* magazine as saying: 'One of the aspects of a growing secular society is that we find ourselves increasingly incapable of seeing anything other than human needs. The attitude of the consumer seeks only to dominate and absorb things in such a way that it is impossible to treat the provisions of nature as a gift for which we might show gratitude.'

Towards sustainability

Current practices are *unsustainable.* So what might be the antidote for these assaults on our environment and our brothers and sisters worldwide? Friends of the Earth's book *Tomorrow's World* sets quantified targets for what is needed to bring sustainable development. It is clear that we must take a long-term and more global view of policies on housing, agriculture, water and transport. Their guidelines for achieving sustainable development are based on two principles:

(i) we should stay within environmental limits;

(ii) everyone has a right to the earth's resources.

Surely this is common sense, but many people would consider these goals impossibly idealistic. I believe it is time to move away from industrial-scale practices and develop biodynamic and organic agriculture (see Chapter 3).

A common misconception, however, is that these farming systems can only ever supply a niche market. In the UK only 0.3% of agricultural land is farmed organically, one of the lowest rates in Europe, and only comparable with those of New Zealand and Australia. So two-thirds of our organic produce is being imported to meet increasing demands; is this proof of a 'niche market'? One of the chief reasons we need to import is the lack of support given to organic farming by the Government and the Department of the Environment, Food and Rural Affairs. The UK has the lowest subsidy rates in the EU for conversion to organic production.

What should we be doing?

If we take global warming and food inequalities around the world seriously and want to restrict our energy use, we shall need to return to a much more localized lifestyle. Buying locally doesn't mean we have to restrict ourselves entirely to produce from a certain area, but to do so as much as possible. When it isn't possible, we can buy the next best (and freshest) option, be it fairly traded or organic. Buying locally means that we are contributing to the local economy, to maintaining traditional crops and varieties, and keeping people employed. We should support local growers, farmers' markets and the small shops who buy locally—*we can keep asking for local food*. We can join vegetable box schemes and encourage all local institutions such as councils, schools and large firms to source all their supplies as locally as possible. If there is a Community Supported Farming scheme near you, find out about it and join! And, of course, I cannot leave out a reminder that we should start growing our own. If we don't return to a local food economy we are compromising the health of future generations.

Do you use Fair Trade products? Under this scheme retail prices include a premium providing funds for investment in environmental and social programmes in poorer countries. The workers are often paid 60% above the minimum salary rate and healthcare is provided on site. Fair Trade has largely been concerned with luxury goods, coffee, tea, chocolate and bananas, but now supports a wider range of goods. Recently it has been supporting a return to traditional ways of growing food and helping with literacy schemes and health centres. It has been said that 80% of farmers in developing countries would not have to change their methods to be certified organic.

Can organic or biodynamic farming feed the world?

The answer to this question will depend on what is meant by the word 'feed'. If it means
(i) a varied diet of grains, fresh fruits and vegetables, pulses, low in saturated fats

or

(ii) a diet that is rich in animal proteins—a 'convenient' diet for a developed world life-style and high in short-term gratification

then the answer would be 'Yes' to the first option and a definite 'No' to the second. (From a paper presented by Lawrence Woodward of the Farm and Food Society.)

I shall develop this further as we look at what answers biodynamic farming could provide.

Dry land farming, Northern Montana

3 WHAT IS BIODYNAMIC FARMING?

My first introduction to a biodynamic farm was over 35 years ago, yet it made such an indelible impression upon me that I can still vividly recreate the memory. Nestling in the

soft East Sussex hills, Busses Farm, run by Jimmy and Pauline Anderson, was a clear demonstration of a living example of bio-dynamics. Walking through the kitchen garden was like being in a Monet painting. The French intensive biodynamic method was being practised, with raised beds and an exuberant riot of herbs, flowers and veg-etables. Patches of marigolds, tagetes and nasturtiums tangled with bright blue bor-age, lavender, rosemary, courgettes, cucum-bers and firm-hearted lettuce. Runner beans busily twined up poles and tomatoes grew warm, sweet and ripe. If you managed to glimpse the soil through this cornucopia it was black and crumbly, the kind that pro-duces happy plants. Bees provided the background hum as they gratefully progressed from flower to flower, spoilt for choice between gardens and orchards. This was the first time I remember hearing about companion planting.

Out in the fields was a herd of horned Sussex cows, most with their calves, for breeding as well as some milk cows; a few fluffy sheep that looked like an advertisement for wash-ing powder, 300 pecking and excitable hens, and a wonderful workhorse that was used for transporting heavy loads. All of these animated the landscape with their variety of shapes, colours, sounds and behaviours. In addition to this huge quantity of mouths and beaks to feed there was usually a group of very hard-working and very hungry appren-

tices who would come to train for 3–6 month blocks. Their healthy appetites meant that Pauline's four-oven Aga was always on the go, full of marvellous dishes. And, as if this was not enough, the inde-fatigable Andersons pioneered a vegetable and wholefood shop in the village of Forest Row, which has continued to go from strength to strength. So many people were enthusiastic about getting biodynamic pro-duce that a number came forward with their various talents, and the next enter-

prise was a restaurant run by a team of good cooks—some days the queues would stretch round the block. The salads fairly jumped off the plates with vitality and we all felt that this was an 'idea whose time had certainly come'.

On the farm were study groups looking at the theoretical side of biodynamics, and reg-ular celebrations of festivals with music, singing and dancing. It was very hard work to be sure, but it made the profound statement of Manfred Klett (former head of biodynamic work in Germany) that 'the farm is the university of the future', a living ideal to be realized eventually on a much wider scale. When it honours the particular piece of land that forms it, in all its true depth of potentiality, the farm is a world of symbiotic relationships and processes. Then the farm becomes the most excellent, cheap and efficient place to study botany, zoology, chemistry, physics, water, soil, chemistry, nutrition, cooking, animal husbandry, crafts, climatology, astronomy and true economy (the Greek *oikos*, meaning house + *nomia*, meaning management); to manage nature's household properly we will need to develop a new and qualitatively different understanding of economic principles).

To bring us back to today, my local biodynamic farmer Richard Smith takes up the theme:

> Walking around a biodynamic garden, or as in my case, over the fields of a biodynamic farm, one soon begins to realize that there is something different going on here. It is usually an impression of vibrancy in the plants, warmth in the soil and a health and contentment amongst the animals. When we look at some of the surrounding conventional farms, the fact that they have become highly specialized will be evident. There will be a small selection of crops spread out over huge fields or there will perhaps be animals, usually cattle or sheep. We rarely see poultry or pigs, because they tend to be kept in barns or feedlots where they stay summer and winter. It is hard to think of the deprivations that they endure. Whereas on a biodynamic farm we will usually see a wide diversity of crops and animals outside in smaller groups, smaller machines (e.g. lighter tractors) and generally a closer connection between human beings and nature.

One of the biodynamic farmer's main goals is to create a balance between plants, animals and humans, and the needs of that particular soil. The aim is as far as possible to grow food for the animals entirely on the farm. No artificial fertilizers are brought in since the fertility of the soil will be derived exclusively from composted plant waste mixed with the different animal manures. If there are so many animals that it is necessary to buy feed in, or the plants do not thrive because there is insufficient compost, then somehow a more realistic and secure ratio of plants and animals has to be achieved. With experience, most biodynamic farmers usually find this to be possible. It is a principle at the heart of biodynamic farming; it is also one of the ways biodynamics may differ from organic farming (where the main aim for some farmers is to be able to grow food without chemicals).

Sometimes, of course, there are difficulties to be faced, such as extremes of weather, which seem to be occurring with greater frequency. A farmer who has a wide spread of plants and animals usually observes that not all are affected with equal severity. Failures are neither total nor ruinous, and there is a measure of security in such an approach. (No biodynamic cattle succumbed to the foot and mouth epidemic. The only cull of biodynamic cattle was in Scotland where the farm was contiguous with an infected farm.) Such security came from diversity, which used to be true of traditional farms before the last World War, but is not the lot of the current conventional farmer who has sacrificed a wide spread of farm products to concentrate on mono-crops or only dairy cows and has to cope with the unpredictable and fluctuating prices of different commodities. This is short-term, high-risk farming because specialization also exhausts the soil, limits the habitat of insects and birds and can open the door to disease.

A biodynamic farmer trying to 'orchestrate' the number and type of animals required to create the ideal and appropriate balance on the farm will need to consider the different types of manures produced by the various animals, and this in a qualitative way. In animal dung there is something of the essence of the animal and its whole relationship with the earth. Each group of animals has a different attribute or gift, and a good farmer will understand how to direct certain animals to specific parts of the farm where they can improve and enliven the soil. Here are some thoughts on various farm animals.

The Pig is a very intelligent creature. It spends a great deal of time rooting in the soil and is inexhaustibly curious, heaving up the soil and disturbing it where it is compact and damp, letting in the air. As an omnivore it is partial to whatever is rich in flavour, especially the taproots of pernicious weeds. With only a sparse coat of hair it likes to grow fat to keep itself warm and it seems to extract all the potential for warmth from its feed, so that its dung tends to be much more earthly and cold (compared to that of the cow). But this type of manure works well on the cold root crops.

Sheep, clothed in the 'Golden Fleece' and famous as the 'Golden Hoof', improve the land wherever they tread. They nibble close to the ground thus allowing light to penetrate the pasture, which responds by the production of a rich clover. Their silica-rich manure encourages the growth of strong stems that help the plant reach up into the air and light. Although the sheep is a ruminant animal with a complex digestion, involving four stomach chambers and a circular process of regurgitation into the mouth for further chewing, its digestion is not as advanced as that of the cow.

The Cow, a ruminant, has a digestive system that has reached a state of perfection. The reach of the cow's senses out into the world, however, is limited; she chews the cud in a state between dreaming and waking. She seems to inwardly experience all the plants of the meadow as she chews and re-chews them in a wonderful reverie. It is not difficult to appreciate why this animal is so venerated by the Hindus as a model of meditative peace. The dung that derives from a digestive tract 22 times the length of the animal is so transformed from the original plant state that cattle are not repulsed by it, as other animals are by theirs. Cow dung has been so well assimilated that it is provides the most nutritionally available dung for manuring plants on the farm or in the garden, when composted. Its effect is strongest on the soil surface; it nourishes leaves—the watery part of the plant—and so balances the earthly and watery realms. The cow is indeed quite central to the proper workings of a biodynamic farm.

So farm animals are connected with the four elements of earth, air, fire and water. If only there were still horses on farms, then the aspect of 'warmth' would be more completely

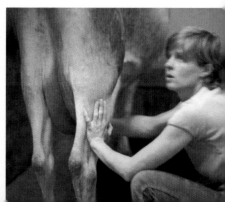

fulfilled. (Horse manure has always been prized by flower growers.) The dung of the pig specially fertilizes root crops and sheep's dung the stems and flowers. Much that we have been describing could be observed on a well-run organic farm, so what is different about biodynamics?

Origins of the biodynamic movement

The biodynamic movement grew out of the deep concerns of a group of farmers in central Europe back in the 1920s. They had noticed an increasing degeneration in seed strains, in many cultivated plants, and in their livestock. They approached Rudolf Steiner in 1924 seeking some insights and practical ideas to offset this decline. (How much has happened to exacerbate this trend since then!) Steiner envisaged what might happen if mineral fertilizers should be used extensively in farming rather than the natural fertility of animal manures and good compost. He said:

> The materialistic farmer who thinks about these matters can calculate how many decades it will be in this century before agricultural products have degenerated so far that they can no longer nourish the human being adequately. With the materialistic world conception, agriculture has come the furthest away from rational principles. (*Agriculture*)

He went on to predict how farm products would become so denatured that people would endeavour to make mineral blueprints of them, and here we are reminded of the growth of the mineral and vitamin supplement industry over past decades. Steiner pointed out that not only was the earth already middle-aged, but it would become increasingly sclerotic (declining in vitality) as a result of the developing materialistic view of the earth as a resource for human beings to exploit. When he was persuaded to offer his insights into agriculture, his aim was to try and correct a largely one-sided, mechanistic view of nature, entrenched as early as the 1920s. Steiner's approach offered a view of life that reconnected the earth and the cosmos, physical life with its origins, in a spiritual world-view—a vision that takes account of the powerful forces that pour down from the cosmos to work within the soil and plant. These forces stimulate the processes vital to agriculture, but in order for these beneficent influences to be fully active, the soil needs to be sufficiently sensitive. This in turn requires the use of natural organic fertilizing materials, to keep it alive. Coupled with this, special potentized 'medicines' (usually known as 'preparations') would be required for the compost heap and for spraying on the land, as well as a renewed understanding of planetary and zodiacal influences, to be creatively harnessed by the sensitive farmer.

The moon and its relation to the zodiac

The forces that come from the zodiac (Greek *zodiakos* means circle of animals) have always been recognized as being connected with the enlivening forces of the four elements, for the earth is indeed a living organism, deriving energy, warmth and light from the sun. The processes of rain, evaporation, day and night, summer and winter all depend on our relationship to the sun. The earth's satellite, the moon, particularly influences the movement of the waters on the surface of the earth, waters that are in constant ebb and flow according to the phases of the moon. As the moon circles the earth it is able to focus the particular aspect of each constellation rather like a lens, according to its passage in front of that sign. So that when the moon is in front of the constellation of Pisces, Cancer or Scorpio (all water signs), it magnifies their influence on the watery part of the plant—the leaves. The earth element (particularly favourable for root vegetables) can be stimulated by the arrangement of planting, hoeing or any work that disturbs the soil, at a time when the moon is in Capricorn, Taurus or Virgo (earth signs). Some bio-

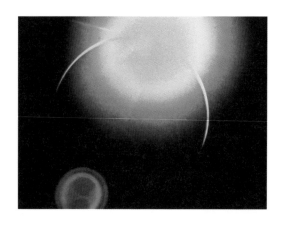

dynamic gardeners arrange their garden rotations so that each year a different plant activity is accentuated on each plot. Flowers should be grown under air signs (Gemini, Aquarius and Libra) and cereal and seed crops under the fire signs (Leo, Sagittarius and Aries).

The Roman scholar Pliny the Elder, in his *Natural History*, examined the influences of the moon's phases on vegetal and animal life. He observed that if one wanted juicy and good-looking fruits and vegetables for sale or for consumption, the optimal time to pick them was at full moon, just when ants were busiest in their hills, even at night, and marine animals such as oysters were in their period of burgeoning growth. At new moon the ants were seen to be listless and the growth of sea creatures slack. 'Fruit,' said Pliny, 'is much less susceptible to rotting at new moon and can be easily and efficiently dried.'

Virgil, born just after the death of Pliny, told in a discourse on agriculture how husbandmen took cues from the heavenly spheres and constellations to tell them when to sow their crops, certain seeds being best put into the ground when 'glittering Taurus opens the year with his golden horns'. Paracelsus—a healer and one of the last of the true alchemists—made much of the connections in astronomy and astrology for perceiving the 'signatures' of plants and to use remedies much more effectively, as did Nicholas Culpeper who saw that each planet was linked to a particular plant species, in turn connected to a particular organ of the body. From the seventeenth century onwards people following such traditional wisdom have been systematically marginalized, so we have lost the link to the cosmos.

Biodynamic farmer Alan Brockman adds:

> Each planet has its own force field; thus each planet can, at some time or other, be seen in every part of the zodiac. The earth can be pictured as being surrounded by seven spheres of force, of which each physically visible

planet is marking out its own particular boundary. These spheres were known as 'crystal spheres' (a description attributed to Ptolemy). Steiner indicated that the various leaf spirals and their positioning around the stem, or 'phyllotaxis', indicates which particular force field the plant is reacting to. So clearly plants and planets have correspondences, as healers such as Paracelsus and Culpepper knew.

The twentieth century—Maria Thun

Maria Thun has been farming with her family for many years using biodynamics in the state of Hessen, Germany. As a young farmer she encountered others who still used traditional methods related to the lunar cycle. She has made it her life's task to research into the influence of the moon on the life and growth of plants, and has been producing a biodynamic planting calendar for 40 years, using the results of her research. This calendar is enormously popular and is used by large numbers of farmers and gardeners. It has inspired similar calendars in at least five other countries. Maria Thun points out that with the ascending moon, plant forces and saps flow upwards more strongly to fill the plant with vitality. But when the moon has reached its highest point and begins to go down again, the plant then orients itself towards the root, making this a time more favourable to transplanting, as it enables 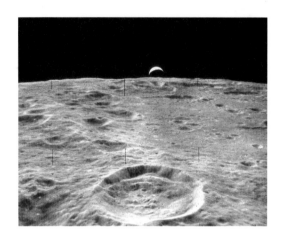 the plant quickly to form rootlets with which to anchor itself. As the sap flow weakens, it is also an appropriate time to prune trees or hedges. When the moon runs low on the horizon, echoing the sun's influence in autumn and winter, the vitality of plants concentrates in their lower parts and this then is a time for manuring, rooting, composting and harvesting root crops.

Richard Smith, who had an earlier career in the classroom, told me that his mind was opened to biodynamics after continued experiences with a pupil whose behaviour was extremely erratic during those full moon episodes. Subsequently he has met many people who admit to a kind of regular 'lunacy'. Gaols provide extra staff at full moon and people know that maternity wards will be particularly busy at this time. Perhaps you have your own observations.

Preparations 500–508

These preparations were born out of Rudolf Steiner's specific insights into the dynamic workings of what can only be called 'life-processes' and the rigorous and patient research carried out by the group of first biodynamic growers who gathered around him. These included Dr Ehrenfried Pfeiffer and Mr and Mrs Kolisko who spent many years researching and developing this important work. The first two biodynamic preparations are known as 'the horn preps'. Though it may sound bizarre, there is an enormous wisdom behind the bringing together of plant and animal 'sheaths', 'ripening' them in some way, and then potentizing them by a specific way of stirring a minute quantity into a large barrel of water.

There are two 'horn preps' and they work as opposite polarities. They are both stuffed into cow horns before being buried—for the winter in the case of the cow manure, and the summer for the Horn Quartz. Steiner pointed out that cow horns are natural attractors for cosmic forces, focusing and concentrating these forces into the preparations during their six-month burial in the bosom of the earth.

Horn Manure Preparation 500

In autumn fresh cow manure is packed into cow horns and they are then buried in winter, a time when the earth is most open to receiving cosmic forces. When dug up in the spring the contents are unrecognizable. A sweet-smelling, friable soil results, which when stirred into a barrel of tepid rain or spring water will be able to treat at a rate of approximately 3 oz per $3\frac{1}{2}$ gallons per acre.

This preparation works on the soil, promoting germination, root growth in the plant and assisting microorganism growth, and making the soil more sensitive. It acts as a regulator for the lime and nitrogen content in the soil and importantly aids the release of trace elements. The presence of many earthworms is another indicator of its effectiveness. This is the foundation remedy supporting all future work on the farm.

Horn Quartz or Silica Preparation 501

This works more in the atmosphere above the soil, helping the processes of flowering, fruiting and maturation, which can be seen more as expanding and contracting processes. The preparation is made by crushing the six-sided crystals of quartz into a fine powder and then placing the mixture again in a cow horn, but burying it this time during the summer months. When sprayed it acts as a growth stimulant that will transmit light forces as well as warmth, thus sensitizing the soil. It improves the plant's ability to form

chlorophyll and thus to photosynthesize, and it also has a beneficial effect on the flavour, nutritional value and keeping quality of food plants.

Richard Smith comments: 'A neighbouring farmer once saw me spraying a mist of the silica/quartz solution, so that it hovered over a field of oats in the early morning, as the sun's power gathered. Later he came back to ask me what I had been doing because he actually could see a difference in the crop.' The cell walls of the plant are largely a silica/cellulose compound and they are strengthened by this preparation, which can counteract an over lush and watery growth that encourages sap-sucking pests. It also deters mildew and fungal diseases. One needs only a tiny amount of this solution as it has great power.

The stirring of the preparations

In homoeopathy tiny amounts of substance are potentized by a process known as succussion, involving a progressive dilution of the substance in water through repeated shaking in a particular way. In biodynamics such dynamizing of tiny amounts of special preparations in a large container of rainwater is carried out by a special stirring process, which takes an hour to complete.

The purpose of stirring is to create a vortex. Through the vortex the maximum amount of water will be exposed to air and oxygen and, through this, to the forces of the cosmos. The repeated stirring and creation of the deeper vortexes open up a greater surface of water. It should be stirred in one direction until the vortex is deep. Having achieved this vortex of orderly swirling water, the direction should be reversed, which causes chaos to begin with, until a smooth, swirling deep vortex is again achieved.

The movement of the water energizes it, with rapid movement at the centre throwing water out to the sides and then, because of the friction at the sides of the container, the solution has to separate into thousands of sheaths, each moving at a different speed and each getting faster as it moves back towards the middle. These 'skins', just a molecule thick, rub against each other and a tremendous energy is built up in the process. The water palpably changes its condition, becoming silkier and livelier. One can feel how the spiral-shaped vortex reflects the whirling galaxies and the orbits of the planets around the sun. This mixture should be used within two hours of completing it.

It is essential to be really calm and concentrated while doing this, as it is a real meditation and reveals a great deal about water and earth processes. The stirring is usually done as a shared task, with friends and co-workers, and becomes a special community-building activity.

Herbal remedies, the Compost Preparations 502–507

The use of specific herbs and flowers for the compost preparations continues a long tradition of using these plants medicinally, some having particular planetary connections.

Space will not permit me to go into details of how they are made but there is much literature that gives the information. I will just list the plants that are used and indicate their properties and planetary connections:

Chamomile

Yarrow Blossoms 502 (*Achillea millefolium*). Specially connected with potassium and sulphur processes. Planetary relationship with Venus.

Chamomile Blossoms 503 (*Matricaria chamomilla*). Helps to stabilize nitrogen and stimulates micro-life. Connected with Mercury.

Stinging Nettle 504 (*Urtica dioica*). Vitalizes and enlivens soil. Rich in iron and silica. Connected with Mars.

Oak Bark 505 (*Quercus robur* or *Quercus alba*). Helps to neutralize alkaline soils, instead of using lime, and so bringing healthy calcium processes. By regulating calcium the oak bark prep also regulates moon forces of lush growth and fungal diseases.

Nettle

Dandelion

Dandelion Blossoms 506 (*Taraxacum officinale*). Also connected with silica (marvel at the silica skeleton of the dandelion clock!). Jupiter.

Valerian blossoms 507 (*Valeriana officinalis*). Valerian flowers draw warmth into their environment. Made into a juice as distinct from the other preparations, it is applied to the outside of the finished compost heap, allowing phosphorus to be used by the soil. Saturn and Mars.

The quality question

You may well ask, 'Why would anyone want to go to all this bother? Is this produce so superior?' From my point of view as a cook who has been using this produce for over 30 years, I would say a resounding 'Yes!' The produce speaks for itself in flavour, appearance, keeping quality (most important) and texture. The farmers that I have met who farm this way have a high integrity and are prepared to do what they do because they believe in it and observe the results. They are also convinced that biodynamics heals the earth.

One place where biodynamic agriculture thrives most successfully in the UK is in the Camphill Villages, created for people with special needs. The food grown is eaten by the community and any surplus will be sold in the farm shop. In these special places, plants, animals, winged creatures and human beings animate the landscape. Festivals that punctuate the year and honour the work on the land bring a warmth and gladness to the heart. I always try to go to my local biodynamic farm before Christmas when groups of people go to sing carols to the cows in their hay-lined byres. It is a truly remarkable experience. There is such a stillness and attentiveness amongst the animals, and the rosy faces of children reveal a glimpse of the original Christmas Eve!

'And what about scientific proof?' I hear you ask. Well, there is by now quite a body of research into the quality of foods produced by this method. You will understand that the reductionistic, materialist methods of modern science can only cope with the visible and measurable. Aroma, for example, is completely ignored as being of any significance to nutritional value (as a cook, I find this quite unbelievable, but a friend who has just returned from Cornell University with a Ph.D. in nutrition assures me that it is so). A method known as sensitive crystallization was pioneered by Ehrenfried Pfeiffer to demonstrate the qualitative aspects of biodynamic foods. In this method a little of the juice or dissolved substance of the product to be tested is crystallized in a solution of copper chloride. The process is carried out under controlled temperature and humidity conditions. The organizing shapes that arise provide information about the object's vital properties, or its 'life forces'. The pictures show rhythmic and integrated structures in plants grown biodynamically and organically, whereas conventionally grown plants often show a denaturing, with gaps in their organization—spaces, which can fill up with water, causing weak cell structure, and weak nuclei. Such plants have poor keeping quality compared to biodynamic or organic produce. Another qualitative method is capillary dynamolysis (using chromatography), developed by Lili Kolisko. This method is used to investigate the life quality of the soil, in addition to its nitrogen, phosphorus and potassium content. (See Bibliography for references for both methods.)

With the increase in trade of organic products, criteria other than those used in modern science have to be used to assess quality, and these picture-forming methods are now becoming more widely acknowledged and used. Assessment is clearer than with other methods. Dr Ursula Balzer-Graf is running a flourishing laboratory in Switzerland where such methodology is in increasing demand.

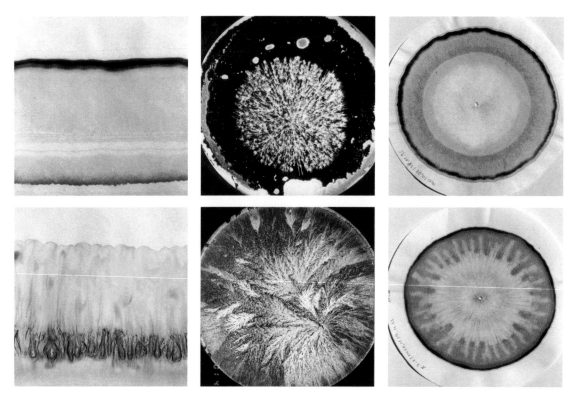

Experiments with 'sensitive crystallization'. The top pictures are the controls with 'metal salts' alone, while the bottom pictures include Demeter quality apples.
(*Journal of the Biodynamic Agricultural Association.*)

The effects of the biodynamic preparations were researched by the United States Department of Agriculture in 1999. Their researchers found that 'use of the biodynamic compost preparations could speed the composting process, better destroy pathogens and weed seeds in the material by maintaining elevated temperatures longer, and change the value of the resulting compost as a fertilizer by increasing the amount of nitrate'. (See Wright, H in Bibliography)

The German physicist Popp believes that it is impossible to measure by conventional means the energies necessary for maintenance of life processes. He has demonstrated that food of the highest quality shows the highest photon transmission, compared with average quality food of identical calorific value. (Photons are stored in the DNA during photosynthesis and transmitted continuously by living cells.) His work might also be applied to examining the essential nature of vitamins and minerals, around which topic much conflicting information exists.

Birth of a Galaxy

The question of sunlight—of 'light photons' being indicators of vitality in plant nutrition—is one of the most important areas of attention in research. Cereals are the most efficient of all traditional crops at assimilating maximum sunlight. As a teenager in the science lab I was astounded at the brilliant light that issued forth when a piece of magnesium ribbon was ignited.

When we think of plants having magnesium as their central molecule, this gives a clue to their light-capturing abilities, and when we begin to see the qualitative aspects of infinitesimally small substances wielding such a mighty force, we may begin to perceive life as organized coherence. The light principle then appears of paramount importance, leading to harmony in structure.

To close this chapter, it should be pointed out that biodynamics has been receiving great publicity recently. In one Sunday colour supplement alone there were three separate articles with references to biodynamics, mainly about restoring the superior quality conferred on the terroir, where grapevines are grown. One grower has been quoted as saying:

> If the best wines from Burgundy start to taste like the most banal wines from Australia because our soils have been made to become so similar, so denatured, from a saturation of the same chemical fertilizers and weedkillers, we will have lost not only our vinous heritage, but our raison d'être as winegrowers, too.
>
> Monty Waldin (*Jnl. Biodynamic Assn.*, Winter 2005)

If this subject is new to you, it will be worth finding some books with more background than I have been able to give here (see Bibliography). The use of biodynamic preparations has been shown to have immense restorative powers on exhausted soils, and biodynamic animals have better resistance to infection. Above all, the sensitivity of relationships between man, earth, animals and plants and the cosmic forces around us seem to me just what we are longing for in our world starved of such warmth and understanding.

I have an eighteenth-century ploughman's cup which bears the following verse:

Let the wealthy and great
Roll in splendour and state,
I envy them not, I declare it!
I eat my own lamb,
My own chickens and ham.
I shear my own fleece and I wear it.
I have lawns, I have bowers.
I have fruits, I have flowers.
The lark is my morning alarmer.
So Jolly Boys now
Here's God speed to the plough,
Long life and success to the farmer.

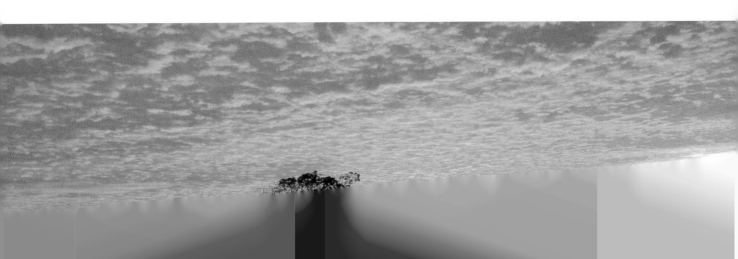

4 CREATING A BALANCED DIET

The issue of protein

In *The Dynamics of Nutrition* Dr Gerhard Schmidt says: 'There is no problem in modern nutritional science that is so hotly contested and so far from being settled as the question of the significance of protein.' So why has this subject become so controversial?

Firstly, what is protein? It can be found everywhere in the body as structural material in muscle, bone, blood, connective tissue and to some extent in cell walls. Protein is the universal 'carrier of life' and is distinguished from carbohydrates and fats by the presence of nitrogen. Protein molecules are the giants of the biochemical world and each one of these macromolecules is composed of a very long chain of building blocks known as amino acids. These chains are characterized by tremendous plasticity, facilitating flexible movement. Protein's nature is half liquid, half colloidal, and thousands of amino acids may be linked together in one chain. Over 20 kinds of amino acids occur in nature.

Until recently, standard sources of nutritional information insisted that there were eight essential amino acids that could not be synthesized by the human body and had to be provided by animal products, if not by meat then certainly by eggs, cheese and milk products. Behind such a view is a belief that plant protein is deficient in certain amino acids and incomplete for the purpose of human nutrition. Much of the research behind this thesis was conducted on rats! However, the fact that approximately two-thirds of the world's population live on foods mainly derived from plants indicates the contrary, i.e. nearly all whole grains, nuts and seeds have amino acid profiles adequate for human needs. Paul Pitchford in *Healing with Wholefoods* says: 'Each human being constructs his own individual protein as the specific forming substance of his own bodily nature. This is an expression of his ego' (the individualized self).

From a reductionist scientific point of view, plant, animal and human protein all appear to be identical at a molecular level. But animal protein is always something of a polar opposite to plant protein, and here we need to be aware of qualitative difference. For instance, in hen's eggs or caviar a reproductive protein predominates. In the plant (e.g. in nuts, seeds and cereals) there is a different kind of reproductive protein. Plant material leaves the nervous system free of the residues found in animal protein, since an animal's sentient life is imprinted upon its tissues and in its blood.

Despite the discovery that a judicial combining of plant products such as grains, legumes, seeds and nuts with some dairy products such as yoghourt can adequately fulfil human amino acid profiles, this tends to be ignored. The question most frequently asked of vegetarians is 'Where do you get your protein from?', showing how deeply imprinted dietary misinformation has become. It has led to synthesized meat being spun out of soya protein by highly costly industrialized processes, and the resulting product— odourless and colourless—is then injected with colourings and flavourings and sold as a meat substitute. Similar technology has led to the creation of new products out of yeasts and other microorganisms. This shows a disdain for any real nutritional wisdom, and as Paul Pitchford states:

'This mega-protein mania symbolizes the consciousness of a society based on continuous growth, as protein is the body's primary builder.'

(Healing with Wholefoods)

The question of vegetarianism

There are now at least four million vegetarians in the UK according to the Vegetarian Society, a number that is steadily growing. Many young people choose to abstain from meat, as did my own daughter. The motives for choosing a vegetarian diet may be manifold, including an ethical view embracing compassion for animals, spiritual discipline, environmental considerations, health, and financial reasons.

We in the West can no longer avoid scrutinizing our lifestyle and the way we impact on the wider environment. Unlike most people on the planet, we do have choices. The way we access and prepare our food is within our own hands. It is amazing what changes and insights come just from moving in the direction of vegetarianism, even if not totally embracing it, and beginning to use biodynamic or organic sources of food.

The current practice of fattening animals or birds indoors, in feed-lots in crowded conditions—fed low fibre diets, given no bedding and very restricted behavioural opportunities—makes for highly inappropriate living conditions both ethically and environmentally. These animals, which have obligingly provided us with milk, meat, wool and leather down the millennia, deserve better. How is it that we have become so alienated from that warm and intimate relationship which once existed between the herdsman and his cows, between shepherd and sheep? It is a real sign of spiritual deterioration in our society that we tolerate the suffering caused to our domestic animals by current intensive farming methods.

Of course there are farmers who still honour their animals and I must say I have been impressed with the special relationships that biodynamic farmers have with theirs. Since domesticated animals are no longer self-regulating, as most wild animals are, we have a special responsibility to respect their intrinsic needs and not over-breed them, for eventually it impacts upon us humans.

Currently the average western diet is composed of more than 50% animal products—in the USA over 60%—leading often to excess fat, cholesterol and an acidic condition in the blood. As a result there are many diet-related diseases such as diabetes and cancer. Meat of the type commonly eaten now would in the Ayurvedic tradition be labelled Tamasic and can fill the mind with dark emotions such as anger, aggression and greed.

Long ago Herodotus said, 'Among our humanity there are those who lead wars against one another, who relate through anger, antipathy and sensual passions. They draw this out of animal nutrition. They have, however, developed bravery, courage and boldness. Other cultures, occupied with more spiritual pursuits, have customarily used mostly plant nutrition.'

Rudolf Steiner, having looked at the physical processes involved in heavy meat-eating, said: 'We find that red blood corpuscles become darker and heavier and the blood has a greater tendency to clot. Phosphates and salts are produced more easily. With predominantly vegetarian food the sedimentation rate of the blood corpuscles is much lower' (*Nutrition and Stimulants*).

A diet too centred on meat products also tends to cause deposits of uric acid, which in excess become toxic in bodily tissues, particularly in the joints. Gout, caused by these deposits, was once considered to be the illness of the rich and idle and is still with us. Excessive uric acid is also implicated in arthritis. Our bodies are normally only able to excrete eight grains of uric acid per day; however, according to Dr Gabriel Cousins, eating 1 lb ($^1/_2$ kg) of meat would leave a residue of 18 grains of uric acid, hence the excess left in the tissues. Uric acid initially has a stimulating effect on the human being as its structure is similar to that of caffeine.

Of course there are few people who live solely from animal products and there are those who, despite attempting to, find themselves incapable of nourishing themselves on a purely vegetarian diet. The work on blood types as researched by Peter d'Adamo may provide us with some insights: 'The story of human survival is reflected in our digestive and immune systems. It is in these two areas that most of the distinctions in blood type are found. Blood provides a keystone for humanity, a looking glass through which we can trace the faint tracks of humanity' (*Eat Right for Your Type*).

Human teeth

Whilst studying the principles of macrobiotics I came across a system that made a lot of sense to me. If we look at the arrangement of the human teeth and the digestive tract we will see that they are intermediate between those of vegetarian and carnivorous creatures. Yet they have a character all their own, allowing the human being the possibility of being an omnivore, of eating a mixed diet.

Of a total of 32 teeth, five-eighths are molars, including pre-molars (from the Latin *molere*: to grind, the motion needed to masticate cereals); a quarter are incisors, best suited for cutting and slicing, particularly fruits and vegetables; and an eighth are canines, best for dealing with flesh foods. Thus in the macrobiotic system such a relationship of function is used as a guideline for choosing cereals, vegetables and fruits together with a small proportion of animal foods. Considering the composition of many traditional one-pot dishes of peasant cookery (like paella, couscous, risottos and cassoulet) it is noticeable that they are structured approximately in these kinds of proportions. In this book, which is not purely vegetarian, I try to follow these principles, but it is directed towards people in transition from an animal-based diet to one where at least two-thirds of the diet is from good plant sources. There is a great deal to learn, but it is interesting and important work involving a certain amount of trial and error.

Finally, we cannot leave this subject without touching upon the Achilles heel of the question of vegetarianism, the issue of the controversial vitamin B12. In healthy people B12 is manufactured in the colon through the action of beneficial bacteria. Small amounts also appear in the mouth enzymes. Foods that contain B12 are live yoghourt, miso and yeast products. The conditions for a healthy gut flora can be created by good nutritional habits.

It is very hard to have too little protein in a diet that consists of well-grown products: grains, vegetables, nuts, seeds, and some dairy produce. We need to demystify the discussion around protein, which has overemphasized the need for animal protein, and do our own experimenting.

The importance of grains in our diet

> I believe a leaf of grass is no less
> than the journey work of the stars …
> and the cow crunching with depressed head
> surpasses any statue.
>
> Walt Whitman

When we look at the composition of cereals we see some similarity to milk—a food that represents complete nourishment and feeds the whole person. To understand the nutritional impact of different foods, and particularly complex carbohydrates, we need to look at their structure. In the starch granules of properly grown cereals it is possible to see a rhythmical concentricity, indicating a harmony. When digested, this structure slowly releases reliable energy (unlike refined sugars, which 'peak and trough').

Wheat, rice and maize are the three most important food crops from the grass family (*Graminaceae*), which boasts some 6000 members; other familiar cereals are barley, millet, oats and rye. These cereals have for millennia provided major civilizations with their primary nutrition. Millet has been the grain of China and parts of Africa, rice was originally cultivated in the Far East, wheat and barley in the Middle East, the Mediterranean and Europe, and maize was the grain of the Americas. Rye, tamed and developed by the Romans, does not have the Neolithic antecedents of wheat or barley and thus is a relative newcomer.

Members of the grass family form a thick matted growth of roots that penetrate the soil, holding it together as turf, which can be seen as a living geological stratum encircling the planet. Anchored into the earth as no other plants are, the new blades of grasses and grains strive upward like spears of light that have taken root. Grains have a particular affinity to sunlight, and the strong vegetative growth is due to their ability to use light more efficiently than any other green plants. Up to 24% of incoming light is used for photosynthesis against 5–10% for other plants. It is no wonder that these crops have been so valued.

According to ancient mythologies each of the seven cereals was the gift of one of the revered gods, whose abodes were the planets and stars. For some cultures they were the gifts of the Seven Holy Rishis. In Greek mythology Demeter was the goddess of fertile cultivated soil who presided over the harvest. Her precious daughter Persephone was abducted by Hades, god of the underworld, for six months of the year. Thus she became the goddess of death and resurrection through her descent into the underworld and subsequent return to the earth, which is beautifully illustrated by the annual rotation of the crop of the Barley Mother, the goddess Demeter. (Demeter is used as the symbol for biodynamically grown produce.)

Wheat

The oldest known cultivated plant, growing abundantly in the Fertile Crescent of the Middle East. The bread wheat known today is now assumed to have been derived from a crossing of wild Emmer wheat and another *Aegilops* grass species. In our present time wheat has been bred specifically to make it contain increasingly higher percentages of gluten, so that the bakery industry can produce an elastic dough that holds a lot of air. This has led to a distortion of the normal balance in this most ancient grain of the sun, so that many people experience gluten allergies. Kamut and spelt are durum-related, traditional wheat varieties, which many people find they are able to digest more easily.

Rice

Developed in the Far East and is the staple diet of over half the world's population. It is the crop requiring the most human labour. Seeds are germinated in a nursery and then each seedling must be carefully transplanted into half-submerged fields. The harvest must also be done by hand. With such a special relationship to water, this plant can be seen to have correspondences with the moon, which affects our watery tides.

Dr Gerhard Schmidt in *The Dynamics of Nutrition* says of rice, 'No culture that is based on rice can be completely materialistic. Rice, unlike the potato, needs little salt. Among the rice-eating peoples of the Far East there is less of a desire for salt.' In addition, the high phosphorus content of rice helps to support the time-honoured spiritual disciplines that still live strongly in these cultures.

However, it is a tragedy that even people suffering from malnutrition insist on eating polished rice, leaving them with nothing more than pure starch. Researching vitamin B, Dr Robert Runnels said: 'Man commits a crime against nature when he eats the starch from the seed and throws away the mechanism necessary for the metabolism of that starch, notwithstanding the loss of the most vital nutritional elements.'

Varieties of rice are: Patna and Basmati, traditional Indian varieties with fine-pointed grains and a distinctive aroma; Arborio, from Italy, is bred for risottos and so is sticky and absorbs the cooking flavours. So-called 'wild rice' is from a different botanical genus, and is harvested by North American Indians where it grows along the low-lying lakesides of Minnesota. It contains higher levels of protein and minerals than the true rice varieties. Both whole short-grain and long-grain rice are very nutritious.

Maize

For the Aztec and Mayan civilizations maize (*Zea mays*) was their principal food. Maize grows taller than a man and has the strongest stalk structure of all the grains. No greater contrast to rice could be imagined, with its heavy ears emerging from several nodes lower down the stalk; only the male flowers carrying pollen appear at the top of the stem and form the tassels. The

varieties are flint corn (now used for cattle feed) and dent corn, used to make polenta, tacos and tamales. Blue corn was indigenous to south-west America and was used by the Hopi and Navajo who planted it in raised mounds together with squash and beans.

Millet (sorghum)

Was used originally in China and is now an important staple in Africa, India and Asia. The long-living Hunza people use millet with yoghourt as a staple food combination and the people of Java grow millet as a border plant around their rice paddies to stimulate the growth of their rice plants. Millet is particularly high in silica. Varieties include foxtail millet, known as Italian or yellow millet; pearl millet, also known as bulrush or cat tail; and broomcorn millet.

Barley

This grain has been fundamental to the ancient Tibetan civilization, it was used as currency by the ancient Sumerians and was honoured in the Greek Mysteries. In Roman times it was used to bake the bread of the poor. The loaves in the biblical 'feeding of the five thousand' were barley loaves. It is a warming and comforting cereal. Barley flour can be mixed in with wheat flours for a good loaf. Pearl barley has been polished, destroying the nutritious aleurone layer, but it is lighter and can be used in soups like Scotch broth.

Oats and rye

These cereals of the north were only taken into cultivation less than three millennia ago. Oats are one of the younger cereal varieties, and have been adopted enthusiastically by the Scots. With the highest fat content of all the cereals (4%), oats are known to protect the heart, balance cholesterol and

help circulation, and have also been useful in treating mild cases of diabetes.

By the Middle Ages rye had become a staple throughout Europe and was especially popular in Germany, Russia and Scandinavia. Ergot, a parasitic fungus that attacks the rye plant, contains LSD (lysergic acid) which attacks the central nervous system and can cause hallucinations.

Rye is lower in gluten than wheat, so the rye loaf will not rise like a wheaten loaf; however, many people may find it more digestible than wheat. Rye groats can be soaked and cooked like rice or cracked and kibbled to shorten cooking time.

Other grains

Coming back into popularity are some other 'grains' that do not belong to the grass family but are nevertheless very nourishing. The seeds of certain species of amaranth, that belong to the love-lies-bleeding family (Amaranthaceae), and quinoa, a member of the goosefoot family (Chenopodiaceae) were once used by the Aztecs. Buckwheat, the beloved kasha of the Russians, is a member of the dock family (Polygonaceae).

Sugar

Few people will deny the need for sweetness; since our first food, breast milk, is immensely sweet (more than 7% sugar), we may understand that sweetness plays a significant role in nutritional needs. The human brain uses the most sugar, in the form of sucrose, followed by the heart and limbs. Sugar is a carbohydrate—metamorphosed sunlight, if you like—and its best source is via the digestion of complex carbohydrates derived from grains, fruits, vegetables, seeds and nuts. Their complex carbon chains are broken down more slowly than sugars, releasing energy in a rhythmical and sustained fashion and bringing their characteristic warmth to the human organism.

Paul Pitchford in *Healing Foods* points out: 'Eating complex carbohydrates maximizes the concentration in the bloodstream of the amino acid L-tryptophan which is manufactured within the brain into the "calming" chemical serotonin. Most people feel calmer within half-an-hour of a carbohydrate snack.' White sugar, on the other hand, is a 'stripped' carbohydrate and consists largely of empty calories. The correct metabolism of sugar will only proceed through the use of all the necessary nutrients involved in its digestion, hence the importance of quality.

I see the 'sweet pole' as the 'heavenly pole', with salt representing the 'earthly pole'. Somehow we must try to mediate our nutritional needs between these two polarities. It is interesting to note that the wonders of the Renaissance were achieved on an average sugar consumption of one teaspoonful per head per year! What a contrast to today, especially in western countries.

The first sugar arrived in Europe in 1319 and England soon became the largest consumer of sugar. Queen Elizabeth was known to be addicted to it. When Napoleon blockaded Europe in 1806, stopping the cane sugar trade, beet sugar was already being developed. We know that the roots of plants are particularly stimulating to the brain and nervous system (see Chapter 5). When we extract sugar from a root source, although apparently chemically the same, qualitatively it is substantially different from sugar derived from stems (cane sugars, maple syrup) and from blossom sugar, i.e. honey.

According to Rudolf Steiner, sugar in its essential state and in appropriate amounts has the potential to awaken the human self and to develop the necessary forces for mental and physical work. But the increasing consumption of sugar appears to be in direct ratio to the increasing per capita income of a nation. Such a high consumption of refined carbohydrate in the form of pure refined sugar places a heavy burden on the liver, which has to regulate sugar concentration in the blood.

Cane sugar is made by first crushing the cane in a press and removing impurities from the juice, which is then boiled down until it begins to crystallize. The liquid is separated by centrifuge, leaving raw sugar. It is further refined using steam to clean it (the industrial process is very heavy on technology, energy and the environment). Beet sugar has a similar but even more wasteful manufacturing process.

Honey

In olden times the wisdom of beekeepers related the whole wonderful activity in the beehive to the life of love, that part of life ruled by the planet Venus. The whole hive can be seen to be permeated with love. Individual bees, however, renounce love and sexual activity, which is reserved for the queen bee and some successful drones. The temperature in the hive is critical and is the same as human blood (37°C). The bees work completely as a unity, arranging all their activity so that everything is in harmony within this special atmosphere of warmth.

In addition to bees' symbiotic relationship with flowers and blossoms, they also receive many influences from the starry worlds. The life of the sprouting, budding love displayed in the flowers appears in the honey. When eaten by humans, honey furthers the beneficial connections between the airy and watery elements and has a favourable influence on the harmonizing of human breathing, particularly in the young child. Honey is a special substance with strengthening qualities that, in small quantities, supports the nutritive health of both young and old. Thus we could see beekeeping as a great help in advancing our civilization. But we must be respectful of how much honey we take from the bees, and not deprive them of their winter supplies.

The hexagonal structure of the cells that the bees create using their wax-secreting glands communicates form to the larvae. The queen bee, however, is bred in a special

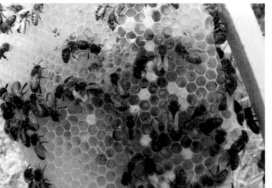

sac-shaped cell and matures after only 16 days; a worker bee requires 21 days, and the drone (male) 24 days. Twenty-one days is the time needed for the sun to turn on its axis, so the worker bee is exposed to all that the sun can give and thus is entirely 'a child of the sun'. The drone, in its slightly longer maturation period, is subjected to earthly forces which give it the power to fertilize.

The queen is much nearer to her more spherical larval state and is, too, a sun-related creature. She produces eggs, which are fertilized by the drones; thus sun and earth forces are united. The fertilization of the queen bee takes place in full sunlight and as high as she can fly towards the sun. Only drones that have the strength to overcome the earthly forces of gravity and can reach her in her marriage flight will be successful. Then the queen returns to the hive to lay her eggs. When a new queen comes into being she needs to form a new community, and so swarming takes place.

> It is not realized how important the consumption of honey actually is. For example, if it were possible to influence the social medicine of today, it would be discovered that if people ate honey as a preparation for having children, the laying down of their bony structure would be enhanced.
>
> (Rudolf Steiner, *Bees*)

Seasonality

The move away from the land, where people only ate what was in season, superficially appears to be liberating. It is now possible to eat strawberries and melons in December, brought from climates completely different to our own. But what do they taste like? And what does eating out of season do to our sensibilities and capacity to be in tune with our environment and ourselves?

For me biodynamic cookery has to begin with seasonality, the most important nutritional and ecological starting point for any menu planning. Each food is a special aggregate, with its own shape and composition of finely tuned substances that are unique to it and its time of maturation in the calendar. The oils, carbohydrates, fibre, cellular fluids, proteins, minerals and, most importantly, the colour represent what can only be described as 'a message from the cosmos'. It also has a basis in tonality, which can present as either harmonious or discordant. Our organisms 'read' a substance through an amazing series of tasting and sorting processes, involving not only tasting in the

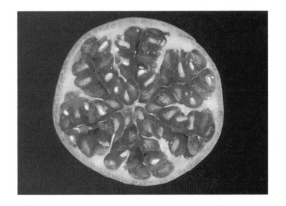

mouth but also in the gut, with its tiny finger-like villi, which if extended would cover an area the size of a football pitch. Then we have to completely destroy the substances in a catabolic (breaking-down) process and build it into our own flesh, blood and bone (an anabolic process). That is why the expression 'You are what you eat' is rather inaccurate, for if we were not able to destroy so completely the form of what we take in as foods we would certainly be walking about looking like lamb chops or beetroots!

The following question is therefore very important: 'What kind of encoded message does your food give to your body and soul?' Is it nature's best seasonal offering, grown with the care and intelligence that biodynamic or organic husbandry confers, or does it consist of cheap, mass-produced, processed and synthetic 'products'? It really depends what we want to align ourselves with. If we choose the latter type of diet the biochemical impulses will inevitably be distorted in such a way that cravings are set up, constantly requiring inputs of those denatured and incomplete substances; and because they tend to be so unbalanced it is unlikely that there will ever be a feeling of satisfaction or repleteness. The result can be the urge for constant snacking.

All products that have been grown with artificial fertilizers and pesticides and then subjected to industrial food processing will be unbalanced to varying degrees. In contrast, nature provides each food with its own nutritional completeness where its unique 'natural packaging' ensures that all the necessary nutrients are there for proper assimilation. Processing usually strips the food of this packaging (often the fibre) and therefore the body has to supply from its own 'metabolic pool' that which has been taken away, in order to complete digestion. (As in the case of polished rice; so many nutritional problems could be overcome if people were to eat whole rice.)

My intention in this book is to put forward a solid case for choosing a large percentage of locally grown food and wherever possible to access biodynamic or organically grown products.

The importance of wild food

> There are few studies which compare the nutritional values of uncultivated wild plant foods with their agricultural cousins grown as commercial crops. However, a study of edible vegetables eaten in Crete found that wild green-leafed plants used in traditional cuisine were rich in phytonutrients, such as antioxidants, flavonols and flavones.
>
> *Food Magazine,* January 2004

At the time of writing, young nettles are coming up and I can feel just how my body soaks up their special qualities when they are lightly-cooked—they are rich in iron, silica and formic acid. The iron activity in the plant stimulates iron activity in the human being. A small amount goes a long way and it is one of the most purifying and detoxing plants you can find. I have been making nettle tea, nettle and oat soup, nettle dumplings and nettle soufflés—delicious! Nettles can be found growing in many places on wastelands and the edges of woods (avoid those which grow anywhere near car exhaust fumes). Take only the tender top shoots—about six leaves. Harvesting, washing and sorting them is helped by wearing rubber gloves.

Other wild foods to be gathered include: sorrel, wild garlic, young dandelions, birch leaves for elixir, elderflowers and berries, rock samphire, purslane, sloes, field mushrooms (fungi), crab apples, black-berries, rosehips and hazel nuts.

Planning a menu

The macrobiotic and Ayurvedic systems favour a balanced diet: 35–60% whole grains; 25% vegetables; 15% fruits and salads; 5–10% legumes, lentils, nuts

and seeds; and 10–15% animal products (dairy, fish and meat). The Ayurvedic system indicates that we need to eat in a way that reflects what we want to achieve in life. For this it outlines three categories, which I think are worth thinking about. First, a Sattvic diet suits the scholar's or spiritual student's way of life, of study, contemplation and meditation as well as some fairly demanding physical work. It excludes any foods that excite the nervous system, i.e. no meat, garlic, onions, spices or wine, but mainly freshly prepared grains, vegetables and herbs, fruits, yoghourt, curd cheese and spring water. The second category is the Rajasic one for kings and warriors, for people doing physical labour, and maybe for today's businessmen. It allows meat, wine, garlic and onions, fruits and vegetables and spices—foods that can stimulate and engender passion, even aggression. The last category is known as Tamasic and refers to dead, pre-served or spoilt food that has no spark of life in it. This category would cover all of our fast and convenience foods, products designed to produce automata—people who would tend not to think for themselves.

In our menu-planning we should be guided by the first two categories. Sometimes we need to be stimulated and sometimes we need to be quiet and contemplative, and we should be aware that children need special consideration when it comes to what they might eat. If we are wise cooks, knowing the individual and collective properties of our ingredients, we can use a wide range of ingredients in moderation and to good effect.

After I trained in Japanese diet and cuisine, I found myself working as part of a team that cooked for 200 people at Emerson College, an adult training centre in Sussex. Our diners represented around 25 different nationalities, of different ages and all with their own food traditions. This was indeed a special challenge. The College had its own bio-dynamic farm so we were fortunate in having a constant supply of freshly harvested farm produce: vegetables, fruits, freshly ground flour, milk, eggs and yoghourt. Some students were studying, some doing artistic and craft work, and some were gardening and farm-ing. Others worked in the offices or were teaching. We had to come up with meals that provided for all these differences. We started to work with a menu-plan using the principle of root, leaf, stem and fruit (cereal being an example of the fruiting process), which evolved from the work of the medical doctor Rudolf Hauschka who had applied Steiner's ideas to the practical matter of daily nutrition. This concept got us away from the dry, reductionist paradigm of measuring foods as proteins, fats and carbohydrates and gave us a living and artistic matrix upon which to plan really balanced, life-giving meals. It involved quite a bit of thinking at first, but very soon became second nature.

We also worked with the seven cereals in a way that each grain corresponded to a day of the week and therefore to a planet: Sunday (day of the sun), Monday (*Lundi*, moon day), Tuesday (*Mardi*, Mars day), Wednesday (*Mercredi*, Mercury day, or Wodan's day) Thursday (*Jeudi*, Jove's, Jupiter's or Thor's day), Friday (*Vendredi*, Venus or Freya's day) and Saturday (*Samedi* or Saturn's day). In mythology, each grain is a gift of a planetary being (see *Foodwise*) and each day has its own particular atmosphere or character. The planning of a meal around a particular grain gave a discipline and rhythm to the week (though we also had potatoes sometimes). We applied the 'root, leaf, stem and fruit' principle to whatever was produced by garden and farm.

It is always a help to have a wide range of dishes from which to draw and to have tasted many different types of cuisine, so that one can be truly creative with ingredients. Ingredients are like paints on an artist's palette—and we seek to stimulate the human palate with its seven areas located on the tongue to register sweet, sour, salty, bitter, oily, astringent and sharp or hot flavours. Then there are temperatures of hot, warm, cold and frozen, and textures that are soft, crunchy, smooth, silky, etc. In addition, there are energetic and qualitative phenomena that a good cook will grow to appreciate; all of these will become part of one's unconscious alchemical dictionary which, once absorbed, becomes practice. As we become more confident we can experiment, discovering little secrets. For example, fresh orange slices bring the fruiting, blossoming quality to an earthy salad of beetroots; a little grated horseradish with cream in the beetroot salad adds the mustard oils that stimulate our thinking process. We can try adding some berries—blueberries, blackcurrants or cranberries—to bring an astringent flavour into a casserole of game. We learn that fennel seeds cooked with the brassica family can stop undue flatulence, that radishes have a diuretic action. These considerations are not just gimmicks, but knowledge that we can gain to enhance food and its preparation.

Let us summarize what the main considerations are when planning a meal: what is in season and locally available (or what you have in your garden); the ages and occupations of your diners (office workers, elderly people, children, farmers?); your budget; the constraints on your time; your cooking capabilities; the weather; the time of day for the meal; and so on. Think of the various textures, colours and flavours—let them sing harmoniously. (It is not a bad idea to build up gradually your repertoire of dishes, but do experiment and be creative. If you choose a recipe and don't have some of the ingredients, understanding their function in the dish will enable you to decide whether you might improvise by using other alternatives, especially when it is a question of fruit and vegetables.)

Most of all we are aiming to achieve a balance in our menu-planning and to retain and enhance the life forces (or vitality) in our food.

The meal

There appears to be a great deal of controversy about what we should or should not eat, but little discussion about how and when and where we should eat. Increasingly, a microwave oven displaces a stove or cooking range, or homes are designed with just a breakfast counter and no space for a dining table. From the dining table to the altar, sacred rhythms and rituals of life that used to bind family and community together are quickly being eroded, and for what? The dining table used to be a magnet in the home where as well as hosting meals and cups of tea with friends, where joys and sorrows were shared, homework was done, Christmas cards created, jigsaw puzzles pondered over and a whole teeming life of activity was played out. It was a place where we learned to care for each other's needs and the art of conversation, to savour the fruits of garden and kitchen, to feel nurtured and satisfied. For most of my family life we were blessed by a large farmhouse kitchen table, which seated eight to ten people comfortably. Every Saturday morning it was ritually scrubbed and fresh flowers were placed in the centre. This table had been witness to many wonderful meals and extraordinary conversations (and some disputes, too, admittedly).

The dining table must return to our lives, our homes, our inner and outer spaces. To enjoy a meal we should sit down, leaving our watches and our mobile phones elsewhere, for the convivial enjoyment of food and companionship. (The word companion derives from the Latin *cum panis*, so breaking bread together we become companions in bread.) Eating together can be a sublime experience, but it rarely is if you are sitting down to factory-prepared meals out of aluminium containers.

It is important to rediscover rhythm. This is different from routine and should be linked into human and natural biorhythms. Mealtimes fall at appropriate intervals and we should therefore come to the table with a healthy appetite. We cast envious glances across the Channel to those slim pâtisserie-eating French women who apparently 'don't get fat'. The *Observer* monthly supplement on food noted: 'They enjoy a sensible, sensuous way of eating. Just watch them dip mussels into marinière broth (made on the premises, of course) at any brasserie in St Germain. They savour their food. They have a natural heritage devoted to and founded upon food. Eating is a life-enriching exploit, not a chore and certainly not a guilt trip.' In France 76% of the population eat meals prepared at home. The markets flourish, showing that food is carefully chosen. A meal is a pleasure to share; small courses give time for a feeling of benevolence to arise and with it stimulating conversation, usually assisted by a glass of good wine (savoured, not slugged down).

Enjoy this comment from a Frenchman observing the British: 'If you want to learn to drink as we do, you must work less, you must learn to cook, learn to love to cook and to want to spend six hours in your kitchen, and to receive friends. You must enjoy being lazy and taking a long time for lunch breaks away from your office. You must learn to love discussing flavours, tastes and smells.' (*The Independent*, 24 January 2005.) A meal in France may take in excess of two hours to prepare. Contrast this with the current average 15 minutes in a British household. A positive backlash to this tendency is the Slow Food Movement, started in 1989. Its literature states the following: 'A firm defence of quiet material pleasure is the only way to oppose the universal folly of fast life... Let us rediscover the flavours and savours of regional cooking and banish the degrading effects of fast food.'

5 THE THREEFOLD PLANT

In order to understand why we might design a menu around the threefoldness of the plant we will look more closely at the plant-human relationship. It was Plato who described the human being as an 'upside-down plant', with roots reaching to the heavens and branches to the ground. Rudolf Steiner carried this metaphor further when speaking about nutrition and agriculture. Humans, animals (including birds and insects, of course) and plants live in a finely tuned symbiosis. The plant stands as a mirror to the human (and animal). The potential for warmth within the plant comes from its miraculous ability to catch and transform sunlight in the chlorophyll process that utilizes the so-called 'porphyrin ring'. Professor Brian Swimme describes this as follows:

> By means of the plants, the sun's rays are transformed into flesh. Alone of all the life forms, plants can not only catch sunlight, but by a unique alchemy [the porphyrin ring] compound it with terrestrial ingredients to make the basis of food and substance of all living things

> *(The Universe Story)*

The plant's 'blood' is its green sap, contrasting with the red blood of the human (these two colours are complementaries). Blood has an iron molecule in its nucleus but the iron cannot act without the presence of magnesium, whereas in the plant it is magnesium that is found in the central molecule but needs the presence of iron for its activity. The human being and animal breathe in oxygen and breathe out carbon dioxide; the plant reverses this process absorbing carbon, turning it into food, and breathing out oxygen. So we are greatly indebted to the plant world and cannot live without it. We live in a stream of vital exchanges that have an intrinsic lawfulness.

There are two main plant groups: the monocotyledons (one seed-leaf) and the dicotyledons (two seed-leaves). The monocotyledons are represented by the lily, and include, among others, bulbous plants, e.g. onions (*Allium* species), and the grasses (Gramineae). The dicotyledons (two seed-leaves) are represented by the rose, and most of our fruit trees—apple, pear, cherry and plum—belong to the Rosaceae family).

Many plants demonstrate a threefoldness: the root; the leafy part where starches are formed; then rising upwards, the blossom and fruits (which include seeds, nuts and cereal grains). It is at this last stage that starches are refined into sugars and sugars become glycosides, contributing to the plant's colour and fragrance. Later the fruit process develops. In contrast to this upwardly refining movement we find plant tissues become more condensed and tending to be ligneous the closer we get to the roots.

Polarity of plant and human being

The root, leaf (including stem) and fruit (including seeds, etc.) have a corresponding polarity in the human being, which can be seen in the nervous system (centred in the head), the breathing-rhythmic system (heart and lung) and the metabolic-limb system (intestines and limbs).

The root

The root of the plant is most sensitive to the earth. It often spreads out over wide distances where its fine lateral rootlets seek out and select minerals, salts and water in the cool depths of the earth. These substances are then lifted up and vitalized through fine capillary systems from the dark into the light. The root is the most dense and mineralized part of the plant; in cutting up a carrot or beetroot we can see crystalline, sometimes star-shaped structures.

The human nervous system, centred in the head, also seeks out, selects and vitalizes thoughts and concepts. The brain depends upon fine amounts of trace minerals such as phosphorus to carry out its activities. It also functions best when slightly cooler than the rest of the body. It shares these characteristics with root vegetables.

The leaf

The leafy part of the plant with its large surface area for assimilating sunlight is where respiration occurs. In a well-grown plant it unfolds rhythmically node by node. Rudolf Steiner compared this to the human heart-lung or rhythmic system. The spine, with the ribs enclosing the chest, is where the lungs are found, and this corresponds to the respiratory function of the leafy plant.

It gives a picture of how the leaf can be particularly helpful in stimulating a proper breathing process in the human being

Blossom and fruit

In the part of the plant where blossom, fruit and seed are created we find warmth and sugar formation. In the human belly we find a greater degree of warmth and activity, indicating that the fruiting part of the plant is particularly nourishing to the metabolic, digestive process.

Naturally these elements all work together, exchanging, reinforcing and enhancing each other when the processes are healthy.

We will now briefly look at some of the main plant families that provide us with a variety of foods:

Umbelliferae (carrot family). These plants demonstrate dense and bulky root systems but above ground we find fine feathery leaves and heads of delicate lacelike flowers (umbels). Members of this family are highly developed in attracting and transforming light forces and provide us with some of our most highly nutritious foods. They generally help with the breakdown of the products of digestion and with the excretory processes (sweat and urine). Carrots are especially worth mentioning; the blossom process that usually produces colour and sweetness in the plant has in this case been drawn down into the root, giving it colour, fragrance and sweetness. Rich in trace minerals, the carrot contains magnesium, iron, calcium, potassium, phosphorus, arsenic, nickel, cobalt, iodine and manganese. In addition we will find considerable quantities of silicic acid with its special relationship to light. This may well justify the old saying that carrots help you see in the dark. Carotene is also one of the important ingredients. Carrots are particularly beneficial in a child's diet, helping to stimulate a proper silica-building process and a sensitive nervous system, as well as strengthening teeth, brittle nails and hair.

Other vegetables in this family include parsnip, celeriac, Florence fennel, Hamburg (or root) parsley. Herbs in this family are: lovage, sweet fennel, chervil, dill, coriander and parsley. Aromatic seeds, which contain essential oils, are produced by: coriander, cumin, aniseed, fennel, and caraway. (The poisonous 'fool's parsley' and hemlock also belong to the Umbelliferae.)

Cruciferae (cabbage family). Plants in this family have evolved from the wild *Brassica maritima* and are recognizable at the flowering stage by the four petals that form a cross. Sulphur, with its warming quality, is a characteristic component of this family of vegetables, occurring in the waxy, resin-like coating on leaves and stems. It gives a plasticity that has allowed different parts of the plant to be developed into many different vegetables, such as turnip (root), kohlrabi (swollen base of stem), white cabbage (solid leaf head), red cabbage (sweet leaf head), savoy cabbage (curly leaf head), kale/spring greens (curly open leaves), Brussels sprouts (swollen leaf buds), cauliflower (single large swollen blossom head), broccoli (several swollen flower buds). Other crucifers that are also rich in sulphur are radish, mustard and cress, watercress, rocket, mitsumi and horseradish; they help to quicken a slow digestion, and stimulate liver processes.

Chenopodiaceae (goosefoot family). Here we find beetroot, similar in properties and value to the carrot, sugar beet, mangel, spinach beet, seakale, Swiss chard and fat hen. These plants are strong in sugars and mineral salts.

Compositae (daisy family). This family includes daisies and has many plants that contribute to both the culinary and medicinal spheres. A harmonious and rhythmical structure is shown in their complex flower-heads. Food plants include the lettuces, endive, chicory and salsify, both Jerusalem and globe artichokes and their relative, the sunflower. Medicinal plants are chamomile and dandelion (both used in biodynamic preparations), arnica, mugwort, wormwood, marigold and tarragon. Globe artichokes are particularly good in stimulating liver processes, arnica for bruising (both internally and externally), and marigold petals are lovely in salads and rice puddings (instead of saffron).

Cucurbitaceae (squash family). This family includes cucumbers, marrows and courgettes, pumpkins, summer and winter squashes, melons, watermelons and gourds. With their high water content they tend to have a cooling effect on the metabolism. All members of this family need warmth and a rich soil for optimum growth.

Polygonaceae (sorrel family). This family features buckwheat (traditionally used in the Balkans and often mistaken for one of the seven cereals), as well as sorrel and rhubarb whose oxalic acid content gives them purgative properties.

Convolvulaceae (bindweed family). This family provides the exquisite blue of the morning glory. Surprisingly, it also supplies us with sweet potatoes, which were first cultivated in Peru and have now spread around the world. In America they are often called yams, but the true yams belong to the Dioscoreaceae family.

The Malvaceae provide the vegetable okra (gumbo) as well as the mallows and hollyhocks.

Labiatae (nettles family). Members of this family are noted for offering themselves (or their lips, labia). Through their leaves and flowers they exude powerful fragrance that help both assimilation and purification of the blood. Examples are the various mints, melissa (lemon balm), marjoram, rosemary, sage, thyme and summer savoury. They demonstrate a very rhythmical growth process connected with warmth and mineral salt formation.

The legume family (Papilionaceae) includes peas, beans, lentils, clovers and vetches. Their flowers appear like 'trapped butterflies', hence the name (*papillon* = butterfly). Like the Solanaceae family they are associated with unusually high levels of nitrogen, that element necessary for the creation of protein. In farming the legumes are known for their properties of nitrogen-fixing and traditionally used in strict rotation with other crops. Rudolf Steiner pointed out that these plants thus have specific functions.

> However, we must learn to see each plant species in relation to the total organization of the plant-world, so that we understand the role of each one in balance. If we lose sight of this, the danger is very great that in the near future, when still more of the traditional ways of agriculture are lost, humans will adopt erroneous paths in the application of the new ...
>
> (*Agriculture*)

In need of special mention in this family is the Soya bean. In China and Japan the soya bean was seen as 'the vegetable cow'. However, raw soya beans are highly indigestible, they contain toxic substances that interfere with the action of trypsin, a protein-digesting enzyme in the intestinal tract. The traditional Japanese, understanding this difficulty, cleverly devised ways of transforming raw soya beans into products highly nutritious for that particular culture. This involved long fermentation processes (up to three years for miso and tamari), using sea salt and a special bacillus.

In recent times soya has become something of a panacea plant, with its properties of mimicking other substances and holding them fast. It is now used in medicines (plant oestrogens), cosmetics, paints, milk substitute, ice cream, sausages and pet food. It is the chief source of lecithin which 'smoothes the way', giving the silky smoothness to chocolate and sauces. It also hinders the crystallization of sugars, and fatty substances are made lighter (e.g. margarine is made to contain 20% water). Soya flour mixed with wheat flour prevents shrinkage in baking. It has this useful capacity to expand and hold water, the volume increased literally by a watering-down of quality. Most of all soya is used as oil-cake for cattle fodder. Many countries dilute their olive oil with imported American soya oil.

A recent book has this warning about soya formula for babies:

> Infants on soya formula may receive the equivalent amount of oestrogen to that found in 5–10 birth control pills each day. Boys on a soya-based formula are also ingesting oestrogen and manufacturing large amounts of testosterone. Receiving these confusing hormonal messages can wreak havoc with a child's emotionality!
>
> (Carol Simontaachi, *Crazymakers*, Putnam, 2000)

> As we witness the proliferation of soya production worldwide, seeing forests in Brazil and Argentina being cut down for its cultivation, we may well need to ask ourselves about the value of this product—'once a veggie option and now the invisible ingredient in most processed foods'.
>
> (*Observer Food Monthly*, No. 44)

Solanaceae (potato family). See page 21-22.

The soya bean

6 What Do We Do When We Cook?

'We can cook a better world.'—Michael Symons

Nowadays we always seem to defer to scientific research, but is it the whole picture? When I was taught domestic science at grammar school instruction was given on food hygiene and the importance of proteins, fats and carbohydrates. Even the Edwardians had reverence for science; here is what Mrs Beaton had to say in her Great New Edition of 1909 about why we cook our foods:

> 1) To render mastication easy; 2) To facilitate and hasten digestion; 3) To convert certain naturally hurtful substances into nutritious foods; 4) To eliminate harmful foreign elements in food (e.g. the tapeworm, or tinea in beef and mutton, trichinae in pork, the ptomaines resulting from tissue waste); 5) To combine the right foods in proper proportions for the needs of the body; 6) To make it agreeable to the palate and to the eye.

We can see here the scientific paradigm given priority, with sensual and aesthetic aspects last on the list. Of course, cooking is a science, it is chemistry, and it has a lawfulness that we should learn before we get carried away with its amazing creative possibilities. But surely there is a limit to how much information we need in order to nourish ourselves? At present we have absurd developments that exploit this 'scientific' approach and play on a lack of insight into our real nutritional needs. For instance, a restaurant that serves a £55 lunch (for the wealthy and weight-conscious) consisting of seven bite-sized courses including soft-boiled quail's egg and watercress with tiny slices of mackerel fillet and a chocolate fondue high in antioxidants. In the advertisement it claims that the foods contain omega-35 fatty acids, essential minerals, fatty acids, lecithin to stimulate cell growth and vitamin C. Where will such trends lead us?

Unless we have the whole picture by pursuing a phenomena-based (that is, taking note of what meets all our senses) and qualitative dimension we will be loaded with information that has little bearing on real food. Learning how to cook in a biodynamic way, to my mind, requires us first and foremost to become sensitized to what we are doing, to the deeper provenance of our ingredients, and to the wider implications of our choices. Tiny amounts of seemingly costly substances such as saffron or pine nuts can have a huge impact on a dish.

Cooking as well as being a science is also a craft that requires us to use our hands. People who use their hands intelligently and skilfully tend to be soundly based in practical wisdom. But nowadays our hands are being ill-used, tapping endlessly at a computer keyboard or priming the keys of a mobile phone. In the craft of cooking our hands become sensitive to weight, texture, moisture, warmth and cold, stimulating our thought processes too if we allow them, and leading to myriad insights into the qualities of our ingredients.

Cooking is also a very social exercise in that what we make we give away. There is no point in hoarding up our cooking; it has to go out into the world. So cooks need to be of a generous nature. Cooking is also a great mystery because we imbue our cooking with qualities of ourselves—something ethereal that goes beyond the sum total of ingredients. It is to do with our attention, our wisdom in the knowledge of what we are doing and how we are doing it, and the love of the activity.

The great systematizer Aristotle saw cooking as the continuation of a natural sun-ripening process: heat influencing matter, perfecting and maturing it. He called the cooking process pepsis, involving a softening, a kind of pre-digestion. As we learn to master fire (and the nearer to real fire we can get the better—a word on the different qualities of fire will come later, on page 67), we begin to perceive that life is calibrated into ever-refining degrees of warmth. We are warmth beings and our bodily temperature of 37°C is no arbitrary matter. A similar temperature exists in a beehive, suited to intricately integrated activities amongst the bees. Temperatures at which certain life-processes occur are also finely determined. For instance the optimum temperature for the activation of yeast in breadmaking is 37°C, the temperature at which bacillus introduced into milk will 'work' to make yoghourt or keffir is 43°C. Even a slight rise in temperature can kill off the yeasts or bacilli whereas lower temperatures render them dormant. The temperature at which sugar turns to caramel or the albumin in an egg solidifies are, again, specific. Heat is a manifestation of movement and when certain molecules collide through the action of heat, a disruption in structure occurs that changes relationships in cells and molecules, binding or disintegrating them.

There is nothing like experience and thoughtful cooking to give us confidence; we learn the powerful laws that underpin life. Standing in the kitchen and orchestrating heat (which includes cooling and freezing), chopping, slicing, kneading, pounding, stirring, we are in a world of *processes*, and in a kind of time-capsule, for each ingredient has its own inbuilt time laws. How long will it take the yeast to rise at blood temperature? How long for the jelly to set? How long for the pot of rice to cook? Certain processes can be speeded up and our culture puts high value on this, as we see in the Chorleywood bread baking process where the maturing of the dough is replaced by a few minutes of intense mechanical agitation in special high-speed mixers (two-thirds of bread in the UK is made like this). But the quality is inevitably changed; our 'staff of life' has become, in general, a highly denatured product, far from providing our basic nutritional needs.

Allowing time for natural processes to be fully developed should imbue us, as cooks, with a sense of calm that can be passed on as serenity to our diners. We really need to free ourselves up from slavery to the clock, which causes time to flee out of our grasp as we try to manage and manipulate it. Our slavery to the clock, to technology and to labour-saving devices is pathological in my opinion and can cause burn-out. Burn-out happens when mind, body and spirit are all pulling in separate directions. We in the West are often workaholics, and a lot of our activity is a distraction. A Chinese Tai Chi master opened my eyes when he said, 'You western people use a great deal more energy to do your physical tasks than an oriental might do. You are often inwardly fighting, having to do the activity and therefore trying to dispatch it with undue haste and resisting it the while. This burns up a great deal of energy and blood sugar.' My advice to myself, after a minor burn-out, when everything ground to a halt, was to do less and enjoy it more, not to resist doing the washing up, but to be at one with it and try to enjoy the experience. It may mean prioritizing life in a slightly different way, but rather than spend the whole day in a kind of embattlement with time one can start with the acknowledgement that when God made time he made plenty of it! How wonderful to luxuriate in process, where time unfolds cyclically, organically.

Our entire organism is intelligently adjusted to biorhythms. When we were much embedded in natural cosmic rhythms we were 'palpated' by the universe. Our daily breathing once reflected the 25,920 earth years of the solar or Platonic year (the time it takes for the sun to complete its backward journey through the zodiac). We can learn to slow ourselves down. When we relax, enjoy, and breathe fully and deeply, the benefits are truly life changing. We are connected in three ways to our universe: through our breathing, our nutrition, and our senses. The kitchen and the garden are wonderful arenas in which to develop our senses.

So let us indulge in the process of looking, not only with our eyes but with our hearts. Our culture is very visually orientated, but when we look, do we really see the whole picture or edit out the bits that we don't want? Snow White was attracted to the appearance of the witch's shiny red apple, but upon eating some a piece stuck in her throat and sent her into a deathlike coma. We should learn not to be taken in by appearances alone, but to develop a picture of quality by using all our sensibilities.

Our sense of smell is one of our first senses to unfold. Aroma is one of the most important clues to the real quality of a foodstuff. It is its most spiritual property, since it arrives in a gaseous, ethereal state when it reaches our senses. Aromas in foods are caused by specific volatile chemicals, characteristic of the particular foods. It is through our sense of smell that, even at an early age, we develop a kind of feeling for morality too. In expressions such as 'This smells fishy', or 'I smell a rat', we equate smells with discrimination about intangible qualities or feelings.

Taste and smell are linked inextricably; the tongue has seven areas to register sweet, sour, salty, bitter, oily, astringent and sharp or hot flavours. A well-planned menu will also take into account the textures and temperatures: hot, warm, cold and frozen, and foods that are soft, crunchy, smooth, silky, etc. A proper enjoyment of all these qualities requires, of course, that we masticate our food thoroughly before swallowing.

The role of our sense of hearing is to be appreciated, too, as we cook: the gentle simmering of a casserole, the sizzle of an egg frying, the sing of a sharp knife on the wooden chopping board as it slices through various vegetables and fruits. My Japanese teacher was very keen to impart to us that this sound of chopping should 'sing' and not have undue pressure or any kind of aggression in it.

If we can 'enter into the cooking pot' as it were, and imagine ourselves going through the various processes, we may better relate to cooking and become sensitive to the fact that heat, light and oxygen all tend to change vitamin and enzymatic value of foodstuffs. The important thing is to know how to minimize any nutritional losses through intelligent preparation and storage.

The qualities of the fire as used in cooking

As a child living with an old-fashioned kitchen fire with a range, occasionally used for baking bread, I grew up with the realization that heat coming from wood or coal was qualitatively different from that of an electric fire. Although the calorific value might be equivalent, there is a huge difference, as is a flame from gas. Later on in my life I had the opportunity to experience cooking with a range (cast-iron, solid fuel or oil-fired), whose qualities, once mastered, had real advantages. Such cookers have a real presence in the home; they also often heat the water and the radiators and transmit a quality to food that will be appreciated. Then, when living on a farm in Mallorca, our bread was made several times a week with a natural-rise fermentation process and cooked in a wood-fired stone oven, into which other dishes were placed after the bread came out. This was the best bread I've ever tasted. It would be covered with flecks of wood-ash and eaten with olive oil, garlic and ripe tomatoes—unbeatable! Our guests immediately spotted the difference to most commercial bread; but it was a real art to get the temperature correct.

Most fire that we have traditionally used, whether released from wood, coal or gas, is directly or indirectly a gift of the sun. All these substances come from a kind of ripening process that has taken place in growing organisms to produce usable energy, so when we cook with awareness we should be continuing that ripening process, making our foods more flavoursome and digestible.

How does electricity compare as a heat source? John Davy, in his book *Hope, Evolution and Change*, described electricity as being 'like a meeting with a mysterious and foreign will, which can shake our body in strange contortions. It is like a trapped energy emerging from the hidden depths of nature, full of tension and buried "violence".' Despite our seeming array of choices, some people only have access to electricity. But even in such cases it is possible to produce excellent meals using skill and love.

I have great reservations, however, about the use of microwave technology. The invention dates from the Second World War and began to be marketed to the public with virtually no research until the 1970s, when histological studies showed what molecular changes took place in food. Swiss food scientist Dr Hans Ulrich-Hertel conducted some of the early research, and he concluded (in 1989): 'Any food eaten that has been cooked or defrosted in a microwave oven can cause changes in the blood indicative of a developing process that is also found in cancer.' He continued, 'When food is microwaved the oven exerts a power input of about 1000 watts or more. The resulting destruction and deformation of food molecules produces a new radiolytic compound, unknown in nature.' The results of this research were suppressed following a complaint by the Swiss Association of Dealers for Electro-apparatus for Households and Industry.

In a microwave oven, a device called a magnetron tube causes an electron beam to oscillate at a very high frequency. Microwave (MV) radiation at 2.45 gigahertz (GHz) is produced. As water absorbs electromagnetic energy quickest at this frequency, food containing water is heated more rapidly. The molecules in the food are *forced* to align themselves with the very rapidly alternating field and to oscillate around their axis. Heat is produced from *intense intermolecular friction*. Microwaves are beamed from the magnetron in the oven compartment where they heat the food *from the inside out*. Apart from being the counter-picture to what we have described in a normal cooking/ripening process, this heating from the inside can give rise to cold spots, hence the need to constantly rotate the dish. Space will not allow more of the more recent research to be shared here, but I urge you to consider carefully whether the microwave has a place in your kitchen. (With thanks to Simon Best; see his article in *What Doctors Don't Tell You*, March 2000.)

Last but not least, a total polarity to the microwave is the hay-box cooker. This is simply a cardboard or wooden box filled with hay where, for instance, you can leave your porridge oats—having brought them to simmering point the evening before—gently to cook in their own heat overnight. It is also a good place to put your pot of grains after cooking to 'rest and expand' for 10–15 minutes.

Methods of cooking

There are the following ways of cooking: steaming, sautéing, stir-frying, boiling, steam-sautéing, poaching, roasting, baking, braising, casseroling, grilling, barbecuing, deep-frying (and to a certain extent smoking and pickling can also be seen as cooking methods). The season of the year will usually be an indication of which cooking methods are most appropriate. Spring and summer call for lighter cooking methods such as steaming, stir-frying, sautéing, grilling and barbecuing; it is also a time for more raw foods. Autumn and winter call for longer, slower casseroling, baking and roasting.

In cooking we transform foods by transferring energy by convection from whichever heat source we use into the foods. Heat is transferred by the movement of molecules in a fluid from a warm region to a cooler one, as in stewing and casseroling, sautéing and steam-sautéing. The relatively subtle flavours of many vegetables and fruits are often intensified, allowing sweet sugars or sour acids to become more prominent by rupturing cell walls and releasing their contents. Aromatic oils also become more volatile and therefore more pungent with heat, starches soften and become more digestible, proteins coagulate and potentially harmful microbes will be destroyed.

Steam-sautéing

This is frequently my preferred way of cooking vegetables. In a sauté-pan put a tablespoonful of olive oil, heat and add a small knob of butter. Next, add the vegetables to be cooked, a sprinkling of sea salt, possibly some garlic and herbs, depending on the dish. Stir the vegetables until they are all coated with some of the oil, then add half a cup of hot stock or plain spring water and cook with the lid on till al dente (differing times for different vegetables), keeping colours and textures bright and crisp. You will have a little liquid at the end, which will be full of wonderful flavour and nutrition, so either include it in a sauce to serve with the meal or it can go into the stockpot. Coating the ingredients with a little fat also significantly improves absorption of fat-soluble nutrients; it also wraps the vegetables in a blanket of warmth before the stock is added. Remember that the enemy of keeping that wonderful emerald chlorophyll green in your broccoli, spinach or cabbage is acid, so alkaline water is preferable; adding lemon juice or vinegar to your cooking water will turn greens a khaki colour.

Steaming

You need a steamer, or a pan of boiling salted water with either a metal or bamboo steamer on top, with a well-fitting lid. This is a favoured method for many people of cooking vegetables. (I personally feel the vegetables to be a little 'naked' done this way.) You will be left with the vegetable tasting of itself, but control of seasoning is somewhat difficult in this method. In order to get an even cooking the ingredients need to be in single layers so that the steam can penetrate them all equally. You can cook French beans, mangetout peas, carrot sticks, peas and broccoli and other vegetables like this. Until fairly recently the Japanese did not have ovens so everything tended to be steamed in many layers. It is an economic and efficient way of cooking.

Stir-frying

The vegetables and other ingredients need to be cut finely and evenly as they will need to be cooked at the same time. The wok or sauté-pan is heated and coated with a film of good quality cold-pressed sesame oil (ideally). Do the vegetables quickly in batches, stirring with wooden chopsticks (if you have them) or a wooden spatula and keeping a high flame. Seasoning is added towards the very end of the cooking. This is a good method for retaining nutrients—they are sealed in by the high temperature—the colour pigments and the crunchy texture of the ingredients.

Boiling

Boiling certain vegetables in water is often one of the best ways to cook them. Potatoes, swedes and carrots, which are dense and fibrous, can be cooked this way. My mother used to say: 'Those that grow below ground need to be cooked in cold water brought to the boil, and those that grow above (i.e. leafy vegetables) need to go into boiling water.' I usually follow this guideline, often adding seasonings and herbs to the water (mint with potatoes, rosemary with carrots) and a splash of olive oil. It is so important not to overcook vegetables. Unfortunately the tradition has been to cook our vegetables to death and throw away all the soluble nutrients down the drain. This way we lose the vitality of the food, not to mention the flavour and appearance.

Baking

When we bake food we are placing it in a heated, enclosed space, relying on a combination of radiation from the walls and hot air convection to heat the food. Oven air is less than a thousandth as dense as water, so the collisions between hot molecules and the food are less frequent in the oven than in the pot, and this explains why we can reach our hand into the oven without immediately getting burnt. Baking cakes, breads, biscuits and pastries generally calls for dry heat. Moderately high temperatures are needed to bring about browning and crisping, creating flavours and textures that we find so appetizing. French scientist Louis-Camille Maillard did much research into this 'browning' process. What he discovered was a combination of complex factors: plant cellulose, sugars, pyrazines, amino acids and sulphides interacting in what is now known as 'the Maillard reactions'. Food chemists have tried to synthesize this process for use in microwaved food.

Exceptions to dry heat are the steam baking of, say, an egg custard in a *bain-marie*, where the dish to be cooked is placed in a container of hot water that modifies the heat of the oven and produces a kind of steaming/baking environment.

Roasting

When roasting—meat, fish or dense, starchy vegetables—lightly coat the ingredients with oil and seasonings and cook at an initially medium temperature (around 180°C/gas mark 4), and then towards the end turn it up quite high to bring about a crisping of the surfaces. Originally this would have been spit roasting.

Grilling or broiling

This uses a dry but fierce heat, as in barbecuing over wood or charcoal. The important key to this method is to position the food far enough from the source of heat for the outer browning rate to match the inner conduction rate; also, keep basting with a marinade, and turn at appropriate intervals. Char-grilled vegetables can be delicious.

Braising, casseroling and stewing

Braising and casseroling are methods generally more suitable for autumn and winter meals. Start off by gently sautéing the ingredients in oil, then add stock, wine, herbs and vegetables. Finish the dish in a slow oven. Stewing involves cooking the ingredients in a flavoured liquid on top of the range at a medium to low heat. These methods are good for tenderizing cheaper cuts of meat, or for bean dishes like *cassoulet* and for whole grain dishes. A tip for adding colour, texture and vitality to slow-cooked dishes is to keep green vegetables, such as courgettes, broccoli, and the green part of leeks or chard, and cook them separately at the very end and add them to the casserole just before serving.

A kind of 'cooking'

There are other kinds of food preparation that involve a type of 'cooking' but don't need more than room temperature: pickling in salt; the lactic acid process used in making sauerkraut; and marinating in oil, wine and spices as in *seviche* (a Spanish marinated raw fish dish).

7 UTENSILS AND THE LARDER

What we use to cook our food in is almost as important as our ingredients, for it is the sheath through which the heat is mediated to our ingredients, and can vary in quality a great deal. There are many fairy tales which feature cooking pots and serving dishes that possess special properties; to be able to eat from and cook with vessels of gold was the very height of good fortune in the royal palace. Dr Rudolf Haushka's research into qualities of cooking vessels found that gold was the optimum material—even stirring a dish with a golden spoon made a qualitative difference. Well, I'm afraid I have none of these and don't suppose that you do either, so let's look for the next best thing.

Utensils

Enamelled cast iron

It will involve spending some money, but some good quality enamelled cast-iron Le Creuset cooking pots are a valuable investment in my opinion and they will last for a lifetime if cared for properly. They provide a steady, even heat and are perfect for cooking grains and vegetables, fruits and soups. In these utensils powdered glass is fused in a thin layer onto the surface of the cast iron. The metal diffuses the direct heat evenly and the ceramic layer is thin enough to expand and contract uniformly; it serves to protect the food from reacting with the iron, which as we know will rust in the presence of air and water. It is important only to use wooden stirring implements as metal could scratch the surface. And do not use abrasive metal cleaners or wire wool, which would also cause damage.

Ceramic

The moulding and firing of simple clay pots goes back some 8000 years or so and enabled increasingly complex cooking methods. Before then it was often pebble-lined pits that served as saucepans! The advantage of clay is that, because it is another aspect of the earth our food has been grown in, there is an energetic correspondence. Fired clay is stable and therefore does not contaminate the food, though some of the lead glazes used by the Romans may well have caused poisoning over the years.

I have several open-bodied clay cooking pots (greixoneras) from Mallorca, which are very cheap to buy and wonderful to use. A deep brown colour of burnt caramel makes them lovely to both cook and serve in. They can be used directly on a flame if you are careful, and they cook dishes like lasagne or a cassoulet in the oven with good results. Stoneware (clay fired at a higher temperature so that it vitrifies) can also be a good cooking medium for the oven.

Copper

Copper is a good heat conductor, but copper saucepans need to be lined with stainless steel or, traditionally, tin, which is not so stable. Copper ions have an alchemical effect of stabilizing egg foams and I have a copper bowl for beating egg whites, but this is not a necessary piece of kitchen equipment. A small, lined copper saucepan is good, however, for making special sauces.

Stainless steel

This was developed in the nineteenth century and is an iron-carbon alloy containing chromium and nickel. (Chrome is responsible for its shininess.) Having stainless steel saucepans with an inlaid copper bottom is very good as this helps the even conduction of heat, but it will also add to the price. I have stainless steel, heavy-bottomed saucepans with glass lids for the cooking of vegetables and fruits. It is useful to be able to see what is going on inside!

Aluminium

Aluminium is never found in a pure state in nature; it is smelted by drastic forcing at high temperatures in electric kilns, making it something of a bogus metal. Despite its low density giving it light weight, cheapness and high conductivity it is an unstable medium in which to cook. It reacts with acid foods, creating over time a pitted surface where elements have leached out and transmigrated into the food—so it is far from ideal. Today many aluminium utensils are anodized and coated with silicone non-stick surfaces. These can be dangerous if heated to high temperatures (about 250°C/500°F), decomposing into noxious and toxic gases. The surfaces can easily be scratched and then food can adhere to these scratches. So in my opinion, these utensils should be treated with caution.

Electric gadgets

Although my cooking students learnt to cook without resort to electric kitchen equipment, I have to say that I do find certain pieces of electrical equipment very useful, and these are:

Food processor. I use a Robot-Chef, for grinding nuts and blending mixtures. It has a liquidizer for soups and purées, but I don't use it for cakes, breads or vegetable slicing, which I prefer to do by hand.

Electric hand-beater. I find this very useful for beating egg-whites (when I'm not doing them by hand in my copper bowl with a balloon whisk), beating yolks and sugar where they need to be really fluffy, and for mayonnaise etc.

Electric hand-blender. For puréeing soups or sauces.

Electric spice-grinder. Although a pestle and mortar is the most authentic way to grind spices, sometimes you need to do something a little more quickly. It should be kept for this purpose alone as the residual spice aromas tend to be hard to get rid of.

Other important utensils

A good selection of sharp knives. My favourites are Japanese vegetable choppers, which are a perfect weight for fine vegetable cutting. I take one whenever I travel.

Mixing bowls. A selection of different sizes, some metal, some ceramic.

Wooden stirring implements. Lots of them, including long cooking chopsticks. Wood is so much better for the pots and for the food; it allows us to be more sensitive to what we do. In cooking, the stirring process is very important (as it is in the biodynamic agricultural preparations, too).

Wooden rolling pins for pastry, pizzas, etc. Best if you can find a heavy one.

Chopping boards. Some good large wooden ones.

Sieves and colanders (I have a very useful ceramic colander which is good for soft cheeses and to make the Russian Easter treat *paskha*).

Mouli-de-legumes for certain purées and for baby foods.

Mini stone flourmill. If you bake regularly and use grain porridges, there is nothing more satisfying than to have your own. This is quite a costly piece of equipment, but you'll find the quality of flour is superior. It would be a good investment for a family.

Suribachi (ridged Japanese pestle and mortar).

A good box grater for cheeses etc.

Porcelain grater for grating ginger root.

Zester for zesting citrus fruits.

Garlic press (a good quality one).

Whisks.

Vegetable scrubbing brush.

Pastry brush.

Bamboo/wicker baskets for draining and drying grains.

Bamboo steamer.

Flan tins and cake tins with spring sides.

Roasting pans and baking trays.

Egg-timer.

Sugar thermometer.

Muslins and cheesecloths for soft cheesemaking and straining yoghourt.

Flame-spreader (non-asbestos).

Pretty serving bowls and plates for salads, pâtés and desserts.

Wooden salad servers.

Metal skewers for kebabs and for testing if a food is properly cooked.

Cocktail sticks for securing things.

Some extras

I'm sure that all keen cooks have special utensils, either handed down in the family or bought on some journey, that are irreplaceable. One of mine is an ancient heavy cast-iron waffle iron in the shape of a four-leafed clover. It has developed a wonderful patina over the ages. For special birthday or Sunday breakfasts it produces the most wonderful waffles. Similarly I have a caste-iron chappati pan which came with a slim decorated rolling pin. Their provenance I don't remember, but they are also good for tortillas. I also treasure an old but still intensely sharp wooden and carbon steel mandolin for slicing potatoes (for a *pommes dauphinoise*). Last is a Georgian marbled glass rolling pin, hollow with a well-fitting cork to hold iced water for best results with pastry.

The Larder

(To be built up gradually!)

Oils

Lots of good quality virgin olive oil, best kept in a dark place or in dark glass.

Toasted sesame oil for stir-fry, Japanese or Thai cookery.

Refined organic sunflower oil for frying and occasional deep-frying.

Walnut and hazelnut cold-pressed oils for special salad dressings.

For sweetness

Organic maple syrup (remember it takes 40 litres of sap to make 1 litre of syrup so, like honey, it is a very high energy substance).

Organic honey (set and runny).

Unrefined cane sugars: Muscovado, Rapadura, molasses, caster.

Date syrup, rice syrup, apple and pear concentrate, barley malt.

Dried fruits

Hunza whole apricots, sulphured and non-sulphured apricots, apricot 'leather' from Middle Eastern stores.

Prunes, Lexia raisins, sultanas and currants, crystallized citrus peel.

For salting

Fine sea salt. Good quality coarse grey *sel de mer* for cooking. Malden salt crystals. Herb salt. Gomasio (sesame salt, home-made). Tamari and shoyu, good quality soy sauce. Miso paste. *Omeboshi* (Japanese salted plums).

Flours

100% wheat (Demeter), 85% wheat flour for pastries, unbleached strong white flour, also for pastry, pizza dough, etc.

100% rye flour for rye bread.

Small quantities of barley flour, millet flour, buckwheat flour (for galettes), maize flour (fine) and polenta (coarse).

Wholegrains and cereal products

Various varieties of rice (Demeter quality wherever possible)—short grain, long grain, Basmati, red Camargue, Arborio for risottos, pudding rice, wild rice.

Wheat—kamut and spelt. Bulgur and couscous.

Barley, yellow millet, red quinoa.

Semolina, oatmeal, porridge oats and rye flakes.

Nuts, seeds, and their products

Hazels, almonds (whole, flaked and ground), pecans, cashews, walnuts (I always try to buy a supply of wet walnuts in the autumn, either local or from France; they really taste like walnuts should), pistachios, pine kernels, pumpkin, sunflower, sesame and poppy seeds.

Dessicated coconut. Coconut milk (in tins).

Nut butters (cashew, almond, hazelnut), tahini.

Pulses

Haricot beans, flageolets (pale green), pinto beans, red kidney beans, chick peas, butter beans, dried broad beans, aduki beans, le Puy lentils, red lentils, green and yellow split peas.

Setting and thickening agents

Gelatine, Vege-gel, organic fruit jelly crystals.

Arrowroot for thickening sauces.

Dried seaweeds

Kombu (kelp), wakame (for salads), nori (sheets of seaweed for sushi).

Yeast

Fresh and dried (check that they are not enzymatic yeasts). Try to get some baking ferment—Bak ferment—or you can make your own starter.

Vinegars

Apple cider, balsamic (aged in oak), raspberry and tarragon, red and white wine vinegars, sherry vinegar, Japanese brown rice vinegar (for sushi rice).

Herbs and spices

Whenever it is at all possible to grow your own herbs, they will of course be of optimum vitality, even if grown indoors in pots. Parsley, mint, basil, coriander and chives can flourish beautifully, and they bring a great sense of life and abundance to your kitchen. You will get a good harvest from a few seeds so it's much cheaper if you grow them yourself. Otherwise, if you are buying dried herbs and spices, try to buy from organic or biodynamic sources, because so many commercial ones have been routinely irradiated.

Here are some I use regularly:

Herbes de Provence, sage, rosemary, thyme, bay, tarragon, lovage (these last two only fresh), fennel seeds, caraway, anise, coriander, dill, star anise, cumin (ground and seeds), turmeric, chilli (powder, flakes and whole), cayenne, Hungarian smoked paprika, cinnamon (bark and powder), whole nutmegs, vanilla essence and pods, cardamom pods, saffron threads, curry paste and powder, Iranian mixed spices, sweet mixed spice, juniper berries, black dried peppercorns and green pickled peppercorns, ground ginger, ginger root (fresh), pickling spices, ground mace, and allspice.

Cooking wines and sherry

Miscellaneous

Pickled capers, olives, *cornichons* (small pickled cucumbers), pickled lemon slices, anchovy fillets, cans of chopped tomatoes, sun-dried tomatoes, bottled preserved red peppers, soba (buckwheat noodles) and a small assortment of pasta (which I would normally make or buy fresh), good quality mineral water and local spring water, cooking chocolate, preserved ginger root in syrup.

For Persian and Middle Eastern cooking: pomegranate syrup, tamarind paste, rose water, orange-flower water.

8 MALLORCA

Before moving to the recipe section, I would like to explain why I refer to Mallorca so often in this book, and why it has been such an influence and inspiration for my own cooking. I first visited Mallorca in 1966. I had been given a letter of introduction to the poet Robert Graves who lived in a breathtakingly beautiful village on the northern coast.

Deya is perched on a hill with a church standing on the summit and a row of cypresses leading up to it. It had quite a biblical atmosphere. The lush tangle of fruit trees, a veritable Garden of Eden, prompted the Spanish writer Santiago Rusinol to write:

> Amongst the branches of a fig tree appear clusters of grapes from a neighbouring vine. From the vine emerge the plums of a tree that embraces it, and the plum tree produces oranges lent to it by an orange tree that has no room to mature. The tones of green are so varied . . . everything grows, blossoms and fructifies as if to relieve its heart of some burden in gifts to this little village, like a latter-day Bethlehem.

Such was the abandoned voluptuousness of the island's fruit trees.

The figure of the great poet was indeed impressive, often wearing a black Spanish sombrero, shading his high forehead but accentuating his graceful Roman nose. He was tall even in his later years, though a little stooped. I admired his hands, sensitive as an artist's but strong as a farmer's, as he pressed his guests to join in some olive gathering with special baskets for the purpose. He demonstrated how to collect the fallen ones, and squatting on haunches we gathered the black pungent and bitter fruits (bitter until cured by pickling in brine), entertained by Robert with stories of the sunken Atlantis, White Goddesses and local lore. How could we notice the discomfort of the procedure? Thus many a useful and entertaining afternoon was spent as the shadows lengthened. I became enthralled with this jewel of an island, and this special introduction to it was part of the enchantment. After spending a childhood growing up in war-torn Britain, with food rationing and clothes only to be had in the drabbest of colours—navy, brown or grey—and the constricting effects of the aftermath of war, it was so stimulating to be in this warm, sundrenched and colourful environment. People smiled and greeted you with 'Adios' ('God go with you'), no matter that you were a stranger. Everywhere one met the horizon, the hyacinth blue of the Mediterranean, cradling this 'Island of Calm'.

I kept going back. The climate seemed to have a positive effect on little Daisy's asthma and so we decided, after a great deal of searching, to buy a small farmhouse on the outskirts of the old Templar town of Pollensa. It had about four acres of *tierra secana*—land with no water, except from the rainfall gathered in great cisternas. It was here that I learnt never to waste water; how precious it was. The trees that did well in this dry soil were a combination of almond, carob and fig trees—all very useful crops. The carob was good for animal feed and to chew on if you were hungry (this is the locust-pod tree that St John chewed in the wilderness). The almonds were delicious and could be used when they were young and milky in the fresh almond gazpacho, while still in their pale green furry overcoats. Later in the season, harvesting them with long bamboo canes, we were well exercised (no need for the gym in this way of life). It resulted in a larder full of these delicious nuts as a snack, roasted and salted, and in numerous savoury and sweet dishes.

The figs . . . what can I say? Nothing can be more sensual than plucking a ripe fig from the tree. This mysterious fruit, whose 'flowers' are to be found inside the fruit as described by D. H. Lawrence:

> It is a glittering, rosy, moist, honied, heavy petalled, four-petalled flower . . .
> Folded upon itself and secret, unutterable
> And milky sapped
> Sap that curdles milk and makes ricotta . . .
>
> ('Figs')

Imagine a lunch plate of figs cut in half and eaten with fresh white sheep's cheese (*requeson*), some crisp leaves of cos lettuce and the *pa pagès* crusty country bread made without salt (there were always olives to supply that). Who could ask for more? Figs dried in the bread oven and sprinkled with Anis liqueur made great Christmas gifts.

In between these useful, shade-giving trees were planted, in alternate years, broad beans and wheat. The beans fixed nitrogen in the soil and were delicious fresh or dried (see recipe for Mallorcan Broad Bean Stew on page 178). After the crop had been harvested sheep were run in to nibble the stubble, thus fertilizing the land with their droppings; nothing was wasted. Even the almond shells were made into charcoal. I met farmers who still planted and harvested attentive to the phases of the moon.

The same principle of no waste was applied to the *Matança*. The beginning of winter was the time to kill the family porker; my little daughters were unwittingly witness to this rather gory event, invited by our neighbours, and I don't think that they have ever forgotten it. But by twelve o'clock noon the porker had been dispatched into salted haunches for hams, strings of *sobrasada* sausages, belly fat, ribs, pickled trotters, and salted ears. (Liver and lights were kept for *frit mallorqui* with fried potatoes, fennel, red chilli peppers and green onions.) This is to my mind a more honest way of eating meat, to take responsibility for rearing and butchering your own animal—if you are trained and efficient in it—and then to eat the whole thing.

In the 1960s donkeys and carts were to be seen everywhere—just about my favourite speed of transport—and later we were to have our own, though in the 'eighties a donkey cart was becoming something of a rarity. We didn't lock the doors of the houses or our cars in the 'sixties. There was such trust; the Mallorcans were tolerant and seemed quite interested, if somewhat bemused, by the carryings-on of the increasing number of artists and 'drop-outs' who were gravitating towards the island. Being of an entrepreneurial character they knew how to make the most of this invasion. They had a long history of invasions and whilst they generously shared the bounty and beauty of their island, they also managed to grow wealthy themselves in many cases. There are, to be sure, some lamentable hotel developments along once pristine coasts, but on the whole the people have a good aesthetic sense that still prevails. Much is retained of what I love and have valued over the years. For me it has been the grounding of an ideal in the art of living: the sun dictates the daily rhythms of such communities and leads to a sensible way of life. Or at least, it used to. Only 'mad dogs and Englishmen go out in the midday sun'. Everything closed down for three hours in the small villages, disdaining the frenzy of the tourist resorts. During this time the families enjoyed the fruits of the senyora's hours in the kitchen, and the smells wafted and met tantalizingly at the top of my street. Mallorcans are born philosophers and raconteurs so eating and talking, followed by a well-earned siesta, made it a time of true sustenance punctuating the long day.

At the bottom of the street in Campanet, my last place of abode on the island, was Montse's little shop. From the outside it looked like any other house save for the metal chain curtain that garnished the doorway. Upon entering into this Breughel-like scene one was aware that thousands of products, from suspender belts to mouse-traps to dishes of fresh *requeson* (white sheep's cheese), black olives, boxes of tomatoes, peaches, melons and the freshest golden-yolked free range eggs I've ever tasted, all jostled for space. Behind a raised counter as on a podium Montse ruled, smiling and helpful. She had everything that you might need—a real supermarket. I also knew that each customer would require a minimum of ten minutes to be served, entailing a discussion of the family, the day's menu, town politics and any up-coming fiestas. There was no need to buy the local paper, you knew it all in greater depth.

The people had little use for psychiatrists, and one of their secrets was that when God invented time he invented lots of it! So to try to press London schedules on people who lived with the rhythms of the sun and the Catholic saints' days was useless, a real short cut to a heart condition. *Mañana*, a word that you heard often, didn't necessarily mean tomorrow or next week, but possibly next year.

Of an evening you would see gaggles of pinny-ed elderly senoras going for a pre-prandial stroll, having fixed the dinner and left it bubbling away, and often waving bunches of fresh basil to keep away the flies and mosquitoes in the summer evenings. Their babble in the local dialect of Catalan made them sound like a flock of excited turkeys.

Despite the growth of supermarkets, I'm very glad to say the wonderful weekly markets in the various villages and towns continue to thrive. I love those markets and they are an indicator that local food is still being cooked in the homes. The produce has usually been harvested that very day and so confident are the stallholders of the quality of their goods that they are often happy to proffer slices of fruit or cheese, or the great variety of olives, caper buds or pickled sea fennel (*fonoll de mar*). This ritual is a necessary prerequisite in the dance of seller and customer, without which there used not to be any real satisfaction for either.

Shopping in these markets was a real education in the cycle of nature as manifested in the fresh produce. In winter large piles of oranges, tangerines and lemons were plentiful and cheap, so we could have large glasses of freshly squeezed orange juice. There were *esclataangs* (wild mushrooms), frothy endive, chestnuts and fresh dates, and mountains of artichokes, which in their abundance can be incorporated into many dishes. (My favourite is the sautéd hearts of young artichokes, sliced thinly with olive oil, garlic and lemon, and chopped flat-leaf parsley.) Then, suddenly, after four months' profusion of plenty, from one day to the next they are all gone, not a single one to be had! But now come other delicacies: in the spring wild asparagus is sought by one and all, rich and poor. It is to be found growing profusely in the hedgerows and around the margins of the fields. This tender, mineral-rich morsel will also find its way onto some market stalls where it is usually ridiculously cheap—wonderful in an omelette! Now came the extraordinary purple carrots (the original carrot, from Afghanistan) with their bright yellow centres, tender broad beans and early peas. Barrels of salted herring, cheeses from Mallorca, Mahon, La Mancha and from other exotic places, next to the honey stall with its gleaming ranks of golden, super-condensed bee-energy gathered from the blossoms of orange, carob, thyme, rosemary, sage and myrtle.

Olive oil commands an important place in the market and in the diet of the islanders. The most proffered snack is a *pà amb oli*, basically a slice of fresh country bread which has been rubbed with the contents of a winter tomato (*ramallets*, a special vine variety that keeps all winter and has a wonderful flavour), sprinkled with coarse sea salt and a generous trickle of good virgin olive oil. Some of the best comes from the oil-producing village of Caimari, with beautiful stone terraces lining the mountain slopes, where grow gnarled, millennium-old olive trees still producing their green-gold bounty. This basic meal—to which can be added slices of dry-cured ham, or the island cheese with a handful of olives—is ubiquitous throughout the island, and even well-attended restaurants have it as their speciality.

The market in the old town of Pollensa was organized on Sundays so that the farmers could bring their produce, go to church and then meet their friends for gossip, dark coffee and cognac. Other towns rotated the days so that all could benefit from this spirit of cooperation, rather than competition, between people whose lives depend upon the soil.

The Mallorcans are traditionally hard workers, but they also know when to stop and celebrate the various saints' days. Some of their fiestas are enormously elaborate and some are interspersed with pre-Christian ritual. Fiestas usually have their own special foods. For the festival of San Antoni at the end of January, the inland market town of Sa Pobla has a particularly spectacular display, its special dish being a pie which contains a mixture of eels fished from the marshy area, mixed with spinach and raisins. The meal was eaten around the family dining table, covered with a thick tablecloth and underneath, on the floor, was a copper brazier full of embers warming our feet and proving very companionable. This festival is about the creation of light in the dark of winter; each street competes with its neighbours to construct a theme fire. If you are a fisherman, you may have an old boat to crown the bonfire. Creative ideas abound and a lot of wood is burnt, mainly carob and olive prunings. Fireworks shoot off in all directions without warning. Traditionally every town had its own firework-maker, who produced amazing creations out of sugar paper and secret potions. I never knew anyone to get hurt.

Old ladies, dressed sedately with pristine hair-dos, sing somewhat 'blue' songs accompanied by the primitive drum, the *Ximbomba*, and the crowd falls about laughing. Children dressed as little *demonis* run about scaring each other. Altogether it seems to be a most lusty and cathartic celebration. On the next day, the air is heavy with wood-smoke and now comes the more religious part of the celebration. All the pets and domestic animals are brought out, from guinea pigs to prancing Arab stallions, to be blessed by the priest who sprinkles them with holy water. It is a most charming spectacle and many towns continue this practice.

The cuisine on the island has French, Moorish, Jewish and Spanish influences, which make it interesting. I have a doctor friend, Felip, who told me one day with a twinkle, 'We are Christians by day, Jews in the evening and Arabs at night!' Such is the cocktail of bloods that pulses through the islanders and emerges in the various interesting names resulting from intermarriage. The cooking also demonstrates some of these influences. Though many of the local dishes are quite simple, relying on good fresh ingredients, there are also to be found

some extremely complex dishes, reflecting the cuisine of the manorial houses. The combination of nuts (pine-nuts or almonds), together with raisins or apricots and saffron in meat and grain dishes, reflects the Moorish influence.

One of my favourite restaurants is the Celler C'an Amer in Inca. The chef-owner, Senora Dona Antonia Cantallops, has devoted much of her life to researching old recipes, which often involve complex stuffings. Mixtures of fruits, nuts and spices go into meat dishes, often accompanied by a grain, usually rice. Her knowledge is impressive and our conversation was enhanced by the setting of an atmospheric old wine cellar, with branches of citrus decorating the stairway. She told me how they used to grow much of their own produce. They still prepare their own olives for the restaurant and have their own almonds to make the famous *gato d'ametles* and the fresh almond ice cream to go with it. Once during our meeting she disappeared into the kitchen (now run by one of the sons, a kitchen bright with copper saucepans and festooned with strings of peppers and chillies), and reappeared carrying a canister with such delicacy and reverence it

might have been gold dust. Well may it have been, as the lid was removed to reveal a cache of precious saffron threads, grown by two old ladies who had a patch nearby. She told me that in the old days everyone had a saffron patch. She also related how, in her childhood, at the fish-market there were special police who at the end of the day would come and chop off the heads of any unsold fish, so the housewife could not be cheated the following day.

We were fêted with a wonderful meal of wild mushrooms, sautéd in olive oil with garlic and lemon and served with *Ca'n Amer*—wonderful bread—and wine. This was followed by courgettes stuffed with prawns in a tomato sauce and *bacalao* (cod) cooked with red peppers and garnished with pine nuts and raisins. For dessert we had the famous Mallorcan almond cake with almond ice cream (see recipes pages 232 and 145). An unforgettable indulgence!

Last Easter I had the incredible good fortune to be introduced to Jaume Moranta, a talented young photographer whose family members—mother, aunts and mother-in-law—were great *aficionados* of Mallorcan cookery. In his enthusiasm to share some of the

secrets of Mallorcan culture, which is quickly being eroded, he opened doors of the inner sanctum, allowing me to cross the sacred threshold of the various family kitchens and be initiated into the Easter specials. This was a rare honour, since the Mallorcans probably don't share the secrets of their recipes with each other, let alone with foreigners. I entered a scene where mother, aunt and neighbour were sitting around the kitchen table making *empanadas*,

Easter lamb pies with spring onions, some including peas. The mother has three grown, healthy sons and their appetites are pretty good. It was real mass-production. They were also making *rubiols*, a special sweet almond pastry filled with apricot confit, or *cabea d' angels* ('angel hair jam') made from spaghetti squash and ginger.

A younger son came in brandishing a long knife. I asked him what he was doing, waving it about and looking dangerous. He said that he was just about to go and slaughter the Easter lamb and would I like to go and watch. I didn't think that I could quite manage

this, so I declined. The meal for Good Friday was made from the blood of the lamb with fried potatoes, hot red peppers, onions and fennel, the traditional Mallorcan *frit* that I mentioned earlier. The brothers were also participating in the Good Friday procession, when most of the town walked up to a sacred hill outside the village, where a very moving tableau took place.

The next lesson was more in my way of cooking: the famous Mallorcan *coca*, a delicious pizza-type open tart piled up with peppers or chard, onions and raisins. The secret ingredient in the yeasted dough is fresh orange juice, and the crust is delightfully crisp and crumbly, not really like pizza dough, but alas they use lard, which I'm not happy to use in my cooking. The best *cocas* are baked in a wood-fired oven, dusted with little traces of wood-ash, which supplies those minerals that people buy in bottles. (Sadly, few people now have access to wood ovens. For more about cooking with wood, see page 67.) You can buy slices of *coca* in bakeries on certain days of the week. Made on the premises, they are great for picnics. Catalina, Jaume's mother-in-law, also prepared *sopas*, a very basic filling and nourishing soup made of

seasonal vegetables and in which a little salted belly of pork is sometimes used. This soup is poured onto specially thin slices of stale bread that soak it up; often a raw egg is added if there is no meat and it cooks in the hot broth.

Jaume's mother-in-law, Catalina. His mother, Margarita, is on the previous page.

A biodynamic farmer in Mallorca

Marie-Luise grew up in Northern Germany, where both her grandparents and parents had been farmers. Her father was, she says, 'a proud representative of the "modern" type, treating agriculture as an industrial input-output system, rational on one level but blind to the subtle realities of life on another'. Marie-Luise studied history and music but one day came across Rudolf Steiner's agricultural lectures and found them a 'revelation and a relief'. Here at last were advice and instruction for a deeper understanding of the life processes in agriculture and a practical way of dealing with them. In due course, her childhood roots in farming called her back to the land. This is her story.

She gave up her life as a baroque musician and started, with the help of friends, to explore and work in the direction that Steiner had indicated. It was like inventing agriculture anew. She tried to look at everything that she undertook in a totally new way, finding that the biodynamic approach answered many of her questions. She saw that soil, plant, animal or human being will all tell their stories if we are prepared to observe and listen to them. Through understanding we can be creative in helping to manage them in such a way that they may be true to their potential and bring forth high quality farm products with optimum nutritional value. Such gifts, received with gratitude and appreciation, carry cosmic building forces, obeying the laws of well-formed organisms (plant or animal). She has found through experience that eating nutritionally superior produce also avoids allergenic reactions.

'Now,' she says, 'on the island of Mallorca, I live with a herd of ten wholesome and healthy cows, a proud and paternal bull, a couple of quick-witted calves and some young oxen. They teach me about the true nature of the cow and I now understand why cows are held to be sacred in India. A cow is like the tongue of the earth that really tastes her rich pastures. She diligently savours all the dynamic forces that build up the plants. Just think of the large animal with her weighty body lying in the pastures, ruminating and chewing the cud—ruminating, chewing and dreaming. Can you imagine a more grounded animal? I watch them in this contemplative activity, then go into the fields to observe the sprouting of the wheat and marvel at these great cycles of the life of nature on the farm. To be in the present moment can inform me of a vaster and wider cosmic and cyclical time in which we all live and play our part.

'A biodynamic farmer needs to be an artist in his or her work, which becomes an unfolding path of self-development. Here we may be gifted in perceiving that numinous but palpably cohesive design and the lawfulness of a world that is teeming with symbiotic exchanges. When I fetch the cows home from the pasture to be milked I have first to *be* with them and become a member of the herd, stroking them and dwelling in their presence for some minutes so they can perceive me. *Then* they will follow me home. Cows certainly challenge my organizational capacities. When I call the cows in for milking I have to think clearly about the path they will take and the order in which they will come, so that they can perceive my intention and then there will be no struggle. This requires a serene attitude. From the outside it might look like the easiest thing in the world, but God help me if I should be dreaming or working with a divided or tense mind. Then it could become really dangerous!'

Marie-Luise has discovered that we not only live in a world of substances and patterns, but also in a dynamic world of processes: creation (anabolic) and destruction (catabolic). In biodynamic agriculture farmers try to understand the essence and forces behind these processes. Once understood, one can work with them, enhancing them in appropriate places and diluting them where their capacities could be damaging. This is clearly in contrast with the warlike attitude of present-day conventional agribusiness that seems to be in constant battle with natural processes. When farmers can act intelligently as true custodians of the land, she feels, they will bring into being a way of treating the earth and her progeny that once more reconnects us with cosmic rhythms via our food.

SEASONAL FOOD CALENDAR

Month	Fruit and Vegetables	Fish and Meat
January	Cabbage, cauliflower, celeriac, forced rhubarb, purple sprouting broccoli, leeks, parsnips, turnip, shallots, squash	Goose, lobster, scallops
February	Brussels sprouts, cabbage, cauliflower, celeriac, chard, chicory, forced rhubarb, kohlrabi, lamb's lettuce, leeks, parsnips, spinach, swede, turnip	Mussels, halibut, guinea fowl, lobster
March	Beetroot, cabbage, cauliflower, leeks, mint, mooli, parsley, broccoli, radishes, rhubarb, sorrel, young dandelions, young nettles	Sardines (fresh ones!), lobster
April	Broccoli, cabbage, cauliflower, morel mushrooms, wild garlic, radishes, rhubarb, carrots, kale, watercress, spinach, rosemary flowers, fennel	Spring lamb, cockles
May	Broccoli, cabbage, cauliflower, gooseberries, elderflowers, parsley, mint, broad beans, rhubarb, new carrots, samphire, asparagus, basil, sugar snap peas, wet garlic	Sea bass, lemon sole, sardines, duck, sea trout, mackerel
June	Apricots, carrots, cherries, elderflowers, lettuce, strawberries, peppers, asparagus, redcurrants, peas, rhubarb, gooseberries, tayberries, tomatoes, courgettes, broad beans, globe artichokes, rock samphire	Welsh lamb, crab, salmon, grey mullet, mackerel
July	Carrots, gooseberries, strawberries, spinach, tomatoes, watercress, loganberries, sage, cauliflower, aubergine, fennel, asparagus, cabbage, celery, courgettes, cherries, lettuce, mangetout, nectarines, new potatoes, oyster mushrooms, peas, peaches, radish, raspberries, rhubarb, tomatoes, French beans	Trout, pilchards, clams, pike, pigeon

SEASONAL FOOD CALENDAR

Month	Fruit and Vegetables	Fish and Meat
August	Carrots, gooseberries, lettuce, loganberries, raspberries, strawberries, cauliflower, aubergines, nectarines, peaches, peppers, courgettes, rhubarb, sweetcorn, greengages, basil, peas, pears, apples, French beans, tomatoes, cucumbers, lettuce, kohlrabi	Crayfish, hare, skate, john dory (that's a fish)
September	Apples, aubergines, blackberries, cabbage, carrots, cauliflower, cucumber, damsons, elderberries, figs, French beans, grapes, kale, lettuce, melons, mushrooms, nectarines, onions, peppers, parsnips, peas, peaches, pears, potatoes, pumpkin, raspberries, rhubarb, spinach, sweetcorn, tomatoes, broccoli	Duck, venison, oysters, sea bass, grouse, mussels, partridge, wood pigeon, brown trout
October	Apples, aubergines, beetroot, boletus, celeriac, cabbage, carrots, cauliflower, calabrese, chanterelles, courgettes, grapes, lettuce, marrow, mushrooms, parsnips, potatoes, squash, tomatoes, watercress	Guinea fowl, partridge, mussels, grouse, oysters
November	Apples, cabbage, celeriac, cob nuts, pumpkin, swede, cauliflower, potatoes, parsnips, pears, leeks, quinces, chestnuts, cranberries, beetroot	Grouse, goose, rabbit, venison
December	Celery, cabbage, red cabbage, cauliflower, celeriac, pumpkin, beetroot, turnips, lamb's lettuce, parsnips, sprouts, pears, pak choi, swede	Wild duck, goose, rabbit, sea bass, turkey

Part Two:
Recipes

THE RECIPES

The recipes in this book have been created using wherever possible biodynamic or organic ingredients. The eggs are free range organic, the meat is organic, the salt is sea salt, the sugars are unrefined cane sugars or other kinds (as specified). Spring water is used where possible (you may be lucky enough to have access to a spring, otherwise do the best you can). Herbs and spices, if dried, come from non-irradiated sources. The milk is organic, green top if possible. Plain flours are refined but unbleached. The amounts are generally for six people, or as stated.

Always cook with a joyful heart. When stirring the pot, just stir the pot; when washing the rice, just wash the rice; when eating give thanks, for there are many who do not have access to good food. If you give priority to food in your budget you will in the end get value for money, and the benefits will be shared by everyone and everything—plant, animal, humans and environment.

Do not waste anything! Vegetable trimmings can go into the stockpot or the compost heap. Leftover grains and vegetables can be recycled into stuffings for courgettes or peppers, or into burgers or soups. And lastly, do not be afraid of difficulties; try to embrace the unexpected fiasco. The kitchen is an exciting laboratory; it is also full of potential dangers, but you will learn about the lawfulness of your ingredients. One day a dish that you have cooked many times does not work out. Such is the mystery of cooking—we put ourselves in the pot!

So I wish you joy and a spirit of adventure.

Some Preliminary Tips and Notes

The use of herbs

If you are using dried herbs it is better to add them at the beginning of cooking, so that their condensed flavours can unfold in the dish. When using fresh herbs, add them towards the end of the cooking. Certainly the woody ones like thyme, sage and rosemary do need a certain amount of cooking, but parsley, chives and mint can all be added right at the end to preserve their delicate perfuming oils and chlorophyll richness.

Vegetable cutting

In Japan and China vegetable cutting is both a high art and a science. It does something, and not only on an aesthetic level; it actually changes the quality of the food. When we cut fruit and vegetables we are rearranging the energy pathways. Done correctly, this can potentize the food. My Japanese teacher told me, 'You can always tell the state of mind of the cook when you see how the vegetables have been cut—is it an orderly mind or a chaotic one?'

The ring of the knife, sharp steel on wood, should also have a musical sound. Too much energy or force suggests aggression. A Japanese vegetable knife, which takes seven years for an apprentice to learn how to fashion, is in my opinion the most efficient and practical tool a cook may have. Mine travels with me. It must be sharp; more accidents occur in kitchens with blunt knives than with sharp ones! Slicing vegetables in a food processor not only heats them up, thereby diminishing their nutritional quality, but wrecks the harmony and order in their intrinsic growth patterns.

If we want the juices of the vegetables to go into the liquid, as in a soup or sauce, we need to cut them up really small and evenly so that cooking occurs evenly. Roots take longer to cook, so in a soup we should keep green and leafy vegetables until towards the end of the cooking time, to retain their life-forces. If your vegetables are to go in a casserole and cook for an hour and a half, you need larger chunks so that they retain their form.

So when this aspect of preparation is given full attention, there is a real conversation with the fruit or vegetable. I am sure you will soon notice the benefits.

| *Half-moons* | *Butterfly wings* | *Roll cut* | *Onion cubes* | *Carrot flowers* |

| *Spring onion tassells* | *The finished product!* | *Carrot matchsticks* | *Preparing an apple* | *The finished product!* |

Measurements

I have a more living relationship with imperial measure, despite living with the metric system for much of my life. That is why imperial measures come first in the recipes. Metric measures are usually rounded up to the nearest whole number.

The stockpot

A stockpot is a must for any serious cook. Stock can be used in soups, sauces and to cook grains. It is a way of extracting optimum nutrition from vegetables by using the trimmings (which can then go to the compost bin afterwards, so no waste at all). A large, heavy-lidded saucepan is best, possibly stainless steel, holding at least 3 litres (6 pints).

Be aware of the colour and flavour of the dishes you are going to cook and make sure your stock is not overpowering.

Vegetable stock

The vegetarian equivalent of meat bones is pieces of kombu (kelp), which contains natural sources of monosodium glutamate (msu). To this can be added clean peelings of potatoes, carrots, onions (but not too much), parsley stalks, bay leaves, herbs, leek trimmings, celery and celeriac (both high in soluble salts) and lemon peel. But do not add stock from the brassica family (cabbage, Brussels sprouts, etc.) because of the high sulphur content which can cause fermentation. Cover with cold water, add a little salt and bring to the boil. Simmer for $1^1/2$–2 hours to extract all the flavours. Strain and refrigerate.

Meat stock

Use bones of lamb, beef, chicken or game carcasses, together with combinations of ingredients for vegetable stock. Simmer for 2 hours. Strain and refrigerate.

Fish stock

Use fish trimmings with herbs and vegetables, as above. Strain into a bottle and put in the refrigerator and it will keep for 2–3 days.

Stirring

A word on stirring. If you know about the stirring of the biodynamic preparations, you may begin to realize how potent is the way we move liquids and other mixtures about. When we stir our food during the course of preparation it should be because it needs to be stirred, and in a consequent way, not just getting rid of our nervous energy. This applies to all our gestures towards the food.

The cooking of grains

The cooking of grains is quite an art and something that needs to be learned if you have not grown up with wholefood cookery. It may take a few scorched cooking pots before your confidence in wholegrain cookery is established. But because grains are an important part of wholefood and biodynamic nutrition, it is worth putting some effort into learning how to do this as well as possible.

The grain is the seed of the plant and has experienced the cycle of the year and the ripening process of the sun; it is the plant's total matrix. During the drying and storing period grains harden, so in cooking we need to 'wake them up'. By soaking some of the harder skinned whole grains—wheat berries, rye, oats, barley and in some cases whole rice—we begin a process in the direction of germination.

The outer bran layer or seed coat is designed to control the passage of moisture and thus slows down the absorption of the cooking liquid. First, carefully pick over the grains for any chaff or tiny stones. (The Japanese and Chinese have lovely bamboo baskets that are good for this.) Then wash the measured grain in a large bowl, swishing it around gently with your hands to release dust and excess starch, and rinse again in a sieve under running water. Then drain it and allow it to dry off in a sieve or a bamboo basket. In the case of these harder skinned grains, cover with twice the amount of warm spring water or, if you are preparing a savoury dish, some well-flavoured stock. You may soak the grains overnight, but don't do this to any polished grains or Arborio rice as you may end up with a very starchy mess.

The next day, approximately an hour before you want to eat, cook the grain by putting it, with its soaking liquid, in a heavy pot. If you are not using stock, add a level teaspoon of sea salt per $^1/_2$ lb/50 g of grain. Bring to the boil, and do not be tempted to stir the grain thereafter (my Japanese teacher told me that to do so was like disturbing the order of the universe!). Then turn the flame down to its lowest; you may need to use a flame-spreader under your cooking pot to diffuse the heat. I prefer a Le Creuset enamelled iron pot with a tightly fitting lid that does not allow steam to escape. The size is important. It should be large enough to allow the swelling of the grain but not so large that the grain is dwarfed within it. (I do not favour pressure cookers.) The grain is cooked when all the liquid has been absorbed and the grains are plump and tender, but still with some 'chew'. A further process is to wrap the pot in a blanket or towel and let it rest for a further 10–15 minutes. This gives the grain time to expand and completely absorb any residual liquid—another kind of 'breathing' in its cycle.

For the cooking of millet and often for a savoury whole rice dish, clean, wash and drain the grain as described above. Then—again in a heavy pot—melt 1 oz/25 g of butter in a tablespoon of olive oil and toss the grains around in this so that each grain is coated thinly, but do not fry or discolour them. This is to help keep the grains separate during cooking. (For a Persian rice dish, I would put in a few cardamom pods and a little cinnamon bark at this stage.) Then add double the volume of well-flavoured stock, continuing as above. Whole rice will need approximately 45 minutes, millet 30 minutes. (Cooking time can vary a little depending on how old the grain is.) This omits overnight soaking but the short resting period after cooking is a good idea.

For polenta, couscous and pasta see individual recipes.

PASTRY MAKING

There are a good number of recipes in this book that call for pastry. Can I hear cries of 'It's fattening!' 'It's too difficult!' and so on? Well, although it is possible to buy ready-made pastry, it is not a patch on a good home-made one using excellent flour, ice-cold water and cold butter. As for the fattening aspect, it depends on how often and how much!

One of the good things about pastry is that it allows us to bring *form* to a dish. And we *need* form—so many lives today lack any meaningful form. A Cornish pasty provides the opportunity for many different nourishing and tasty fillings, and makes a welcome change in the lunch-box. Pasties and pies provide a lovely sealed, steamy atmosphere for the fillings to cook, whilst giving the contrast of a crunchy exterior. They can, of course, be sweet or savoury.

My mother was very proud of her pastry and passed on some valuable tips. She kept a cool marble slab upon which to roll it. Traditionally, everything about pastry-making (except for a hot pork pie crust) has to be kept cool. In a traditional French restaurant the *patissière* always arrived before the other chefs, to be able to work before the kitchen heated up.

Having a good, light touch with the fingertips is an advantage; hot hands and over-handling the dough can make it unduly hard when baked. This is something that needs to be learned with patience and practice. I don't know about you, but I learn best from watching. So if you see pastry-making as somewhat daunting, find a friend who has developed the skill and watch them, or treat yourself to a day's workshop at a cookery school. It will form the basis for many interesting dishes.

Pastry crusts are cooked at relatively high temperatures, which partly gelate the starch and dry the matrix of gluten, producing a crunchy, crisp texture and a golden exterior. If the heating is too slow the butter in the dough melts and the flour's protein-starch network collapses before the starch gets hot enough to absorb water from the gluten and set the structure.

In the 1970s when I first started to study wholefood cookery, pastry was made with 100% wheat flour, which tended to be rather heavy. More recently I have used a mixture of flours, or white unbleached flour for dessert pastry and for lighter, crispier results. Flours that are organically grown and stone-ground are superior, and it is possible now to buy 82% or 85% flours, which have had some of the bran removed. But you may still wish to use a mixture of half white, half '85%'. If you sift out some of the bran this can be used in bran muffins or bran pickles.

For my fats I use butter. Try to avoid margarine, as it is such an unnatural product and uses lots of technology to achieve the saturation of what are normally unsaturated oils. To me the flavour is much inferior. There are some pastries, however, that can be made with sunflower or olive oil. For water, I use ice-cold spring water.

The procedure

You need a large mixing bowl to give yourself plenty of room to do the required rubbing motion. This involves lifting up the flour and butter (cut into small cubes) and, as you rub quickly with fingertips, allowing it to fall back into the bowl, letting in as much air as possible, until the mixture resembles fine breadcrumbs. Add a pinch of salt.

Now is the time to add the ice-cold water (use an ice-cube to chill it). Add the water very gradually, and only just enough to bind the dough together, but not to become sticky. The more water you add, the less crispy will be your pastry. Letting it rest in a plastic bag in the fridge for half-an-hour allows the butter to harden. Bring it out about ten minutes before you wish to roll it out. Use a heavy rolling-pin if you can and start to roll briskly up and down. Then turn the pastry at right angles and continue to roll up and down until you have an even thickness. Do not be tempted to roll in all directions, e.g. diagonally. Pastry has a warp and a weft and as it shrinks during baking it will do so unevenly if it has been pulled in many directions.

To transfer it to the flan tin or pie dish pick it up *confidently* on one end and insert the rolling pin in the middle, so that it drapes over the rolling pin. Then you can gently place it where you want it. A good-tempered pastry should be fairly easy to handle, but if it is made of 100% wheat flour (i.e. less gluten) it may be less cohesive.

To bake blind

Line the flan tin with pastry, trim off excess and crimp the edges. Prick the bottom evenly with a fork. Return to the fridge for five minutes to re-harden the butter. Then line the pastry shape with a circle of parchment paper that comes up the sides and fill with dried beans (kept for this sole purpose). It can then be placed in a hot oven (200°C/gas mark 6) for 15 minutes, till the edges start to turn golden. Take the flan case out of the oven and remove the beans and paper. Replace in the oven for another ten minutes until it is pale gold all over and firm. Now it is ready for your filling.

Different kinds of pastry

Crumbly pastries: short crust, pâté brisée; flaky or rough puff; laminated pastries such as filo or strudel that consist of very thin layers of pastry with butter or shortening between the layers. There are also pastries with chopped nuts that require you to put the pastry crumbs into your flan tin and just press them together with the finger-tips to cover the bottom.

Basic Shortcrust Pastry

This can be used for all manner of dishes: quiches, pasties, en croûte dishes, etc. I allow just over half butter to flour, which makes it crisp and delicious.

8 oz/225 g plain flour, sifted together with pinch of salt

5 oz/150 g cold butter, cubed

1. Rub butter into flour and salt until a fine breadcrumb consistency.

2. Add 3 tbsp (approx.) ice-cold water. Mix to a dough, which should be neither sticky nor so 'short' (there's no such thing as 'long-crust') that it is full of cracks. This takes a bit of practice.

3. Wrap in clingfilm and refrigerate for at least 20–30 minutes.

Quick Flaky Pastry

This really does work and cuts out all the rolling, dabbing, folding and resting that I learnt in my domestic science class!

8 oz/225 g plain flour, sifted together with pinch of salt

6 oz/175 g butter which has sequestered in the freezing compartment of your fridge for $^{1}/_{2}$ hour, wrapped in foil

ice-cold water to mix

1. Peel half the foil back from the butter, dip the exposed end into the flour and grate on a coarse grater. Keep dipping the end into the flour until you have managed to grate it all into the bowl. Rather than using your hands, which will soften the butter, use a palette knife to distribute the grated butter until it has all been coated.

2. Carefully add just enough water to bring the dough together, leaving the bowl clean.

3. Put it into a polythene bag and chill for 30 minutes.

If you want to have puffy, flaky layers you can still do the rolling into a long rectangle roughly 12 x 8 in (30 x 20 cm). Mark into thirds. Fold in one-third with the other on top. Press the edges to trap the air. Rest the pastry for 5–10 minutes. Lift it, flour the board, give a quarter-turn and repeat the process three or more times. Wrap in polythene and chill, overnight if possible. When using it for mille feuilles or vol-au-vents, for example, give it time to return to room temperature.

Filo Pastry

I have never attempted to make this, so on the rare, but nice, occasions that I use it—for spanokopita or boreks (Greek dishes)—I buy it. It must be stored in the fridge.

Sweet Pâté Brisée

With ground nuts and icing sugar (see individual recipes).

FESTIVALS

Finally, a note on festivals and rituals, which have traditionally been born out of the need to be in contact with the gods—higher powers—ancestors, and spirits of nature (or elementals). At certain auspicious moments barriers are broken down between the visible and invisible worlds and are reflected in the pulsing rhythms of nature. The great dramas of death and rebirth are manifested in the dying back of vegetation in winter and then there is the anticipation of its renewed fertility issuing forth in spring—indeed a cause for celebration.

Many rituals grew up for the period between the summer and winter solstices, to ensure continuing good harvests by placating the gods and elementals. These rituals fell largely into two categories. The first might be seen as purification through fasts, abstinences and lamentations—indeed a kind of emptying process. Secondly would come feasting and rejoicing with special foods, music, dance, poetry and drama. This symbolized the 'filling up' process and was accompanied by magic—splashing water to bring about rain, lighting fires to bring warmth, and leaping high so that the crops might grow tall. When performed with intense focus, these became powerful group activities.

Mother Earth also had to be consciously united to the moon and her time-keeping phases. The moon represents the dark side of nature, her unseen side, and the intuitive, irrational and subjective aspects of the human soul. In contrast, the 'dying god' of vegetation was seen as the sun god who died in winter and was reborn at the solstice to vanquish the power of darkness with the triumph of the light. These opposing polarities were later dramatized as performances in the Dionysian Mysteries, and later in the still-performed dramas of Christmas, Whitsuntide and other mystery plays. Aristotle considered that the importance of these mystery dramas lay in the impressions, images and emotions they generated, not as forms of instruction.

I have followed with great interest the festivals of Mallorca; some have their roots in pre-Christian times. I was able to experience some of the effects of the tableaux on the souls and personalities of this island people, who are deeply connected to their many and diverse festivals. In Britain, however, erosion of what were originally pagan feasts—inspired by nature—was brought about by Puritanism. Then followed the Industrial Revolution, where efficiency and pragmatism further enslaved humankind and separated it from cycles of the natural world.

We need festivals to nourish community, to reinvigorate our ties with the land and each other. In a nation where many people spend their Sundays shopping in a supermarket, we surely need to consider whether in losing traditions and our mythology we have also lost a great deal of the richness and texture of life. I found that the people of Mallorca knew how to work hard but also how to celebrate. Every week seemed to have a saint's day. I was always impressed, for instance, by the fact that on All Hallows (*El dia de los Muertos*) it is traditional to have a special service *in the cemetery*, and everyone goes with beautiful bouquets of flowers to honour and talk about their dead relatives. Later, special foods are eaten.

As I think the celebration of festivals is so important to modern life, I have mentioned some of the most important at the beginning of each seasonal section of recipes. These are meant only as an indication, and are largely derived from the Christian tradition—although their timings often coincide with pre-Christian festivities.

Spring

Craving for Spring

The Gush of Spring is strong enough
     to toss the globe of earth like a ball
     on a fountain

At the same time it opens the tiny
     hands of the hazel
     with such infinite patience . . .

The power of the rising, golden, all-creative
     sap could take the earth

And heave it off among the stars, into the invisible
The same sets the throstle at sunset on a bough
     singing against the blackbirds . . .

**Blossoms—Nettle soup—
Wild garlic pesto—Rock samphire—
Sorrel soup—Pink salmon—
Artichokes—Green tender asparagus spears—
Soba noodles—Crunchy radishes—
Soft white cheese**

FESTIVALS

Mimouna, is the end of the Passover celebration that originated with the Jews of Morocco, and falls in April.

> It was the custom, in Morocco, for Jews to visit each other at night and dance in the street. The whole community, in every city, held open house. It was also an occasion for the public demonstration of friendly relations between Jews and Muslims. Muslims would bring flowers, ears of grain, greens, honey, milk, bread and fresh butter to their Jewish friends and Jews would invite Muslims to partake of the Mimouna delicacies. The festive table of the night of the Mimouna is garlanded with leaves and grasses and green ears of wheat, symbolizing the renewal of nature after winter. A platter of flour in which lie five broad beans, five dates, five ears of wheat and five coins symbolizes the hope for plenty. Some have a fish on the table, representing fertility. The table is laden with dairy foods and great platters of fruit, confectionery, and pastries. All the food is sweet, there is nothing sour or salty.

> (Claudia Roden, *The Book of Jewish Food*)

Easter is the great annual festival of the Christian Year commemorating the death and resurrection of Christ. Through its relation to the spring equinox it corresponds in the daily cycle to sunrise, the return of the light. Easter Day occurs on the first Sunday following the first full moon after the equinox (21 March). Thus it must fall on or between 22 March and 25 April. Despite many attempts (notably by Pope Gregory XIII) to hold it on a fixed date, it is the one Christian festival which truly links us to the cosmic rhythms of the sun and moon and so is a 'movable feast'.

Ostra, the Risen Light, the Teutonic goddess of spring, and Eostre, the Anglo-Saxon goddess of dawn, had their rites celebrated at the vernal equinox. Spring-cleaning heralds this festival and in Ireland animals' byres were cleaned and whitewashed in preparation. It was a festival of renewal, the old could be thrown out, but there should also be something new, such as a new Easter bonnet (which then became an essential tradition for the ladies).

The Easter egg became an important feature of the festival since eggs, forbidden during the fast of Lent, were eaten again at Easter. An egg is also clearly a symbol of new life, and eggs laid on this day were attributed with special properties. They can be dyed, blown and painted and hung on an Easter Tree, or hard-boiled and decorated and eaten in celebration as a symbol of new life, fertility and continuity. In Russia on Easter

Saturday the *koulich* (Easter bread) is taken to church to be blessed by the priest along with the *paskha*, a moulded cream cheese, and some of the decorated hard-boiled eggs. After the midnight liturgy the family go home to an Easter table groaning with special foods. The eggs and the *paskha* have XB written on them, the Cyrillic initials for 'Christ is risen'. Then the battle of the eggs takes place, where each person pits their hard-boiled and decorated egg against their neighbour's. The loser's egg cracks and the winner continues to challenge the others. Eventually dessert is presented— the *koulich* and the *paskha*.

In Britain on Easter Sunday we hide eggs in the garden for the children to find, or roll them down a steep hill. The winner's egg is the one that remains intact. Of course there are also lots of chocolate Easter eggs and hot cross buns.

May Day (1 May) is an occasion for the rites of spring to be celebrated with morris dancing and dancing around the ribboned maypole. It is the festival of vegetation. Houses and porches and holy wells were decorated with fresh flowers and wreaths that often had a golden and a silver ball (symbolizing sun and moon) suspended within them. A May Queen or May King was chosen in certain traditions and was richly garlanded to represent burgeoning vegetation. Fires were lit in Celtic Beltane rituals from the sacred *Tein-eigin* (Gaelic for 'forced fire').

SAMPLE MENU

Nettle Oat Cream Soup

Asparagus Tart with Wild Garlic

Green Salad

Carrot Relish

Honey, Saffron and Pistachio Rice Bavarois or Rhubarb Fool

Soups

V Nettle Oat Cream Soup

SERVES 6

6 oz/175 g nettle tops (tender ones, picked in springtime), clean and dry

4 shallots, sliced

8 oz/225 g leeks, washed and sliced

3 sticks of celery, finely sliced

3 cloves of garlic, minced

1 large onion, chopped finely

2 oz/50 g oat flakes soaked in $^1/_2$ pt/275 ml cold milk

$2^1/_2$ pts/1.5 l good stock

1 oz/25 g butter

2 tbsp olive oil

Nutmeg

Salt and pepper

Method:

1. Soak the nettles in $^1/_4$ pt/150 ml boiling stock for 5 minutes, then whiz in a food processor till puréed.

2. Sauté onions, leeks, shallots and garlic in the butter and oil till translucent

3. Add celery, 2 pts/1.2 l) stock and whisk in the oats and milk and half the nettle purée. Season. Cook gently till the vegetables are soft and the soup has the consistency of thin cream. Add a little nutmeg.

Serve with a generous swirl of emerald green nettle purée, a splash of double cream if you like, and garlic croûtons. Or serve with crusty rolls and the award-winning Cornish Yarg cheese.

A note on Cornish Yarg

This cheese, which has a distinctive nettle-leaf rind, is based on a recipe of the thirteenth century—a time when people clearly knew the benefits of using nettles in the diet. It is made by hand using the milk from the pedigree Holstein herd that graze the lush pastures of the beautiful Lynher Valley below the rocky outcrops of Bodmin Moor.

Helen's Monkfish Chowder

SERVES 6

Helen is a dedicated cook. Having raised six children with husband Tom, she has continued to fly the banner for good, healthy, delicious organic/biodynamic food—for all, not just a few. She works in the excellent project of Ruskin & Horsley Mill, two reconditioned watermills that have become a centre of excellence, providing highly skilled training in crafts, farming and gardening for young people who are socially ill-adapted. She is the only community cook that I have seen to slosh BD wine into her soups. Here is one which is a real treat and unforgettable—a meal in itself.

Required: large heavy pan with lid

2 medium onions, finely chopped

3–4 cloves garlic, crushed

1 chilli pepper, de-seeded and finely chopped

2 tbsp olive oil

³/4 lb/350 g waxy potatoes, cut into small cubes

³/4 lb/350 g monkfish or sea trout

1 large red pepper, sliced into small strips (if you have time this is better roasted and skinned first)

1 pt/570 ml good stock

1 tin (400 g) organic coconut milk

1 tin (400 g) chopped tomatoes

zest and juice of 2 limes

handful of chopped fresh coriander

2 tsp Hungarian smoked paprika

1 heaped tsp ground coriander

salt and pepper

¹/2 tsp turmeric

Method:

1. Heat the olive oil in a large heavy saucepan. Add onions, garlic and chilli and cook gently until translucent, but do not brown. Add a little salt ($^1/2$ tsp).

2. Add cubed potatoes and spices. Stir and continue to cook another 5 minutes.

3. Add sliced red pepper and 1 pt stock. Cook for further 10 minutes.

4. Now add coconut milk and tomatoes with their juice, zest of limes and cook another 5–10 minutes.

5. Add the monkfish cut into 1-inch cubes and half the fresh coriander. Bring to the boil and cook for 5 minutes. Turn off heat, put on lid and allow the chowder to cool, so flavours penetrate. Reheat briefly before serving, adding lime juice and rest of coriander. Adjust seasoning. A tsp of sugar is good.

Serve with lots of country bread and olive oil, and fresh green salad.

 Miso Soup with Buckwheat Noodles and Spring Vegetables

SERVES 6

1 onion, sliced into half-moons

1 carrot, sliced in 'carrot flowers' (see page 93)

4 oz/110 g young broad beans, or

4 oz/110 g mange-tout

1 stick celery, sliced finely on the diagonal

$^{1}/_{2}$ tsp grated fresh ginger root

2 oz/50 g soba noodles

2 pts/1.2 l good vegetable stock (not salty), heated

1 tbsp miso paste (can be mugi miso—barley— or brown rice miso)

pinch of salt

a little cold-pressed sesame oil

spring onions, finely chopped, for garnish

Method:

1. In a heavy pot splash a little sesame oil and heat. Add onion and sweat, stirring with long cooking chopsticks. Add carrot and celery and grated ginger. Stir briskly, then add hot stock and cook for 5 minutes. Add peas or beans and noodles. Cook for another 5 minutes.

2. Prepare the miso, in a suribachi if you have one. Add a little of the hot stock to dilute the miso paste to a pouring consistency. Add this to the soup and remove from heat. As miso contains a live bacillus boiling will destroy the living enzymes. Garnish with spring onions and eat immediately.

V Nettle Dumplings to go with Soups

SERVES 6

These emerald-green dumplings both look and taste dramatic!

4 oz/110 g young nettle tops

2 oz/50 g breadcrumbs

2 tbsp vegetarian suet

2 oz/50 g self-raising flour

1 tbsp finely chopped parsley

4 spring onions, finely chopped

$1/2$ tsp grated nutmeg

grated zest of one lemon

1 egg

salt and pepper

1 pt/570 ml stock for poaching the dumplings

The breadcrumbs and wheat flour can be replaced by fine maize flour plus $1/2$ tsp baking powder

Method:

1. Steep the nettles in $1/4$ pt/150 ml boiling, lightly salted water. Pour off excess water after 5 minutes, but keep this for the poaching stock as it is full of goodness, including mineral salts.

2. Purée the nettles. You should have about 3 oz/75 g when the liquid is squeezed out.

3. Add to all the other ingredients. The consistency should allow you to form walnut-sized balls, which you then drop into the boiling stock and cook for 10–15 minutes. Drain, but keep the stock for nettle and oat soup (see above).

V David's Fresh Pea and Mint Soup

SERVES 6

2 lb/1 kg fresh peas

2 tbsp olive oil

2 oz/50 g butter

1 large onion finely chopped

3 cloves of garlic

1 bunch fresh mint leaves, chopped

$1^1/2$ pts/750 ml good stock

4 oz/100 g cooked potatoes

2 sticks of celery

Salt and pepper

2 oz/50 g freshly grated Parmesan cheese

extra virgin olive oil for garnish

Method:

1. Shell peas (pods can be used to make stock).

2. Melt the butter and olive oil in a heavy pot. Sauté the onions and garlic for 10 minutes, or until translucent and soft.

3. Add $3/4$ of the mint, $3/4$ of the peas and stock and cook until tender but not discoloured (5–8 minutes).

4. Press this mixture to a thickish purée. Return to the pot, add the fresh uncooked peas and cook a further 5 minutes.

5. Garnish with the remaining mint, sprinkle with Parmesan and dribble a little green-gold olive oil on the top.

Serve with foccaccia and a fresh tomato and basil salad.

Meat and Fish Main Dishes

Lemon Chicken with Almond Sauce

SERVES 6

An Iranian recipe

1 free range chicken, jointed

2 sticks celery

2 white onions

2 pts/1.2 l good chicken stock

wineglass of white wine

3 oz/75 g ground almonds

1 oz/25 g butter

For the marinade:

2 tbsp crème fraîche

3 cloves garlic

^{1}/2 tsp sea salt and freshly ground pepper

2 tsp Iranian chicken spice (see below)

zest and juice of 1 large lemon

4 spring onions, chopped,

plus 4 spring onions and 2 tbsp fresh coriander for garnish

For Iranian spice mix (if you can't buy ready-made):

1 tbsp cumin seeds

1 tsp whole cloves

3-inch cinnamon stick

2 tsp black cardamom

1 tsp peppercorns

2 tsps ground turmeric

(Roast all together in a skillet for 5 minutes to release their oils, then grind.)

Method:

1. Blend together all marinade ingredients in a food processor, pour over the chicken joints and marinate overnight.

2. Peel and slice onions and finely chop celery.

3. In a heavy casserole, sauté the onion and celery in the butter and oil until transparent but not brown.

4. Add the chicken, marinade, stock and wine.

5. Cook with the lid on until chicken is tender (approx. 45 minutes).

6. Remove chicken pieces, then reduce the cooking liquid and add the ground almonds. The sauce should be a coating consistency.

7. Adjust the seasoning, then replace the chicken.

Serve garnished with more chopped spring onions and chopped coriander, accompanied by jasmine rice, sautéd fennel and courgettes.

Salmon en Croûte with Ginger, Rhubarb and Currants with Watercress Sauce

SERVES 6

Required: baking tray

Oven at 220°C/gas mark 6 for first 20 minutes, then 160°C/gas mark 3 for 20 minutes

$1^{1}/_2$ lb/700g fresh salmon fillets, skinned

4 pieces crystallized ginger

3 oz/75 g softened salted butter

1 tbsp currants

4 oz/110 g rhubarb, stewed with a little sugar and drained

10 oz/275 g shortcrust pastry

salt and pepper

squeeze of lemon juice

For the pastry:

6 oz/175 g flour

4 oz/110 g butter

3 tbsp cold water

salt and pepper

egg wash

Method:

1. Make pastry (see pages 97-8) and allow to rest.

2. Remove any bones left in the salmon with tweezers and cut fish into two equal parts. Season with a little salt and pepper and add a squeeze of lemon juice.

3. Make filling: finely chop the crystallized ginger and add to softened butter. Then add currants and rhubarb purée (as free of juice as possible). Combine all into a soft paste.

4. Spread on one of the salmon fillets and sandwich both together. Dab any moisture from the salmon with kitchen paper (it would make pastry sticky).

5. Roll out pastry into a large rectangle and brush the edges with beaten egg. Fold it over the salmon, in a parcel, closing the ends. Decorate with pastry leaves or a little fish cut out of pastry. Brush all over with egg wash.

6. Bake in hot oven (220°C/gas mark 6) for first 20 minutes or till pastry starts to turn golden, then turn oven down to 160°C/gas mark 3 and cook for a further 20 minutes.

Watercress Sauce

1 bunch watercress (stalks removed), covered with boiling water and whizzed to a purée

$^{1}/_2$ pt/275 ml single cream

3 finely chopped shallots

2 oz/50 g butter

2 oz/50 g white flour

1 tsp Dijon mustard

egg yolk (white with a tiny drop of yolk can be used for egg wash)

1 tsp lemon juice

$^{1}/_4$ pt/150 ml white wine or milk

salt and pepper

Method:

1. Heat cream and white wine together, but do not allow to boil.

2. Melt butter and add shallots in a second pan, gently cook until translucent (5 minutes), but do not brown.

3. Add flour and stir thoroughly to make sure there are no lumps.

4. Gradually add hot cream and wine, whisking all the time. Next add mustard, squeeze of lemon juice and seasonings. Then add egg yolk. Lastly add the watercress purée (no more than $^{1}/_4$ pt or 150 ml). Continue to heat, but not to boiling which would curdle the egg and spoil the emerald green of the watercress cream sauce.

Serve with the salmon.

This dish is also delicious cold. We had new potatoes with mint, a beetroot and celeriac salad and a crisp green salad.

Vegetarian Main Dishes

Watercress, Goat's Cheese and Asparagus Roulade

SERVES 6

The White Hart on the Dartington estate is my favourite local restaurant. You can either eat informally in the bar or in grand style in the great medieval dining room. The food is exciting, sourced locally, often organic, and local Sharpham wines are on offer. It is very reasonably priced. This is a version of one of their vegetarian dishes.

Required: a 15 x 10 inch/25 x 38 cm baking tray, lined with parchment

6 eggs, separated

bunch of watercress, roughly chopped

$^{1}/_{2}$ lb/500 g lightly cooked asparagus, coarse parts of stem removed

1 goat's cheese, chopped into small pieces

$^{1}/_{2}$ lb/500 g cream cheese or ricotta

1 tbsp crème fraîche

2 spring onions, finely chopped

salt and pepper

Watercress, Goat's Cheese and Asparagus Roulade cont.

1. Whisk egg whites to a stiff peak.

2. Mix egg yolks in, then watercress. Season lightly.

3. Fold egg whites into mixture.

4. Spread evenly over baking tray.

5. Put in oven for 8 minutes at 200°C/gas mark 6.

6. Allow to cool in the tray.

7. Loosen the cream cheese a little with 1 tbsp crème fraîche and mix in spring onions. Season and spread onto the base.

8. Lay the asparagus across the short length and dot with chopped goat's cheese.

9. Roll up like a Swiss roll, using the parchment as a support.

To serve, cut into 1-inch slices and gently reheat. Decorate a platter with pretty salad leaves. Can be eaten cold. This dish goes well with new potatoes, carrot and celeriac salad with orange-flavoured vinaigrette, and garnished with rocket and other salad leaves.

Wild Garlic or Ramsons (*Allium ursinum*)

A native bulb prolific throughout the British Isles in damp woods and lanes. The fresh young leaves can be used in salads or cooked as in this wild garlic and asparagus tart. Wild garlic pesto is excellent used on pasta. The flowers are clusters of pearly white star-shaped umbels, sweeter than the leaves and good in salads and the asparagus goat's cheese roulade (see above).

Asparagus is most delicious. 'A delicate vegetable which had the reputation, according to Culpepper, of increasing seed and stirring up lust' (*The Englishman's Flora*). The Romans grew it in elaborate ways and Pliny wrote about its popularity. It prefers sandy, well-drained soil. In Mallorca I noticed that our donkey Eureka, when suffering from laminitis from eating too much alfalfa, would seek out wild asparagus in the hedgerows. She was particularly fond of it when it had become ferny and rather thorny.

The Bretforton Asparagus Auction takes place on the last Sunday in May behind the Fleece Inn, Bretforton, Vale of Evesham. Bundles of 10–20, 60 and 120 spears are auctioned by the Bretforton Silver Band.

Asparagus Tart with Wild Garlic

SERVES 6

Required: loose-bottomed, buttered 10 inch/26 cm flan case

Oven 200°C/gas mark 6 to begin

For the pastry:

6 oz/175 g strong white flour

2 oz/50 g 100% wheat flour

$^1/_2$ tsp sea salt

5 oz/150 g cold butter cut in small pieces

1 tbsp sesame seeds

4 tbsp ice-cold water

For the filling:

8 oz/225 g onions, sliced in half moons

$^1/_2$ bunch spring onions

1 bunch young asparagus

generous handful wild garlic, shredded

1 oz/25 g butter

1 tbsp olive oil

6 oz/175 g soft curd cheese

5 eggs

3/4 pt (425 ml) single cream

3 oz (75 g) grated mature cheddar

salt and pepper

Method:

1. Make the pastry. In a large bowl sift together the flours and salt. Work in the butter with finger tips lightly, lifting mixture up to let in air as you do it. (The mixture should resemble fine bread crumbs.) Carefully add the ice-cold water. Now the pastry should stay together in a ball but should not be too sticky (too much water makes pastry hard). Cover and allow to rest in the fridge for half an hour while preparing the filling.

2. Trim fibrous ends from the asparagus and poach in slightly salted water—enough to just about cover—for 5 minutes (to blanch them). Drain.

3. Sauté onions in butter and oil until translucent, with a pinch or two of salt. Add garlic leaves and remove from heat.

4. Beat the eggs in a bowl large enough to hold all the filling. Add cream. Make this mixture up to $1\frac{1}{4}$ pt/725 ml with the eggs and cream. Add a little milk if necessary.

5. Add cheeses, onions and wild garlic to the egg mixture. Test the seasoning. Add salt and freshly ground black pepper.

6. Roll out the pastry case and line a 9-inch loose-bottomed flan tin. Crimp pastry edges and place on a baking tray.

7. Pour in the filling. Then arrange the asparagus all round with the tips pointing inwards like the spokes of a wheel. Press them in a little so they are covered with a little of the egg custard but still visible.

8. Cook for 15 minutes at 200°C/gas mark 6 to seal the pastry, then turn heat down to 180°C/gas mark 4 for further 40 minutes or until firm and a little golden. Allow to rest 10 minutes before slicing.

This tart could be served with new potatoes, or baked potatoes, and a large tossed salad.

Millet, Leek and Walnut Patties

SERVES 6

10 oz/275 g millet

3 oz/110 g walnuts

2 tbsp millet flakes

8oz/225 g cleaned and finely sliced young leeks

2 tbsp Quark or cream cheese

1 large egg for binding

1oz/25 g butter and 2 tbsp olive oil for sautéing

1–1^1/2 pts good vegetable stock

1. Measure millet in a measuring jug. Wash and pick it over carefully. Allow to dry. Melt butter and oil in a heavy bottomed pot and sauté millet for 2–3 minutes until grains are coated (this keeps them from clogging together too much). Pour on the double amount of hot vegetable stock, which should be appropriately seasoned. Allow to come to the boil, then turn down flame to minimum (perhaps use a flame-spreader to prevent scorching of the bottom of the pot). I use a Le Creuset pot for grains and it is important to choose the right size pot. The grain will double in size, so make allowances for this, but at the same time the pot should not be too large because this will not bring good results. Do not stir during cooking. After 30 minutes the stock should be absorbed and the grains plump and fluffy. Add raw millet flakes (for binding). Allow to rest until cool enough to handle.

2. While the millet is cooking, lightly roast the walnuts in a dry frying pan (again, a cast iron one is best). Then grind them in a food processor, not too finely, leave some texture.

3. Sauté shredded leeks in a little butter with oil until softened and the emerald-green colour is still retained.

4. Add leeks, walnuts, Quark, egg and adjust seasoning. The mixture now should be easy to form into firm patties (8–10). Dust with millet flakes and rest for ten minutes. They should be cold now.

5. Fry in olive oil approx. 5 minutes on each side. They should be golden brown.

Serve with Tamari, Ginger and Green Onion Sauce (see recipe on page 216).

Tricoloured Pasta with Saffron Cream Sauce

SERVES 6

This involves a basic béchamel sauce, which is very useful to have for soufflés, lasagnes, Welsh rarebit, etc.

12 oz/350 g tricolour pasta shells or tassels

1 tbsp olive oil

For the sauce:

1^1/2 pt/900ml whole milk

infusion: 2 bay leaves, 2 tsps whole black peppercorns, a few slices of onion, carrot, celery, parsley stalks

3 oz/75 g butter

3 oz/75 g unbleached white flour (for roux)

^{1}/4 pt/5 fl oz single cream

wineglass of Amontillado sherry (or white wine)

1 tsp saffron threads, soaked in small quantity boiling water for 10 minutes or so

salt and pepper to taste

bunch of spring onions, finely sliced and sautéd in butter

To make the sauce:

1. Put milk and infusion ingredients in a heavy-bottomed saucepan. Bring slowly to the boil. Turn off heat and allow to infuse for 10 minutes.

2. Melt butter in a saucepan, add flour and cook gently, stirring with a wooden spoon until it thickens. Start straining the hot milk into the roux (flour and butter mixture). Now you need a strong whisk to keep stirring this mixture briskly so that it does not lump. Keep adding the milk until it has all been absorbed. You should now have a thick, velvety sauce free of lumps. (This is your basic béchamel sauce, which can be used in many ways.)

3. Add cream, sherry and saffron. Season carefully and continue to cook until bubbling gently. Add the sautéd spring onions.

Cook the pasta:

4 Into a large pan of boiling salted water, to which you have added 1 tbsp olive oil and a bay leaf, drop the pasta and return to the boil and cook for 8 minutes, or until pasta is al dente.

5 Strain in a colander, return to the saucepan.

6 Pour sauce over pasta and mix gently.

Serve with Bouquet of Vegetables (see page 227) and a three-leaf salad.

I always try to finish the meal with something sweet. This will often be a piece of seasonal fruit, but sometimes it is nice to make a dessert. It should be more in the way of a treat because, as we all know by now, too much sugar in the diet can be damaging to health. However, the quality and amount of sugar affects how it will be metabolized.

To find a proper balance requires some insight and artistry. I avoid beet sugar and use raw cane sugars—Rapadura, Muscovado or molasses—which retain moisture in the baking process, but for certain lighter cakes I use unrefined caster sugar. I also use maple syrup, rice syrup, date syrup and honeys (though cooking with honey is a waste of the more subtle elements that make it a truly healing substance).

Honey, Saffron and Pistachio Rice 'Bavarois'

SERVES 6

The idea for this dish came from a special Indian dessert made by Satish Kumar at Schumacher College: rice sweetened with honey and flavoured with cardamom and saffron and studded with pistachios. Then my daughter Daisy told me of a creamy, moulded Rice Bavarois dish they made in the smart restaurant where she cooked. I have joined the two concepts together to make a beautiful primrose-tinged rice dish, to celebrate the primroses coming out. But if you prefer not to bother with the gelatine part you could just serve it warm.

8 oz/225 g pudding rice

3/4 pt/425 ml water

a pinch of salt

1 pt/570 ml milk

6 cardamom pods

2 generous pinches of saffron

2 1/2 tbsp runny honey

grated rind of 1 lemon

2 oz/50 g pistachios

4 egg yolks

and optional—

1/2 pt/275 ml milk

2 packets gelatine

small carton of whipping cream

Honey, Saffron and Pistachio Rice 'Bavarois' cont.

Method:

1. Wash and drain the rice and parboil it in $^3/4$ pt water with a pinch of salt for 15 minutes, when the water will be taken up. (We do this because cooking rice with milk often catches the bottom of the saucepan.)

2. Put 1 pt milk, the cardamom pods, the saffron and lemon zest into a saucepan and bring to the boil. Turn off the heat and let it infuse for 10 minutes or so. Then bring to the boil again and fish out the cardamoms.

3. In a large bowl beat the egg yolks until frothy, then add the honey and pour on the hot milk infusion. Return to the saucepan and to the heat, which should be low (there's little more susceptible to burning than sweetened milk). Whisk all the time until it starts to thicken a little. When it reaches simmering point you may add it to the rice and gently cook for another 10 minutes, stirring, until the rice is fully cooked.

4. Add the sliced pistachio nuts and taste to see it is sweetened to your liking. You could serve it like this, but if you want a dish to turn out and decorate, let the mixture cool right down.

If you wish—

5. Take $^1/2$ pt milk and heat to nearly boiling point. Sprinkle on the 2 packets of gelatine powder, stir to make sure that it has properly dissolved, then add to the cooling rice. It may take half an hour to cool.

6. Whip the cream and fold into the cooled rice mixture. Line a ring mould with clingfilm and spoon in the rice-cream mixture until it is full (you will have a good $2^1/2$ pts). Chill 1–2 hours, then un-mould and garnish with pistachios and primroses, if you have some.

Rhubarb and Custard Ice Cream

SERVES 6

Throw physic to the dogs ...
What rhubarb, senna or what
purgative drug
Would scour these English hence?

Macbeth, Act V, scene 3

14 fl oz/400 ml milk

$^1/3$ pt/200 ml single cream

1 vanilla pod

2 large eggs

1 tbsp custard powder

a little powdered saffron (optional)

$^1/2$ lb/700 g trimmed rhubarb

4 oz/110 g light brown sugar

Method:

1. Bring milk and cream to the boil with vanilla pod.

2. In a bowl blend 1 tbsp cold milk with the eggs, custard powder, sugar and saffron. Then stir in another tbsp of milk.

3. Pour on the warm milk and cream, then return the mixture to saucepan. Bring mixture gently to boiling point, stirring. As soon as custard thickens, take off the heat and beat to prevent curdling.

4. Allow to cool, covered with a piece of wet greaseproof paper or butter paper to prevent a skin forming. Remove vanilla pod.

5. Meanwhile stew the rhubarb with very little water or bake with no water for about 20 minutes, watching it to prevent drying out.

6. Cool and mash up a little, making sure there are no large lumps of rhubarb, but not making it completely smooth.

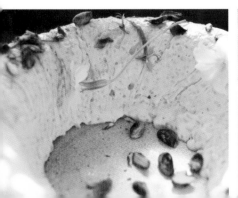

7. Place both mixtures in the freezer, and when they begin to freeze mix them together so there are still small pockets of pink rhubarb in the mixture.

8. Put back in the freezer, removing from time to time to beat the mixture to prevent big ice crystals from forming. Alternatively, use an ice cream maker, following the instructions.

9. Serve in tall sundae glasses with whipped cream and almond thins.

Rhubarb and Ginger Tart with Almond Pastry

SERVES 8

Required: an 8 inch/20 cm loose-bottomed flan tin

Oven 190°C/gas mark 5 to begin with

For the pastry:

6 oz/175 g unbleached white flour

3 oz/75 g ground almonds

1 tbsp icing sugar

5 oz/150 g cold butter, chopped

4 tbsp ice cold water

a few drops almond essence

For the fruit filling:

1¹/₂ lb/700 g young rhubarb

6–8 oz/225 g light soft brown sugar

3 pieces finely chopped crystallized stem ginger and some syrup

zest and juice of 1 lemon

a wineglass of ginger wine or cranberry juice

1¹/₂ packets Vege-gel

whipped cream to decorate

a few toasted flaked almonds

Rhubarb and Ginger Tart with Almond Pastry cont.

To make pastry:

1. Rub the butter into the flour until the mixture resembles fine breadcrumbs.

2. Stir in the icing sugar and ground almonds.

3. Mix to a dough with the water and almond essence.

4. Allow to rest, covered to prevent it drying out.

To make fruit filling:

1. Gently cook the rhubarb with 6 oz/175 g sugar, the ginger, lemon juice and zest, and ginger wine/cranberry juice. Use as little added liquid as possible. Leave to cool.

2. Strain and reserve $^1/_2$ pt/275 ml of liquid. Adjust the sweetness of the juice.

3. Add the Vege-gel to the liquid and bring to the boil, following instructions on the packet.

4. Cool and stir in the fruit.

To make pastry case:

1. Roll out the pastry and line the flan tin, making an extra thin strip of pastry to strengthen the sides, sticking it on with water. Crimp the edges.

2. Chill.

3. Bake blind at 190°C/gas mark 5 (see method on page 97).

4. After 15 minutes remove the paper and beans, or foil. Return to the oven until golden brown (5–10 minutes).

5. Leave to cool.

Putting the tart together:

1. Spoon the fruit mixture evenly into the pastry case.

2. Decorate with whipped cream and toasted almonds, and perhaps some rosemary flowers.

3. Chill before serving.

Apricot Hazelnut Torte

SERVES 8

This was a recipe off a sugar packet, which we have developed into something quite luscious.

Required: 10 inch/25 cm loose-bottomed flan tin

Oven 180°C/gas mark 4

For the base:

4 oz/110 g unbleached white flour

3oz/85g raw cane sugar (Rapadura or Muscovado)

6 oz/175 g butter

6 oz/175 g roasted, finely chopped hazelnuts

1 tbsp water

For the filling:

1 lb/450 g dried apricots (sulphured apricots give better colour)

zest and juice of 1 orange

2 oz/55 g Rapadura raw cane sugar

For the topping:

4 oz/110 g unbleached white flour

4 oz/110 g butter

4 oz/110 g Rapadura raw cane sugar

1 tsp ground cinnamon

1. Soak the apricots overnight with strips of orange peel (use a zester for this). Then cook in half a pint of water with the orange zest and 2 oz sugar until syrupy.

2. Prepare the base by rubbing the butter into the flour until a texture of fine breadcrumbs is obtained. Add sugar and chopped hazelnuts and 1 tbsp water. Pat into an even layer on the base of buttered flan tin.

3. Prepare topping by rubbing the butter into the sifted flour with cinnamon and sugar, till like fine breadcrumbs.

4. Assemble the torte by spreading the apricots evenly over the base and sprinkling the topping over them (to cover).

5. Bake in a preheated oven, 180°C/gas mark 4 for 40–50 minutes, or until golden brown.

Serve warm or cold, with clotted cream.

Apricot Tart with Almond Pastry and Crème Patissière

SERVES 8

You cannot be faint of heart to tackle this creation, with its four different layers, requiring four different processes: crisp almond pastry reveals luscious crème patissière, and moist apricots with a hint of orange clad in a glistening layer of jelly. It is a dish to prepare when the apricots just start to come in and are firm and a little tart—for who would want to cook something as perfect as a ripe apricot?

Required: a 10 inch/24 cm flan tin

Oven 200°C/gas mark 6

For the pastry:

6 oz/175g unbleached white flour

3 oz/85 g ground almonds

1 tbsp icing sugar

5 oz/150 g cold butter, chopped

4 tbsp ice cold water

a few drops of almond essence

For the crème patissière:

15 fl oz/425 ml whole milk

1 vanilla pod

4 egg yolks

$3^1/2$ oz/80 g caster sugar

2 level tbsp ($1^1/2$ oz/40 g) plain flour

1 level tbsp (1 oz/25 g) cornflour or arrowroot

Fruit and glaze:

$1^1/2$ lb/700 g firm apricots (dried ones could be used, 12 oz/350 g, but they should be of the bright orange variety)

zest of 1 orange, in strips

$3/4$ pt/425 ml water

1 tbsp maple syrup

1 tbsp cane sugar

1 packet Vege-gel

Apricot Tart with Almond Pastry and Crème Patissière cont.

To make pastry:

1. Rub the butter into the flour until the mixture resembles fine breadcrumbs.

2. Stir in the icing sugar and ground almonds.

3. Mix to a dough with the water and almond essence.

4. Allow to rest, covered in the refrigerator to prevent it drying out.

To make crème patissière:

1. Mix together the flour, cornflour or arrowroot with just enough cold milk to make a smooth paste.

2. Bring the remaining milk to the boil with the vanilla pod and leave to infuse.

3. Beat together the egg yolks and sugar until thick, creamy and nearly white.

4. Add the blended flour mixture, making sure there are no lumps.

5. Reheat the milk until just below boiling point and pour onto the egg and flour mixture, whisking continually.

6. Return to the clean saucepan and continue whisking until thickened, simmering for 3 minutes.

7. Cover with a butter paper close to the surface of the custard, to stop a skin forming and to allow to cool.

Method for fruit:

1. Boil together the water, honey, orange zest and sugar to make a syrup.

2. Halve the apricots and remove stones.

3. Add halved apricots and a few kernels to the syrup and poach until tender but not squidgy.

4. Drain, reserving the orange zest for decoration and leave syrup to cool.

To make pastry case:

1. Roll out the pastry and line the flan tin, making an extra strip of pastry to strengthen the sides. Crimp the edges.

2. Chill for 10–15 minutes.

3. Bake blind at 200°C/gas mark 6 (see page 97) Return to the oven until golden (5–10 minutes)

4. Leave to cool.

Assembly:

1. Pour or spoon the crème patissière evenly into the pastry case.

2. Arrange the halved apricots on top and sprinkle with the orange peel.

3. Add the packet of Vege-gel to the cooled syrup and bring to the boil following the instructions on the packet.

4. Pour quickly and evenly over the apricots as soon as it has thickened. (Beware: Vege-gel sets extremely quickly!) If you choose gelatine instead, follow instructions on the packet.

5. Chill.

If you don't want to bother with the jelly, use 2 tbsp good quality apricot jam, diluted with 2 tbsp hot water and sieved. This will also give a nice glaze.

Paskha

SERVES 6-8

An Easter celebratory dessert (*Paskha* means Passover and also Easter).

Required: a muslin-lined, sterilized flower pot approx. 9 inch/23 cm high, or a ceramic bowl with a hole in the bottom

^{1}/$_2$ pt/250 ml double cream

^{1}/$_2$ pt/250 ml whipped double cream for decoration

1 vanilla pod

3 large egg yolks

1^1/$_2$ lb/700 g curd cheese

zest of one lemon, finely grated

4 oz/110 g dried apricots stewed till soft

2 oz/50 undyed glacé cherries

2 oz/50 g seedless raisins

1 oz/25 g chopped crystallized angelica

1 oz/25 g chopped preserved ginger

4 oz/110 g softened unsalted butter

small bunch of green grapes for decoration

2 tbsp ginger wine

4 oz/110 g roasted almonds, blanched and chopped

Paskha cont.

On the previous day soak the fruits in the ginger wine.

Method:

1. Put cream into a saucepan. Split the vanilla pod down the middle and add to the cream. Bring gently almost to the boil.

2. Meanwhile, place egg yolks (whites can be used for macaroons) and sugar in a bowl and whisk until thick and creamy, using an electric hand-beater.

3. Then pour on the hot cream still whisking.

4. Return to the saucepan, which you have cleaned out, and continue to heat gently, stirring to prevent curdling or the bottom catching. Do not allow to boil. When thickened remove from heat and allow to cool thoroughly.

5. Cream the butter and blend in the curd cheese.

6. Fold in the cooled custard, lemon zest, then the chopped fruits and almonds (reserve 1 oz for decoration, plus a little of the angelica).

7. Line a mould or flower pot with some muslin or cotton sheeting. There should be a small hole to allow whey to drip away. Fill the mould with the mixture, which should be quite stiff. Fold in the muslin and place a saucer plus a weight on top. Refrigerate overnight.

8. The next day, before serving, unmould onto a festive plate. Pipe whipped cream around the top and decorate with almonds, angelica and green grapes.

This is traditionally served with *koulich* (sweet Easter bread). It is a very rich dish, so small slices only!

Crème Caramel

SERVES 6

This is a favourite pudding, and a good one to use up the blown Easter egg contents, but serve it with some stewed fruit (rhubarb is good) to offset the richness.

Required: soufflé dish or ovenproof Pyrex dish, 2 pint/1.2 litre capacity

Oven at 150°C/gas mark 3

For the caramel:

4 oz/110 g unrefined granulated sugar

2 tbsp hot water

Method:

Mix sugar and water together in a small saucepan and heat. The mixture will bubble and start to turn golden. Allow it to become a deep amber colour and start to smell of caramel. If you boil too long it will become dark and bitter, so keep your eye on it, swishing the saucepan around to distribute the colour. Be very careful as this mixture is seriously hot. Quickly pour it into the base of your soufflé dish and tip it around so that the sides get some of the caramel. It will splutter.

For the custard:

5 large eggs

2 oz/50 g light soft brown sugar

3/4 pt/425 ml single cream

1/2 pt/275 ml whole milk

1 vanilla pod or 1/2 tsp vanilla essence

1. Combine milk, cream and vanilla pod in a heavy saucepan and let it gently heat while you beat the eggs and sugar together.

2. When the milk is steaming hot pour it onto the egg mixture, whisking vigorously. Pour this mixture through a sieve to catch the vanilla pod and any 'threads' in the eggs. Squeeze vanilla pod into the mixture, to make sure you have all the flavour.

3. Set the dish into a baking tray filled with hot water, and then bake gently in the oven for 1 hour. Cool and then chill. Unmould by loosening the sides with a knife and inverting it onto a pretty serving plate.

Summer

May the wind blow sweetness

The rivers blow sweetness

The herbs grow sweetness

For the People of Truth!

Sweet be the night

Sweet the dawn

Sweet be earth's fragrance

Sweet be our Heaven!

May the tree afford us sweetness

The Sun shine sweetness

Our cows yield sweetness—

Milk in plenty!

Rig Veda

**Blue sea with breezes and white sails—
Picnics—Squid and prawn paella—
Mallorcan cocas—Huge green and red
crispy lettuces—Tomato and basil salads—
Peaches and apricots—Tennis—
Charentais melon**

Festivals

Hag Shavuot, which falls in June, is Hebrew meaning Feast of Weeks; in Greek it is called Pentecost. The feast normally includes dairy products, in remembrance of the lands flowing with milk and honey. It might also include cheese blintzes, cheese *kreplach* (stuffed pasta), borscht with sour cream, cheesecake, *pashkha*, cheese filas and *sutlage-muhallabeya* (fragrant milk).

Summer Solstice (June 21-22) is the longest day of the year. Midsummer eve bonfires are in honour of St John's Day, that follows. Jumping over the fire was common, or throwing a garland into it that carried one's sins and diseases. Also, parading the fields with flaming torches to preserve the harvest.

Lammas Day (1 August) was when bread for the mass was made from the newly milled corn from the harvest. It seems to derive from Lughnasad, a much older Celtic observance held at the beginning of the harvest, in honour of Lug, a god of agriculture. In Ireland it was known as Lughnasa.

Fraughan Sunday, or Bilberry Sunday, the nearest Sunday to 1 August, which was celebrated by open-air jollifications on hilltops, by holy wells, rivers or lakes. The celebrants weave their own baskets out of rushes to collect the bilberries.

Aquarids (meteor showers) can be seen from 15 July to 25 August with an approximate zenithal hourly rate at maximum of 8.

Sea Bass at Thurlestone Sands

SAMPLE MENU

Sea Bass cooked over embers, stuffed with rock samphire and lemon, with Japanese sushi (various fillings), globe artichokes, aduki bean pâté, cucumber, radish and wakame salad and dipping sauce.

The sky was hyacinth blue, the sun benevolent, silver undines flickered amongst the waves and Jeb, the Welsh sheepdog, lay in the dunes watching and waiting patiently. We came with our supper, the special treat were two plump sea bass and the location had been chosen not only for its rocky beauty but because there were many great clumps of salty rock samphire growing there with which to stuff our fish. This plant is succulent and has a fennel-like flavour. We harvested some and washed it in the sea. We filled our fish, stitching up the cavity with twine, using a curved needle. The whole was massaged with sesame oil and cooked in a skillet over glowing embers. The smell of woodsmoke mingling with the sea, and the activity of collecting wood and throwing sticks for the dog, all sharpened our appetite.

The sea bass was served as part of a Japanese meal, accompanied by sushi with varied fillings, aduki bean pâté, wakame seaweed and radish salad, and a large bowl of globe artichokes. Dessert was a ruby-coloured tayberry jelly, a bowl of strawberries and slices of Charentais melon.

Sea Bass Cooked over Embers, Stuffed with Rock Samphire and Lemon

SERVES 6

2 fresh sea bass, approx. 1¹/₂ lb/1 kg each, cleaned but with heads on

2 lemons in slices

salt and pepper

shoyu or tamari (soy sauce)

enough rock samphire to fill the cavity of the fish (can be substituted by a mixture of chervil and chopped Florence fennel)

4 tbsp roast sesame oil or olive oil, for cooking

curved needle and strong thread for stitching

Method:

1. Wash the fish and scrape off scales without damaging the skin. Dry and sprinkle lightly with sea salt.

2. Cut 3 incisions in the sides of the fish and insert slices of lemon. Sprinkle the inside of the fish with lemon juice, salt and some freshly ground pepper.

3. Stuff with rock samphire and sew up the cavity. Massage or brush the fish with sesame oil.

4. Cook over wood embers if possible (I used a cast iron skillet to ensure the fish kept its form) 10 minutes each side. Alternatively, bake covered in foil in the oven at 190°C/gas mark 5. Unwrap and expose to a hot grill for 5 minutes to brown.

Sushi

Ayoko used to make sushi for our local fish shop. I looked at it admiringly, so much neater than the kind I make! I asked her to come and do a demonstration for photographs for this book. I watched her graceful fingers smoothing the ivory-coloured rice onto the sheet of ebony-coloured nori seaweed, placing tiny strips of green cucumber, pink smoked salmon and yellow flaky omelette in the centre and rolling it up, then slicing this piece of edible sculpture. What culture could invent this, for which our nearest equivalent is a sandwich?

Required: a bamboo mat for rolling up the sushi

8 oz/225 g sushi rice

1 pt/570 ml good stock

1 tsp sesame oil for sautéing

¹/2 tsp sea salt

1 packet nori seaweed (in sheets)

For vinegar bathe:

1 tsp cane sugar

2 tbsp rice vinegar

1 tbsp mirin or sherry

¹/2 tsp sea salt

Bring to the boil together, then turn off the heat.

Method:

1. Wash the rice carefully and let it drain

2. In a heavy-bottomed pot with closely fitting lid heat up the sesame oil. Sauté the rice for a few minutes, but don't brown.

3. Add 1 pt/570ml of good flavoured stock to the rice and bring to the boil. Turn down the heat to the lowest possible and leave to simmer until all stock is absorbed (about ¹/2 hour).

4. When the rice is thoroughly cooked and the stock absorbed turn it out onto something flat and wide—a large shallow bowl or plate would do. Then sprinkle with the rice-vinegar mixture to flavour it and make it stickier. Allow it to cool whilst preparing fillings.

Fillings:

Fine strips of carrot, spring onions (halved), watercress, parsley, thin strips of cucumber. Sauté in a little sesame oil with 1 tsp grated fresh ginger and 1 dsp tamari sauce. Try to keep colour and crispness of the vegetables.

Smoked salmon

Thin strips of omelette.

Assembly:

1. Take each sheet of nori, allowing one per person, and lay it on your sushi mat, shiny side down. Then cover with a layer of rice, leaving 1 inch at the top and ¹/2 inch as borders either side of the nori seaweed. Be careful not to allow grains of rice onto this area.

2. Make an indentation across the centre with a cooking chopstick and fill this with a layer of filling and press well down.

3. Moisten the strips of nori with water and then roll up in the sushi mat. Let it rest on the join.

4. Chill for one hour and then cut into slices with a sharp knife on a clean board. Arrange on a ceramic plate, and serve with dipping sauce.

Dipping sauce:

1 tsp sesame oil

2 tbsp tamari

1 dsp grated fresh ginger

1 tsp wasabi (powdered horseradish)

¹/2 pt/280 ml dashi (stock)

Bring to boil and then allow to infuse for a few minutes before serving in individual dishes.

Cucumber, Wakame and Radish Salad

1 cucumber

1 bunch radishes

2 oz/50 g dried wakame seaweed

sea salt

2 tbsp rice vinegar

Method:

1. Wash the seaweed, making sure no grit is left.

2. Soak for 30 minutes in warm water to cover. Then rinse, remove the thick spine and chop.

3. Peel strips of skin from cucumber.

4. Cut cucumber into four lengthwise and de-seed.

5. Slice finely on the diagonal (known as butterfly wings).

6. Sprinkle lightly with sea salt and leave for 10 minutes, then drain.

7. Wash, top and tail and slice radishes finely and then add to the cucumber.

8. Remove the seaweed from the water, saving the liquid for a dipping sauce.

9. Chop the rest and add to cucumber and radish.

10. Sprinkle with rice vinegar (you could substitute white wine vinegar or cider apple vinegar) and sea salt.

Serve with fish and aduki pâté.

Soups

 Almond Gazpacho

SERVES 6

Created by the marriage of Spanish and Moorish influences, this is a delicate ivory-white soup with freckles of golden olive oil and white grapes floating atop. Traditionally made with young, milky almonds, this is a very nutritious soup.

Serve chilled, as a starter.

6 oz/175 g blanched almonds

8 oz/225 g chopped onion

1 pt/570 ml milk

1 pt/570 ml good stock

1 tbsp sherry vinegar

1 leek (white part only), finely sliced

1 stick celery, chopped finely

3 cloves garlic

3 oz/60 g white bread

¼ pt/50 ml olive oil

12 peeled white grapes (optional)

salt and pepper

Method:

1. In a heavy saucepan sauté the onion, leek and celery in 2 tbsp of oil until translucent. Add a few pinches of salt.

2. Add milk, stock and almonds. Bring to the boil, then simmer on low heat for 30 minutes.

3. Add crumbled up white bread and leave for 5 minutes.

4. Whiz all this in a blender. If the almonds are not fresh you will need to sieve the soup and rerun the residues through the blender or a coffee-grinder (but remove any smell of coffee first!), until you have a smooth purée.

5. When cool, add finely minced garlic (use a garlic press), and whisk in the rest of the olive oil, sherry vinegar, finely grated zest and juice of lemon and chill for 2–3 hours. Serve with peeled, halved grapes floating on top.

Roger Law's Knockout Fish Soup

SERVES 6

Roger Law (he of the *Spitting Image* team) and I were in the same class at Cambridge School of Art in the late 50s, early 60s. One of my first memories of Roger was watching him devouring what looked to be a half leg of lamb that his mother had provided for his packed lunch. He was a giant of a young man with an appetite like Desperate Dan.

It has been great to reconnect with Roger and his wife Deidre, now we are all grandparents. He has become an amazing cook and made this memorable fish stew for me, the recipe featuring somewhat Desperate Dan quantities of fish and shellfish, which I have scaled down a little. I've also added carrot to give body and to help balance the acidity of the tomatoes. I served it with a dish of *rouille*, which you can spread on your bread and dunk in this delicious and fiery fish stew. Despite the various processes, it does not take too long to prepare.

Cooking time about 1^1/2 hours.

Method:

For fish stock:

1^1/2 lb/700 g fish trimmings, bones, prawn shells

^{1}/2 onion, sliced

1 stick celery, sliced

^{1}/2 tsp salt

3 pts/1.5 l water

bouquet garni

Fish contents:

About 2 lb/900 g mixed fish and shellfish (I used 12 oz/350 g fish pie mix—salmon, monkfish, smoked haddock, etc.)

4 oz/110 g white crabmeat

4 scallops, sliced

8 oz/225 g prawns (half shelled and shells used in stock, the rest whole)

For soup base:

3 fl oz/75 ml olive oil

2 medium onions, sliced

1 large bell pepper, red

8 oz/225 g carrot, sliced thinly

8 cloves garlic, roughly chopped

6 ripe tomatoes, chopped, or
400 g tin of chopped Italian tomatoes
(if fresh ones not in season)

1^1/2 tsp fresh thyme, chopped

3 generous pinches of saffron threads

6 oz/175 g fresh Florence fennel, sliced

zest and juice of 1 orange

3 pts/1.5 l fish stock

1 tsp Cajun mixed spice

salt and pepper

1. Make fish stock in a large saucepan by adding
   3 pts cold water to the fish trimmings with salt.
   Bring to the boil, skim off any scum, and add
   vegetables and bouquet garni. Simmer for 20
   minutes and strain.

2. Soak saffron in a little of the hot fish stock to
   release colour and fragrance.

3. For soup base, heat about two thirds of the olive
   oil in a heavy-based saucepan, add sliced onion
   and bell pepper and a few pinches of salt. Sauté
   till tender but not brown.

4. Add garlic, thyme, fennel, carrots and tomatoes,
   and sauté over low heat for 5 minutes.

5. Pour in the 3 pts fish stock. Check seasoning
   and simmer with the lid on for 45 minutes.

6. Strain through a sieve and put remaining solids
   through a mouli-de-legumes, which will keep
   back the fibres and skins. You can also whiz
   these solids in a blender and return them to the
   strained soup.

7. Slice the fish and scallops into generous bite-
   sized pieces. Heat the rest of the olive oil in a
   sauté or frying pan and sear the fish and prawns
   with a very little salt and sprinkling of the Cajun
   spices. Stir for 5 minutes, then add to the soup
   and bring briefly to the boil.

Serve with a sprinkling of parsley and some rouille
if you like.

For rouille:

3 large red peppers, roasted, de-seeded and
skinned (may be bought in jars)

^{1}/2 tsp salt

1 fresh chilli, de-seeded and chopped finely

3 fl oz/75 ml water

4 garlic cloves, chopped coarsely

2 tbsp fine breadcrumbs

5 tbsp olive oil

1. Cook red peppers, salt and chilli in the water
   till tender (5–8 minutes).

2. Add garlic and breadcrumbs and whiz in a
   blender or stir with an electric hand-blender.
   Gradually beat in the olive oil little by little.
   You should now have a thick paste.

Serve with crunchy bread and the soup.

V Cold Jellied Tomato, Cucumber and Basil Soup

SERVES 8–10

1 lb/450 g juicy ripe tomatoes

1 large onion (red, if possible), chopped—approx 6 oz/175 g

6 oz/175 g piece of cucumber, peeled and sliced into small cubes

3 cloves garlic, finely chopped

$1/2$ wineglass sherry

1 pt/570 ml good stock

1 pt/570 ml Vegetable Cocktail with tomatoes, or plain tomato juice (bottled)

grated zest and juice of 1 lemon

2 tbsp olive oil for sautéing

1 tbsp tomato purée

salt and pepper

a few dashes of Tabasco or Lea and Perrins Worcester sauce (optional)

a few torn basil leaves for garnish

2 sachets gelatine (animal source) or 2 sachets Vege-gel (a seaweed compound), to set the soup

Method:

1. Prick the tomatoes with a fork and plunge into a pan of boiling water for a few minutes till the skins start peeling off. Drain and peel. Pare out fibrous core and chop small.

2. Put the olive oil in a saucepan and heat. Sauté the onions and garlic until translucent but *do not brown*. Add a sprinkling of sea salt.

3. Add tomatoes, cucumbers, purée and $1/2$ pt/275 ml of stock. Bring to the boil and simmer for 10–15 minutes, or until the vegetables are fairly tender but still have a little texture.

4. Add sherry, Tabasco or Worcester sauce, zest and juice of lemon and whiz until smooth in a blender. There should still be a little texture from the cucumber. You should get $1^1/2$ pts/800 ml approx.

5. Add the 1 pt/570 ml of vegetable cocktail or pure tomato juice. Adjust seasoning. Now you should have $2^1/2$ pts/1.2 l of tasty, very red liquid.

6. The $1/2$ pt/275 ml of unused stock is needed to dissolve the gelatine or Vege-gel.

(I divided my mixture into two batches to experiment and set one with gelatine and the other with Vege-gel. I preferred the results with gelatine; it was clearer and brighter. But I understand some people will not wish to use gelatine and the Vege-gel is a good alternative.)

For gelatine (2 sachets of gelatine will set 3 pts liquid):

Heat the $1/2$ pt/275 ml stock and sprinkle the powdered gelatine on top. Continue to heat and stir until dissolved. Add the $2^1/2$ pts/1.2 l soup, stir thoroughly and chill for 2–3 hours, till set. (A 'soft set' is required.)

For Vege-gel

Put 2 sachets Vege-gel into $1/2$ pt/275 ml cold stock and bring to the boil, stirring. Then add to the $2^1/2$ pts/1.2 l soup. Combine thoroughly and chill (Vege-gel can set while still warm).

You can serve the soup hot or cold, but having a jelly is quite a nice and novel texture on a hot day. Garnish with basil leaves. Any leftovers can be frozen and served at a later date as a kind of ice slush—good for palate-cleansing between courses.

Meat and Fish Main Dishes

Seafood Paella

SERVES 6–8

This dish from Valencia is also very popular in Mallorca, and is often made on the beach—usually by the men. It lends itself to being cooked and enjoyed outside (it's good inside as well!). Son Barrina, the organic farm on Mallorca where I stayed for a month, had a frequent visitor, Mario, who arrived with a paella pan as big as a swimming pool and boxes of ready-prepared seafoods and vegetables. Watching him make a paella for 20 people was real theatre. The aromas were tantalizing. People watched and chatted, drinking cold beer. The cooking part takes about half-an-hour.

Required: 15 inch/38 cm paella pan or shallow sauté pan

12 oz/350 g paella or Arborio rice

1 squid (8 oz/225 g) washed and cleaned by fishmonger

12 mussels, washed and de-bearded

6 tiger prawns

^{1}/2 lb/225 g fish pie mix (assorted pieces of fish)

7 fl oz/200 ml olive oil

400 g can chopped tomatoes

2 onions, finely chopped

3 cloves garlic

1 leek

4 oz/110 g shelled peas

4 oz/110 g French beans, broad beans or sliced courgettes

For fish stock:

any fish bones and trimmings from fishmonger

2 bay leaves

1 stick celery

leek trimmings

1¹/₂ pts/750 ml water

¹/₂ tsp saffron threads

1 tsp paprika

salt and pepper

To serve: lemons and 2 tbsp chopped parsley

Method:

1. Make a good fish stock by simmering the ingredients with the saffron threads for 30 minutes. Strain juice from chopped tomatoes into stock (makes 2 pts/1.2 l).

2. In half a pint of stock, poach cut-up fish for 5 minutes. Strain and use the same liquid to poach the raw tiger prawns till they turn pink. Keep this liquid to poach the mussels at the last minute (they take 5 minutes to cook).

3. Into the paella pan pour the oil and fry the squid, cut up into strips (they turn opaque after 3–5 minutes). Remove and set aside with the other fish.

4. Sauté onions in remaining oil, add garlic, paprika and flesh of the tomatoes.

5. Add rice and stir. You should have 1¹/₂ pts (750 ml) of gold-red, well-flavoured fish stock and—this is very important to the success of the dish—it must be kept hot. Start adding it to the rice on a medium heat. Stir continually and keep adding the stock as the rice absorbs it. Make sure it doesn't catch on the bottom of the pan.

6. When the liquid is all absorbed, quickly poach the mussels (having de-bearded and scrubbed them). They are cooked when the shells open, any that don't open discard. Reheat the fish and prawns in the poaching broth and then add to the paella. Add peas and blanched green beans and lay the mussels on top. Sprinkle with parsley and serve with lemon wedges.

V For a vegetarian version you could omit fish and add 4 chopped hard-boiled eggs, or whole almonds or cashews (4 oz/110 g) towards the end of cooking.

Salade Niçoise

SERVES 6

A wonderful summer salad—a one-pot meal full of delicious surprise flavours and bright colours.

2 lb/900 g new potatoes

2 red peppers, roasted, peeled and de-seeded

7 oz/200 g can of tuna fish

^{1}/2 can anchovy fillets

1 oz/25 g black olives

2 tender sticks of celery

4 oz/110 g blanched green French beans

4 spring onions, finely sliced

2 hard-boiled eggs

^{1}/2 pt/275 ml lemon mayonnaise (see page 215)

1 oz/25 g pine kerenels, pan-roasted till golden

1 tbsp capers

2 tbsp parsley, finely chopped

1 tbsp chopped chives

4 sprigs of mint

1 tsp salt

crispy lettuce leaves and cherry tomatoes for garnish

Method:

1. Scrub new potatoes and cover with cold water. Add 1 tsp salt and 2 sprigs of mint. Bring to the boil and cook in covered pan until tender but not soft. They need to be 'waxy' and hold their form. Drain and cool.

2. Chop hard-boiled egg, celery, spring onions, parsley and sprigs of mint. Slice red peppers into strips. Reserve a little of each vegetable and herb for decoration. Break up the chunks of tuna fish.

3. Cut potatoes into fairly even chunks.

4. In a large bowl combine all the ingredients with the mayonnaise.

5. Take a salad bowl and line it with washed and dried lettuce leaves, allowing the green to frill round the edges. Carefully spoon in the salad. Decorate the top with the reserved vegetables and herbs, olives, capers and anchovy fillets.

Serve chilled with hunks of crusty bread.

V The fish can be omitted; the salad is also lovely and nutritious without it.

Mackerel with Gooseberry Sauce

SERVES 6

Avoid the really big mackerel for this dish (the smaller ones are sweeter).

2–3 mackerel, filleted

For the marinade:

2 tbsp olive oil

juice of ^{1}/2 lemon

salt and pepper

Combine these in a bowl.

For the gooseberry sauce:

8 oz/225 g gooseberries

3 oz/75 g unrefined granulated sugar

^{1}/2 tsp salt

1 shallot, finely sliced

1 tbsp white wine vinegar

^{1}/2 cup water

Method:

1. Marinate the mackerel fillets for ^{1}/2 hour.

2. Prepare sauce by cooking all the ingredients together till tender (about 10 minutes), then whiz in a blender to a paste or dropping consistency.

3. Grill or pan-fry the mackerel for 5 minutes on each side (depending on size).

Serve with a tablespoon of the sauce on each fillet. I served it with beetroot risotto and a tossed green salad.

Janet's Lavender Chicken with Orange Sauce

Janet has always grown flowers in with her vegetables to put in her salads and in her cooking. For some time she tried to persuade me to stuff with lavender. I didn't quite warm to the idea. Last year with lots of lavender in our garden I decided to try it out. It was so delicious, so subtley fragrant I urge you to try it. A wonderful dish with a delicate perfume of lavender and orange.

SERVES 6

5 lb/2 kg free range chicken

1 lemon

sea salt and pepper

3 oz/75 g softened butter

2 large organic oranges

small bunch of fresh lavender with stalks

2 chopped shallots

2 whole shallots

2 tbsp olive oil

stock made with chicken giblets, onion, carrot, 2 bay leaves and a stick of celery

Method:

1. Wash and dry the chicken.

2. Sprinkle with salt and lemon juice and set aside whilst preparing the marinade.

3. For the lavender butter, take the zest from the oranges and reserve half for the sauce. Add the other half to the softened butter, the chopped shallots, half the lavender heads and some twists of freshly ground black pepper.

4. Smear this over the chicken breast and thighs. Squeeze the oranges and keep the juice for the sauce. Pop one squeezed orange and the lemon remainder into the chicken cavity with some of the lavender butter and the two white shallots.

5　Press several lavender heads and stalks onto the breasts. Trickle the olive oil over the chicken and wrap it up in foil. Roast in a medium oven 1 hour. Then take off the foil and brown at 200°C/gas mark 6 for $^1/2$ hour.

For the sauce:

Take **2 tbsp of the chicken juices** and heat in a small saucepan. Add **1 tbsp plain flour** and cook up, stirring. Add $^1/2$ **pt/275 ml giblet stock**, **1 tbsp marmalade**, **1 tbsp Grand Marnier** (optional), juice and remaining **zest of the 2 oranges**, **splash of tamari** and heat together. Whiz in a blender and serve with the chicken. Serve with the chicken and a dish of white rice or sautéed potatoes and a crisp green salad.

Vegetarian Main Dishes

Cathy's Carrot Roulade

SERVES 6

Required: a Swiss roll tin lined with parchment

Oven 200°C/gas mark 6

1¹/₂ lb/700 g carrots

2 oz/50 g butter

6 eggs

3 tbsp chopped fresh coriander

6 oz/175 g cream cheese

2–3 tbsp crème fraîche

2 small cloves garlic

selection of fresh herbs, e.g. parsley, chives, dill, fennel, mint

1 tsp ground cumin

salt and pepper

watercress or other salad leaves

sprigs of dill to garnish (optional)

Method:

1. Preheat oven to 200°C/gas mark 6.

2. Line a Swiss roll tin with non-stick baking parchment.

3. Wash and coarsely grate carrots.

4. Melt butter in a saucepan, then add grated carrots and cook gently, stirring frequently, for 5 minutes or until they have changed colour slightly.

5. Transfer carrots to a bowl and allow to cool a little.

6. Separate eggs. Put yolks with the carrot and combine well, and the whites into a large, spotlessly clean bowl.

7. Into yolks and carrot mixture put chopped coriander, cumin, salt and pepper.

8. Whisk egg whites until they form peaks. Stir a spoonful into the carrot mixture to loosen it up, then very carefully fold in the rest of the whisked egg white with a large metal spoon.

9. Spread the mixture evenly into the tin and bake 10–15 minutes until risen. It should be a very pale gold colour and firm to the touch. Allow to cool.

10. Meanwhile prepare the filling. Chop the herbs and garlic very finely and beat into the cheese. Stir in enough crème fraîche to make a consistency that spreads easily but won't ooze out of the roulade. If using marscapone cheese you may not need any crème fraîche.

11. If necessary trim off any crispy bits that may be on the edges. Spread the filling evenly, using a palette knife or spatula, leaving about ¹/₂ inch (1 cm) gap round the edges.

12. Using the paper underneath, roll up the roulade and let it rest on the join for 10 minutes or more to firm up.

Serve on a beautiful flat plate garnished with sprigs of fresh dill if you have them, or a few interesting salad leaves. You will need a sharp knife to cut the roulade into slices.

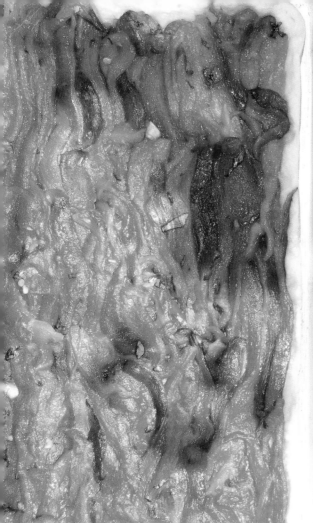

Coca Mallorquina

SERVES 6

This open vegetable tart can be found in bakeries all over Mallorca on certain days of the week. Some are still cooked in wood ovens and they are especially delicious.

The telltale sprinkling of pine nuts and raisins points to its Arabic provenance.

It is rather like a cheeseless pizza and is great for picnics and packed lunches. It is cheap to make and my children loved it. Here is my version.

Required: 2 baking trays

Oven at 200°C/gas mark 6

Bread dough for base:

14 oz/400 g plain unbleached bread flour

1 oz/25 g fresh yeast (or dried)

1 tsp salt

^{1}/4 pt/150 ml tepid water

1 tsp honey

zest and juice of one orange (approx. ^{1}/8 pt/75ml)

3 tbsp olive oil

For topping:

8 oz/225 g washed and chopped chard or spinach

8 oz/225 g assorted peppers, red and green, chopped small

10 oz/275 g onions, chopped finely

1 oz/5 g pine kernels

2 oz/50 g Lexia raisins, soaked in boiling water for ^{1}/2 hour

4 oz (110 g) chopped tomatoes

^{1}/2 tsp smoked paprika

3 tbsp olive oil

3 cloves of garlic, minced

salt and pepper

Coca Mallorquina cont.

Method:

For the yeast dough follow basic bread instructions on page 197. The secret ingredient is the zest and juice of an orange. The dough should be soft but not sticky. Preheat the oven.

To make the topping:

1. Grease 2 baking sheets with olive oil. Divide the dough into 2 pieces. On a floured surface roll the dough out very thinly, divide in halves and flip onto the trays. With your fingers, spread dough out to fill the whole surface and put in a warm place while preparing the topping.

2. In a heavy saucepan heat 3 tbsp olive oil and sauté the onions for a few minutes. Add garlic and paprika, then the peppers, chard or spinach, and salt and pepper. Just toss them around to start the cooking process.

3. Spread your topping ingredients equally on the two trays, making sure they are evenly distributed. Leave the edges free—about $1^1/2$ in/4 cm.

4. Bake in a hot oven for about 20 minutes, when the dough should be risen and golden and the pine nuts golden too. If you think that the cooking is going too fast and there is a danger of overcooking the topping, turn the heat down to 180°C/gas mark 4–5 to finish off. The initial hot temperature is to set the dough.

Tumbet from Mallorca

SERVES 6

This is something like the French *ratatouille*. It is interesting to see how each of the Solanaceae foods are cooked separately, with salt and oil, which balances out their tendency to be so *yin* (expanded, airy, acidic).

Required: an ovenproof dish (I use a greixonera)

Oven 180°C/gas mark 4

1 lb/450 g red peppers, de-seeded and sliced into strips

1 lb/450 g potatoes, peeled and sliced—fairly thinly—in ovals

1 lb/450 g aubergines, sliced into rounds

$1^1/2$ lb/700 g ripe tomatoes, skinned and chopped, or 400 g can

1 onion, finely chopped

6 cloves garlic, chopped fairly roughly

2 bay leaves

a little thyme

$^1/2$ pt/275 ml good olive oil

salt and pepper

Method:

1. Sprinkle the aubergine rounds with salt and stack in a colander, cover with a plate to weight them down. Leave for $^1/2$ hour.

2. Rinse them under running water and pat dry with kitchen towel.

3. Heat a quarter of the olive oil in a sauté or large frying pan and fry the potatoes with a *little* salt and pepper. When they start to go golden turn them out on a plate.

4. Add some more oil to the pan and fry the red peppers. Season lightly and stir until they are soft. Try to retain the juices and golden bits on the bottom of the pan by stirring with a wooden spatula. Turn them out onto another plate.

5. Add some more oil, reserving a little for the last stage, and fry the aubergines with some of the roughly chopped garlic. *Don't salt them*, as they will have retained some from the salting process. Turn them out, when golden, onto a plate.

6. Pour in the last of the oil and fry the onion and the rest of the garlic. Add tomatoes, bay leaf and thyme and cook down until you have a thick sauce.

7. For assembly, oil the dish and layer in the aubergines, potatoes and lastly peppers and pour over the tomato sauce. Cover and bake for a further $^3/4$ hour in the oven. This is a rich dish, which oozes delicious red oil.

Serve with whole rice to help balance out the acidity, and a crisp green salad with radishes.

For non-vegetarians—the Mallorcans often tuck slices of loin of pork in the layers.

Stuffed Courgettes

SERVES 6

This is an idea for left-over cooked vegetables. It is one of Pauline Anderson's recipes used in biodynamic coffee shops.

courgettes, as many as needed

butter

1 onion, chopped fine

oil for sautéing

ready-cooked vegetables: celery, carrot, pepper, leek or what you will, all cut fairly fine

cooked grain

a few olives

herbs

salt and pepper

well-flavoured white sauce made with rice flour, vegetable stock and a little milk, garlic, apple juice and seasoning, plus a dollop of cream.

grated mature Cheddar cheese (can be part Stilton)

Method:

1. Cut courgettes in half lengthwise and scoop out seeds to make little boats. Place knob of butter in each boat and cook on greased baking tray in hot oven until *just* done (about $^1/_2$ hour).

2. Sauté onion in a little oil and add pre-cooked vegetables.

3. Fold into cooked grain.

4. Add a few olives (halved), herbs and seasoning. Check for taste.

Vegetarian Pasties

SERVES 6

These make an excellent picnic or packed lunch item. Crispy and golden on the outside with a number of tasty fillings on the inside. Here is one version.

Required: a baking tray, greased

1 lb pastry

Oven at 200°/gas mark 6

For filling:

8 oz/225 g dry red kidney or pinto beans, which are soaked overnight, drained, and then cooked in stock with a piece of kombu (will make approx. 1 lb/450 g cooked beans)

$^1/4$ pt/150 ml cooking liquid, left over from beans

8 oz/225 g onions, sliced

4 oz/110 g grated carrots

4 oz/110 g grated courgette

1 leek, carefully washed and finely sliced

2 cloves garlic, minced

1 oz/25 g butter, for sautéing

1 tbsp olive oil, for sautéing

1 tbsp tamari or 1 tsp Vegemite (yeast extract)

2 oz/50 g breadcrumbs

1 tbsp chopped parsley or fresh coriander

salt and pepper

1 lb/450 g shortcrust pastry (see pages 97–8)

milk to brush the outside

1 tbsp sesame seeds to sprinkle on

Method:

To make filling:

1. In a sauté pan or large frying pan melt butter and oil.

2. Add sliced onions and garlic and fry until brown, adding tamari towards the end.

3. Add cooked beans with their $1/4$ pt/150 ml cooking liquid and cook together till flavours mingle and beans are soft enough to be mashed with a potato masher. Leave some beans whole and mash the rest.

4. Add sliced leek and cook for 5 minutes. Remove from heat.

5. Add grated courgette and carrots (could be some lightly cooked French beans or garden peas—whatever is available).

6. Add breadcrumbs and allow to soak up all the liquid. Cool. Check seasoning and add a few grindings of pepper if you wish.

To complete:

7. Roll out 6 circles of pastry about 6 in/15 cm across, and not too thinly or the filling might push through.

8. In the lower half of the pastry circle, place enough filling to leave a margin of $1/2$ in/2 cm, which you paint with milk. Fold over the blank side of the circle to completely cover the filling. Crimp the edges and make 3 small slits in the top to allow steam to escape. Paint the whole with milk and sprinkle with sesame seeds.

9. Place on a baking tray and bake for approx. 15 minutes at 200°C/gas mark 6 and 10 minutes at 180°C/gas mark 4. Serve hot, warm or cold.

Desserts

French Lemon Tart

SERVES 6

Required: an 11 inch/28 cm loose-bottomed flan tin

Oven heated to 200°C/ gas mark 6

For the pastry:

8 oz/225 g plain flour

1 oz/25 g icing sugar

pinch salt

5 oz/150 g butter

3 tbsp ice cold water

For the filling:

zest and juice of 3 lemons

4 large eggs

5 oz/150 g caster sugar

1 tbsp ginger syrup from crystallized ginger

¹/2 pt/275 ml double cream

Method:

1. Make the shortcrust pastry (see pages 97–8), roll it out and line the flan tin. I usually strengthen the sides with an extra thin strip of pastry stuck on with milk. Chill in the fridge for ¹/2 hour. Prick the base. Now bake the pastry case blind (see page 97).

2. Meanwhile, take zest from half of one lemon with a zester and infuse strips in ginger syrup for a garnish.

3. Grate the rest of the lemons and then juice them.

4. In a bowl beat the eggs and then strain them through a sieve to remove any threads. Add sugar and continue to beat.

5. Add cream, grated lemon zest and finally the lemon juice, beating so that the mixture will not curdle.

6. Pour this filling into the cooked pastry case and bake for 30–40 minutes in a coolish oven (170°C/gas mark 3) until set.

7. Chill. Then sprinkle with ginger-soaked lemon threads and a little sieved icing sugar. Serve with crème fraîche.

Blackcurrant Ice Cream

SERVES 6

1 lb/500 g blackcurrants

5 oz/150 g unrefined caster sugar

12 fl oz/350 ml whipping cream

Method:

1. Cook the blackcurrants with the sugar, using as little water as possible to keep the flavour concentrated. I bake them in a shallow dish without any water, but taking care not to let them dry out.

2. Purée the blackcurrants and sieve to remove skin and pips.

3. When absolutely cold, stir in the cream and follow the instructions for your ice cream maker.

Lemon Ice Cream

SERVES 6

3 lemons (unwaxed)

4 oz/100 g unrefined caster sugar

8 fl oz/225 ml water

8 fl oz/225 ml double cream

Method:

1. Scrub the lemons, then using a very fine grater take off the zest, taking care not to include any of the bitter pith. Squeeze out the juice.

2. Put the zest with the water and sugar into a small saucepan and bring to the boil for 2 minutes. Leave to cool, then add the lemon juice and cream.

3. Follow the instructions on your ice cream maker.

Note

If you don't have an ice cream maker you can use your freezer compartment, chilling both the whipped cream and a 1¹/2 pt/800 ml freezer-proof container. Place the ice cream in the freezer and before it hardens whisk it to get rid of the ice crystals. Return to the freezer for 3 hours. Remove the ice cream 15 minutes before serving and place in the main body of the fridge so it will be easier to scoop out.

Easy Raspberry or Tayberry Jelly

SERVES 6

This is an easy, good-tempered jelly—it came on our picnic and didn't melt!

Required: sundae glasses

1 lb/450 g raspberries or tayberries

1¹/2 pts/800 ml water

2 packets vegetarian raspberry jelly crystals (seaweed base, available from health food shops)

juice of ¹/2 lemon

1 tsp honey

Method:

1. Boil water, add honey and raspberries. Leave them a few minutes to release some of their juices.

2. Strain fruit off and make liquid up to 2 pts/1.2 l including lemon juice. Heat up and dissolve the jelly crystals in it. Allow to cool somewhat but not to setting point.

3. Divide raspberries between the sundae glasses and pour on the jelly mixture. Refrigerate and serve cold.

Gooseberry and Elderflower Fool

SERVES 4–6

1 lb/450 g gooseberries

4 oz/110 g unrefined caster sugar

1 packet Vege-gel

3/4 pt/400 ml double cream for whipping

2 heads of elderflowers

1/4 pt/150 ml water

Method:

1. Top and tail the gooseberries and cook with water and sugar for 5–8 minutes, or until tender but not mushy.

2. Strain off the liquid (you should have 1/2 pt) and purée the fruit.

3. Dissolve the Vege-gel in the strained liquid and return to the fruit pulp.

4. Divide the mixture into two bowls.

5. Whip cream until soft peaks form (not too stiff). Add to half the purée. Sprinkle the elderflowers into both bowls, then spoon in alternating layers into 4–6 sundae glasses, making an interesting contrast. Finish off with some whipped cream and elderflowers.

Perfect for a summer evening.

Apple Rose Petal Jelly

SERVES 6

This jelly can be prepared with any kind of fruit. Children usually love jelly.

1¹/₂ lb/700 g eating apples, peeled and sliced (the peel can be used for apple tea)

¹/₂ pt/275 ml elderflower cordial (could also be blackcurrant or rosehip syrup), with the same volume of water

zest of a lemon

honey or maple syrup if needed

1 tsp rose water

1 sachet (6 g) Vege-gel (vegetarian gelatine substitute, seaweed based)

Method:

1. Cook apple slices in the syrup water (1 pt/570 ml altogether) until tender.

2. Strain off the fruit and taste the remaining juice for sweetness. Add maple syrup or honey if needed. Allow to cool.

3. Add the Vege-gel to the juice (1 pt) and bring to the boil, stirring vigorously. It should start to set if you test a little on a cold plate.

4. Pour the jelly onto the apple slices arranged nicely in a glass bowl and decorate with crystallized rose petals.

To make crystallized rose petals:

Paint the petals (pink looks good) with egg white and dredge them with unrefined caster sugar. Leave in a dry place to harden. They will keep for two days in an airtight box. They do look pretty and children will enjoy preparing them.

Almond Ice Cream

SERVES 6

This ice cream is made at the restaurant C'an Amer and is usually served with the Almond Cake. It is traditionally made with almonds that are still young and milky. (You can also use ready ground almonds.)

1³/₄ pts/1 litre whole milk

1 stick of cinnamon

Thin strips of zest from 1 large lemon

5 oz/150 g unrefined caster sugar

9 ozs/250 g raw blanched almonds

Method:

1. In a heavy bottomed saucepan bring the milk to the boil with the cinnamon and lemon zest.

2. Remove from the heat, add the sugar and leave to cool.

3. In the meantime crush the almonds until you have a creamy paste.

4. Remove zest and cinnamon from the milk and add the almonds, stirring thoroughly.

5. Follow the instructions on your ice cream maker or see note at the end of Lemon Ice Cream.

Autumn

Blackberry and apple pie—
mulberry-stained fingers—bonfires—fungi—
crispy leaves that children love to kick around—
chestnuts—roasted pumpkin—spice apple pie—
dark venison casseroles—red quinoa—
sloe gin!—jams and chutneys—dark, malty rye
bread—quince paste (membrillo)—hazelnuts,
walnuts and nutcrackers.

To Autumn

Season of mists and mellow fruitfulness

Close bosom friend of the maturing sun:

Conspiring with him how to load and bless

With fruit the vines that round the thatch-eves run;

To bend with apples the mossed cottage-trees,

 And fill all fruit with ripeness to the core;

To swell the gourd, and plump the hazel shells

With a sweet kernel; to set budding more

 And still more, later flowers for the bees,

Until they think warm days will never cease

For Summer has o'er-brimmed their clammy shells.

John Keats

FESTIVALS

Michaelmas (29 September) is the feast of St Michael, patron saint of the sea and maritime lands, of ships and boatmen, of horses and horsemen. As Michael nam Buadh, Michael the Victorious, he is known as the conqueror of the powers of darkness—the archangel who hurled Lucifer down from heaven for his treachery. Folklore in England holds that the devil landed in bramble bushes and therefore one must not pick blackberries after Michaelmas. (But we can celebrate with a blackberry and apple pie, for the blackberries will have been picked before! See recipe on p. 167.) The festival was important in Celtic Christianity, particularly for the dedication of churches. From St Michael's Mount in Cornwall to Mont St Michel in France, Michael steadies the dragon under his foot, taming him. In contrast St George slays the dragon. Harvest festivals at Michaelmas celebrate the gifts of the earth. We had a wonderful picnic lunch at Derek's biodynamic Velwell Orchard in Devon. (See page 148.)

Hallowe'en (31 October) and the festival of Samhain. Hallowe'en is a very popular festival for children, who love to go round neighbours' houses dressed up as witches or warlocks and perform 'trick or treat'. Pumpkin lanterns are made, so recipes for pumpkin soup and pumpkin pie are appropriate. This festival is also known as 'Nutcrack Night' from the custom of cracking nuts. It is also 'Colcannon Night' where an Irish dish of mashed potato, onions, kale and sausages is eaten. Apple-bobbing is a game played at this time, and if you are clever enough to catch in your mouth an apple that bobs in a bowl of water, you should peel it in an unbroken spiral and throw it over your left shoulder where you should then be able to discern the initial of the one you will marry.

All Saints and All Souls (1 and 2 November) have been celebrated since the third century by a midnight vigil with cakes and wine prepared for the return of the dead. Soul cakes were eaten by all and lights burned to help guide the dead to their earthly homes. Children 'Soulers' went round to houses 'a-souling', and soul cakes were given to them. This is one of the songs that they sang:

> Soul, soul, for a soul cake,
> I pray, good mistress for a soul cake,
> An apple, or pear, a plum, or a cherry,
> Any good thing to make us all merry.
> One for Peter, two for Paul,
> Three for Him who made us all.
> Up with the kettle, down with the pan,
> Give us good cheer and we'll be gone.

J.C. Cooper, 1990

I was inspired to create a recipe for this cake, which would tempt down souls (see page 235). Celebrating the element of fire (fires were also burnt to guide the souls of the dead home) now seems to have been transferred to Guy Fawkes night, where bonfires and fireworks are lit to commemorate the capture of Guy Fawkes who attempted to blow up the Houses of Parliament. My mother always made Yorkshire parkin for bonfire night and toffee apples—dark burnt sugar and treacle!

SAMPLE MENU

Michaelmas Picnic

Beetroot Borscht (hot or cold)

Vegetarian Pasties

Butter Bean Pâté

Vegetable Crudités

Four Grain Bread

'Snail' rolls

Plum Brioche

Soups

Parsnip, Celery and Apple Soup *(slightly curried)*

SERVES 6

1 lb/450 g parsnips, peeled and chopped

8 oz/225 g white onion, sliced

6 oz/175 g grated eating apple

8 oz/225 g potatoes, peeled and diced

3 sticks celery, chopped

4 cloves garlic, chopped

2 tsp medium hot curry powder

$\frac{1}{2}$ tsp ground cumin

2 bay leaves

1 tsp chopped rosemary

$\frac{1}{4}$ pt/150 ml single cream

2 pts/1.2 l good stock

1 oz/25 g butter, for sautéing

2 tbsp olive oil, for sautéing

some finely chopped parsley for garnish

Method:

1. In a heavy saucepan heat the oil and butter. Add onions and garlic and sauté till translucent.

2. Add celery, parsnips, potato, spices and garlic. Sauté for a further 5 minutes.

3. Add hot stock, bay leaves, chopped rosemary and cook for 30–40 minutes, or till all vegetables are tender. Grate the apple in and then add cream. Remove bay leaves and blend till smooth. Adjust seasoning. If too thick, add a little milk. Garnish with parsley.

Dartmoor Mushroom Soup V

SERVES 6

It was early October and my neighbour Valerie was taking me to a secret place. We walked through leafy lanes gathering berries, then across sheep-filled fields and over stiles to the crest of a hill where we came upon what looked like a miniature space station of white domes—huge fresh field mushrooms, and lots of them. I'd never seen anything like it! Our baskets were filled in no time.

Afterwards we had a 'mushroom feast'—soup, stuffed mushrooms, mushrooms in an omelette, and grilled mushrooms with garlic and parsley.

Yields 3 pts (approx. 1$\frac{1}{2}$ l)

14 oz/400 g sliced wild or organic mushrooms

8 oz/225 g onion, diced small

4 oz/110 g diced potato

4 oz/110 g white part of leeks, finely sliced

2 sticks of celery, finely sliced

2 cloves garlic, chopped

1$\frac{1}{2}$ pts/scant litre well-flavoured stock

1 tsp herbes de Provence

4 fl oz/100 ml sherry

1 tsp Dijon mustard

$\frac{1}{4}$ pt/150 ml single cream

2 tbsp parsley, finely chopped

2 oz/50 g butter, for sautéing

2 tbsp olive oil, for sautéing

Method:

1. In a large saucepan melt 1 oz/25 g butter and 1 tbsp olive oil and sauté onions till translucent. Add celery, leeks and potato. Add herbes de Provence and a little sprinkling of salt. Then add stock and let the vegetables cook until tender.

2. Meanwhile in a large frying pan melt the rest of the butter, add the olive oil and sauté the mushrooms and garlic with a little salt and pepper. (Reserve a few mushroom slices for garnish.) Add sherry and cook another 3–5 minutes.

4. Combine mushrooms and the rest of the vegetables. Add 1 tsp Dijon mustard. Then whiz in a blender. Add the cream and gently reheat. Adjust seasoning. Serve garnished with chopped parsley, the reserved mushroom slices and garlic croutons, if you like.

Cinderella Pumpkin Soup

SERVES 6

A traditional peasant dish from Central France that looks dramatic when served. Use an orange Hubbard squash, but not too large as it has to fit into your oven. The wet French walnuts are preferable, as so many walnuts today taste bitter.

Oven 180°C/gas mark 4

a whole pumpkin, 5 lb/2kg or more

4 oz/110 g breadcrumbs (wholewheat or white)

2 oz/50 g roasted sunflower seeds or pumpkin seeds

4 oz/110 g fresh walnuts, roughly chopped

2 pieces of preserved ginger, chopped small

3 oz/75 g Gruyère cheese, grated

3/4 pt/425 ml single cream

6 spring onions, finely chopped

1 tbsp parsley, finely chopped

salt and freshly ground pepper

milk to top up if necessary

a little olive oil for basting

Method:

1. Wash the pumpkin and cut the top off (the growing end with stem) and set aside. This will form a lid with a handle.

2. With a spoon scoop out the seeds and fibrous parts and season the inside with salt and pepper (the innards can be used in the stockpot).

3. Mix all the dry ingredients with the cream. Season lightly and ladle into the pumpkin shell. Top up with milk until it is three-quarters full. Put the lid on and brush the whole thing with a little olive oil.

4. Bake in a moderate oven for about 2 hours, stirring the inside occasionally and topping up with more milk if necessary. (This is not a soup in the usual sense, it will be quite thick.)

5. To serve, sprinkle some roasted sunflower seeds on top and dribble in a little cream. You can spoon some of the softened pumpkin flesh into each portion.

Accompanied by some good crusty bread and a green salad, this is a winner and worth sacrificing the jewelled carriage for, on a rainy day.

Red Hot Soup

SERVES 6

This soup has become my family's favourite to put in a flask and take on a walk on the moors or by the sea on a less-than-warm day. It certainly restores some fire in the belly! We drink it out of little terra-cotta mugs, which enhance the flavour.

2 largish red peppers

2 tbsp olive oil

1 head of garlic, sliced through the middle

2 onions, finely chopped

2 leeks (use the white parts) sliced

2 sticks of celery, chopped

1 red chilli de-seeded and finely chopped

2 sprigs of rosemary or 1 dsp dried rosemary

8 oz/225 g carrots, diced

8 oz/225 g potatoes, diced

1¹/₂ pts/750 ml well-flavoured stock

400 g can of chopped tomatoes

salt and pepper

croutons and parsley or fresh coriander to garnish

Method:

1. Brush the peppers and garlic with olive oil and sea salt, sprinkle with the rosemary and roast in the oven at 200°C/gas mark 6 until soft. Allow to cool (approx. 20 minutes).

2. Sauté the chopped onions in the rest of the olive oil until translucent.

3. Add all the other vegetables, including the chilli, and cover with the stock. Bring to the boil with the lid on, then simmer for 20 minutes, or till vegetables are tender.

4. Meanwhile skin and de-seed the peppers, keeping any juices to add to the soup, then chop them. Scrape out the roasted garlic from its skin and with the rosemary add, with the peppers, to the vegetables.

5. Add the tin of tomatoes and bring to the boil. Allow to bubble gently for 5–10 minutes. Cool a little and blend with a blender. Adjust the seasoning and serve with garlic croutons and chopped parsley.

For a more robust meal, earlier in the year, you could add some nettle dumplings poached in the stock. They only need to be warmed through.

A note of caution about chillies. They vary enormously in heat strength, so be careful initially. You can always add more. One was enough to give this quantity of soup a real kick.

Meat and Fish Main Dishes

Lamb and Quince Koresh with Spiced Rice

SERVES 6

This is a traditional Persian dish which features a wonderful perfumed saffron and turmeric flavoured stew, with tiny lamb meatballs and fragrant rice with apricots.

> **V** (If you want a vegetarian dish you can just omit the meatballs.) It has three stages: the compôte, the meatballs and stew, and the spiced rice. I happened to have a last quince of the season, but if you can't find a source you could use thinly sliced carrots or Hubbard squash cooked in the same way.

For quince compôte:

1 quince, peeled and cored (or sliced carrots or squash)

1 tbsp honey

$^{1}/_{4}$ pt/150 ml water

zest and chopped up flesh of 2 tangerines

$^{1}/_{4}$ tsp salt

Simmer all together until quince is tender.

For meatballs:

1 lb/450 g ground lamb

2 finely minced shallots

1 dsp mint (fresh if possible, 1 tsp if dried)

$^{1}/_{2}$ tsp sea salt

pepper

1 tsp turmeric

1 dsp ground rice flour

$^{1}/_{2}$ tsp ground mixed spice

2 oz/50 g butter, for frying

1 tbsp olive oil, for frying

1 tbsp plain flour

$^{1}/_{2}$ pt/275 ml stock

Method:

1. Whiz the ground lamb, minced shallots, seasoning, rice flour, mint and spices together in a food processor.

2. Make little balls the size of walnuts and fry in the butter and olive oil. Set aside.

3. To the frying juices in the pan add 1 tbsp plain flour and cook for 2 minutes, stirring. Then add the stock to make a gravy.

For the stew:

2 oz/50 g butter/ghee

1 tbsp oil

1 oz/25 g blanched and toasted almonds

1 large onion finely chopped

2 leeks, washed carefully and sliced (keep green parts to use at the end)

6 oz/175 g piece of celeriac, cut into small cubes

6 oz/175 g piece of Hubbard squash

3 sticks of celery, sliced on the diagonal

3 courgettes, sliced, with strips of skin removed, for decorative appeal

$1^{1}/_{2}$ pts/800 ml good stock

2 pinches of saffron

1 tsp turmeric

Lamb and Quince Koresh with Spiced Rice cont.

$^1/_4$ tsp ground mixed spice

1 tbsp pomegranate syrup (apple concentrate would also serve)

juice of $^1/_2$ lemon

salt and pepper

Method:

1. Melt butter and oil in a large heavy-bottomed pot.

2. Sauté onion until translucent, add salt, ground spice, chopped squash, leeks then celery, celeriac and stock. Bring to a boil, then turn down the heat so the pot simmers. Add saffron, meatballs and thickened gravy and cook for 30–40 minutes, allowing the sauce to reduce to two-thirds of the original.

3. Now add the quince compôte and pomegranate juice or apple concentrate. Cook together for a further 10 minutes, to let the juices combine. Adjust seasoning and add lemon juice.

4. I tend to cook the sliced courgettes and green parts of the leeks separately with a little mint to keep their delicate colour and texture, adding them right at the last minute before serving.

Sprinkle with toasted almonds.

Spiced Rice with Apricots

SERVES 6

4 oz/110 g dried, orange apricots

8 oz/225 g long grain rice (a wild rice combination is also good)

6 cardamom pods

3 inch piece of cinnamon quill

$^1/_4$ tsp sea salt

1 pt/570 ml good stock

2 oz/50 g butter

Method:

1. Rinse and soak the apricots, just covered in boiling water, overnight if possible. Stew until tender but not mushy (about 20 minutes).

2. Wash rice carefully and allow it to drain and dry.

3. In a heavy pot (with closely fitting lid) melt the butter, sauté the cardamom and the broken up cinnamon quill (keep pieces large so that they are visible and can be removed later). Pour in the rice and gently stir until all the grains are coated. Add salt and stock. Bring to the boil and turn down to minimum, allowing the rice to simmer for 35–40 minutes, when all the liquid should have been taken up.

4. Chop up apricots and slip them in when you fluff up the rice before piling onto a warm dish for serving.

Moussaka
(Lamb and Aubergine Bake)

SERVES 4–6

This is a Middle Eastern one-pot meal, rich and exciting, with different layers.

> **V** Omit the lamb for a vegetarian version.

Required: a 10 inch/25 cm ovenproof dish

Oven 180°C/gas mark 4

3/4 lb/350 g minced shoulder of lamb

2 large onions chopped into small dice

3 cloves of garlic, minced

2 tsp ground cumin

1 level tsp ground cinnamon

1 pt/570 ml thick béchamel sauce (see page 114)

1 egg

2 oz/50 g grated Parmesan

2 large aubergines

3 tbsp olive oil

sunflower oil for deep frying

1 pt/570 ml rich tomato sauce (see page 214)

2 lb potatoes thinly sliced

oregano and some slices of tomato to finish

Method:

1. Slice aubergines fairly thinly, place in a bowl and sprinkle with salt. Put a weighted plate on top and leave for 1/2 hour to 'weep'.

2. Make béchamel sauce and add beaten egg when cold.

3. Make rich tomato sauce.

4. Slice the potatoes evenly and blanch for 5 minutes in boiling salted water. Drain.

5. Fry onions in 2 tbsp olive oil until browned, add garlic, cumin and cinnamon. Then add minced lamb and 1/2 tsp salt. Cook for 15 minutes, stirring the while.

6. Rinse aubergine slices and pat dry with kitchen paper. Sprinkle with white flour.

7. Heat some sunflower oil (1/2 cup) in a frying pan until hot, but not smoking. Test by dropping in one of your aubergine slices—it should sizzle. Then carefully put in more slices until the surface is covered, but do not let them overlap. Flip them over when golden brown and when done both sides drain in batches on kitchen paper.

You now have the five elements with which to construct this dish. Assemble in an oiled ovenproof dish—I use my Mallorcan greixonera.

Assemble the dish in this order:

1. The tomato sauce (should be thick and not runny)

2. The lamb mixture (for vegetarian version add cumin and cinnamon to the tomato sauce)

3. Layer of aubergine slices

4. Half of the béchamel sauce

5. Layer of potatoes

6. Finish with rest of béchamel sauce, more aubergines and the tomato slices. Sprinkle with Parmesan and oregano.

Finally, cover with foil and bake in oven at 180°C/gas mark 4 for 3/4 hour. Take off foil and turn heat up to 200°C/gas mark 6 and brown for 15–20 minutes. Serve with salads.

Pigeon Breasts in Blackcurrant Chocolate Sauce with Shallots

SERVES 4–6

2 pigeons

12 shallots

2 carrots

2 sticks of celery

bay leaf/thyme/rosemary

1 onion, sliced

2 rashers streaky bacon

¹/4 pt/150 ml red wine

1pt/570 ml good stock

salt and pepper

1 tbsp tamari or shoyu

¹/2 pt/275 ml home-made tomato sauce or medium can chopped tomatoes, drained

2 tbsp olive oil for sautéing

knob of butter

2 oz/50 g dark chocolate

1 tbsp blackcurrant jam

Method:

1. Remove pigeon breasts, season with salt and pepper and rub with olive oil. Set aside in the fridge.

2. Place the pigeon carcasses in a saucepan with the red wine, celery, herbs, onion, carrot and stock and simmer for at least an hour. Strain and then reduce over heat to leave 1 pt stock.

3. Sauté the chopped bacon in oil. Add the shallots and brown. Finally add the pigeon breasts and cook for 5 minutes on each side (they should still be pinkish on the inside). Lift the breasts out and keep warm. Add reduced stock to shallots and bacon. Next add the tomato sauce, not too liquid. Then add the blackcurrant jam, tamari and chocolate, which should thicken the sauce to a coating consistency.

4. Simmer together and adjust seasoning. Add a squeeze of lemon. Slice the pigeon breasts and return them to reheat quickly.

I served them with red Camargue rice, sautéd Florence fennel, and a watercress and chicory salad.

Kedgeree

A great supper dish that can be cooked in half an hour.

SERVES 4–6

8 oz/225 g smoked, undyed haddock

2 sticks celery

1 medium onion, finely chopped

1 leek, about 6 oz/175 g, washed thoroughly and sliced finely

1 carrot, about 6 oz/175 g, cut into julienne strips

piece of pumpkin 6 oz/175 g, also in julienne strips

1 courgette

1/2 bulb of Florence fennel

8 oz/225 g Basmati or Arborio rice

1/2 pt/275 ml whole milk

1/2 pt/275 ml stock or white wine

2 tsp curry powder (medium hot)

1 tbsp capers

2 hard-boiled eggs, chopped

2 oz/50 g butter

1 tbsp olive oil

1 tbsp chopped parsley

2 bay leaves

Method:

1. In a large, heavy-bottomed saucepan or sauté pan melt 1 oz butter with the olive oil. Sauté the onion till translucent on low heat.

2. Meanwhile, put the fillet of haddock in a frying pan and cover with milk. Add 2 bay leaves and some parsley stalks. Simmer for 8 minutes, or till the flakes fall apart easily. Strain and keep the milk residue.

3. To the sautéd onions and curry powder add the celery, sliced white part of the leek and thinly sliced fennel. Continue to sauté together for a further 5 minutes. Add a little salt now. Add the washed, drained rice.

4. Add stock or white wine to the liquid from the haddock. This should make about 1 pt of cooking liquid. Heat it in a separate saucepan, not quite to boiling. Taste it for saltiness (haddock is already salty).

5. Start to add this liquid to the onions and rice mixture, stirring. If it is Arborio rice you will need to add it in about three batches, whilst you stir. If it is Basmati rice add all the liquid and allow to come to boiling point and then turn the flame down to its lowest and cover with a tightly fitting lid. Cook for 20 minutes, or till tender.

6. Blanch carrots, pumpkin, green part of the leeks for 2–3 minutes in some boiling salted water, with a little ginger sliced in it. This is to keep the colours fresh and the texture al dente.

7. Skin and flake the haddock and remove any bones. Add it to rice and blanched vegetables, capers and the rest of the butter, with a squeeze of lemon. Check seasoning and pile into a warmed serving dish. Garnish with chopped egg and parsley.

 Omit the haddock.

Vegetarian Main Dishes

Parsnip and Shallot Tatin

SERVES 6

A rich, delicious light supper dish, which is a savoury version of the famous French Apple Tarte Tatin. It will be helped by having a tatin dish, which is one that can go both on top of the stove and in the oven. I have an enamelled Le Creuset one, 10 inches (25 cm) in diameter, which is a very valuable piece of kitchen equipment.

For the pastry:

3 oz/75 g white unbleached flour, and

3 oz/75 g 85% wholewheat flour, sifted together

4 oz/110 g butter

pinch of salt

3 tbsp ice cold water

For the filling:

1 lb/450 g shallots, peeled and halved

1 lb/450 g parsnips, after peeling

1¹/₂ oz/40 g butter

2 tsp Rapadura raw cane sugar

1 tbsp balsamic vinegar

2 tsp soya sauce

1 tsp fresh thyme leaves, or ¹/₂ tsp dried

salt and pepper

Method:

1. Make the pastry by rubbing the cold butter into the sifted flour, together with a pinch of salt. The result should look like fine bread-crumbs. Add 3 tbsp ice-cold water carefully until the mixture holds together in a ball. Allow to rest in the refrigerator for ¹/₂ hour.

2. Meanwhile prepare the parsnips by halving first and then slicing fairly thinly into triangular pieces, cutting off the bottom thin end if too long. The pieces should measure around 5 inches in length (half the length of the dish).

3. In the tatin dish melt the butter together with the sugar, vinegar and soya sauce until it starts to bubble. Remove from the heat.

4. Arrange a layer of shallots to cover the bottom, sitting in the liquid which will caramelize during cooking.

5. Then carefully arrange a layer of parsnip slices evenly like spokes of a wheel. Season with a sprinkling of sea salt and pepper and the thyme leaves.

6. Return the dish to the heat and cook for 5–8 minutes on a gentle heat—being careful not to let it burn at this point—until the juices are heated through.

7. Cover with foil and bake in a moderate oven (180°C/gas mark 4) for 50 minutes, or until the vegetables are tender.

8. Meanwhile roll out the pastry into a circle 11–12 inches in diameter.

9. Remove the dish from the oven and increase the temperature to 200°C/gas mark 6.

10. Cover the parsnips and shallots with the circle of pastry, tucking in the edges. Work quickly as the pastry can start to melt on the warm vegetables.

11. Return to the oven for approx. 30 minutes, until pastry is golden.

12. Rest for about 15 minutes. Turn out carefully onto a flat plate. If any vegetables stick to the pan they can be eased off with a spatula and returned to their vacant spot in the lovely mosaic.

Cabbage Parcels Stuffed with Chestnuts

SERVES 6

12 blanched green cabbage leaves with the toughest part of the stem removed in a V-shape.

For the stuffing:

8 oz/225 g whole rice cooked in 2 cups of good stock

1 oz/25 g butter and 1 tbsp olive oil for sautéing

1 red onion finely chopped

4 oz/110 g wild mushrooms (or chestnut mushrooms), finely chopped

zest and juice of 1 lemon

2 heads of roasted garlic cloves

8 oz/225 g cooked chestnuts (either fresh or dried and rehydrated), chopped small

salt and pepper

1 tbsp finely chopped parsley

1 tbsp finely chopped sage

Method:

1. Sauté the onion in the butter and oil until soft but not brown.

2. Add mushrooms, garlic and lemon. Season.

3. Add the rice, which should be fairly sticky, the chestnuts and the herbs. Check the seasoning. It should hold its shape when moulded.

4. Place a tablespoon (or more, depending on the size of the leaf) on each cabbage leaf, just about the V. Fold the flaps upwards and roll the leaf into a cigar shape. Tie with fine string or secure with toothpicks.

5. Pack the cabbage parcels into an ovenproof dish. Any leftover stuffing can be cooked in a separate dish or used to stuff vegetables (see below).

6. Pour a little stock into the bottom of the dish. Cover and bake in a moderate oven (180°C/gas mark 4 for 30 minutes).

Serve with tomato or parsley sauce and maybe a beetroot and orange salad, with any extra stuffing on the side.

Stuffed Courgettes and Bell Peppers

This same stuffing can be used, with the addition of a beaten egg, to the flesh scooped from blanched courgettes or bell peppers (cut in half lengthways, blanched in boiling salted water for 5 minutes and drained). Sprinkle with Parmesan. Bake in a moderate oven for $1/2$ hour.

Piroshki Stuffed with Wild Mushrooms and Walnuts

SERVES 10 PEOPLE

Small Russian/Polish pies with rich pastry and various stuffings

For the pastry:

6 oz/175 g softened butter

6 oz/175 g cream cheese/marscapone

12 oz/350 g unbleached plain flour (10 for recipe and 2 for rolling out)

1 tsp sea salt

3 tbsp double cream

egg for glazing

1 dsp sesame seeds to sprinkle on top

For the stuffing:

3 oz/80 g roasted and chopped walnuts

1 red onion, finely chopped

6 oz/175 g chestnut mushrooms, finely chopped

4 cloves of garlic

2 oz/50 g wild mushrooms (like porcini or chanterelles), steeped in $^1/4$ pt/150 ml boiling water

4 oz/100 g breadcrumbs

$^1/2$ tsp paprika

2 hard-boiled eggs, chopped finely

1 tbsp sherry

2 tbsp sour cream

4 spring onions, finely chopped

1 tbsp chopped coriander leaf

salt and pepper

Method:

To make pastry:

1. Sift flour and salt together in a large bowl

2. Rub in the butter and cream cheese

3. Add the 3 tbsp cream. It should make a firm ball. Chill for $^1/2$ hour.

To make stuffing:

1. Strain dried mushrooms from their soaking water, check for grit and chop. Sieve the mushroom water through a muslin or fine sieve.

2. Soak breadcrumbs in this liquid.

3. Sauté chopped onions, garlic and chestnut mushrooms in some olive oil with a little butter. Add porcini and brown them. Deglaze the pan with the sherry.

4. Add these to the breadcrumbs. Add walnuts, then paprika and sour cream. Adjust seasoning.

5. Add spring onions and coriander (or parsley) and hard-boiled egg.

Piroshki Stuffed with Wild Mushrooms and Walnuts cont.

To make up the piroshki:

1 Roll out the pastry into squares approx. 4 x 4 in (10 x 10 cm) (this quantity should make 10 piroshki).

2 Place a spoonful (approx. one-tenth of the mix) of filling in the centre and brush around the edges with beaten egg. Bring the points together in the centre and bring all four edges together, crimping them as you go along.

3 Brush with beaten egg and scatter with sesame seeds. Place on an oiled baking sheet and bake at 200°C/gas mark 6 for 15 minutes, or till golden, then turn oven down to 180°C/gas mark 4) for a further 15 minutes.

Serve with grated cucumber and sour cream (tzatziki), and spiced red cabbage. I also served red quinoa.

Non-vegetarians can add some chopped chicken to the filling.

Garlic and Mushroom Bulgur

SERVES 6

From Pauline Anderson's recipes used in biodynamic coffee shops. Plain, simple and delicious

1 medium onion, chopped

2^{1}/2 oz/60 g butter

^{1}/2 lb/225 g bulgur, rinsed

1 pt/570 ml hot stock

2 oz/50 g mushrooms (organic, preferably brown)

2 cloves garlic, chopped

^{1}/4 red pepper, chopped fairly fine

salt and pepper

fresh parsley, thyme and chives, chopped

Method:

1. Sauté onion in 1^{1}/2 oz/40 g butter. Add bulgur and sauté for a few minutes.

2. Add hot stock and bring gently to the boil. Take off heat and set aside in warm place with lid on for 15 minutes (grain should then be cooked and all liquid absorbed).

3. Sauté mushrooms, garlic and red pepper in 1 oz/25 g butter for 2 minutes. Pour onto cooked bulgur. Add salt, pepper and squeeze of lemon. (Taste for the right balance.) Fold in chopped herbs.

Can be served cold as a salad, with other salads and perhaps filled eggs.

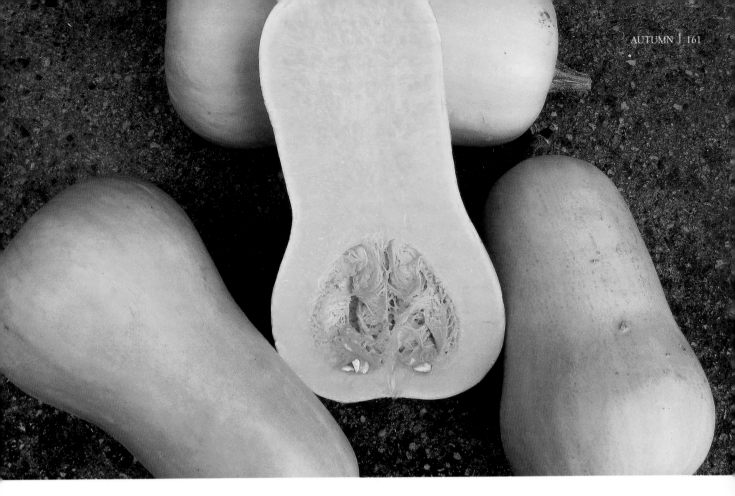

Butternut Squash and Semolina Gnocchi

SERVES 6

This is a light, easy-to-make supper dish completed with a crunchy salad of carrots, lettuce and cashews.

Required: buttered baking dish

Oven 190°C/gas mark 5

1 lb/450 g butternut squash, baked with garlic and rosemary the day before (yields ¹/2 lb/225 g)

6 oz/175 g yellow semolina

³/4 pt/425 ml stock

¹/2 tsp salt and generous grinding of pepper

¹/2 tsp freshly grated nutmeg

2 oz/50 g butter

2 oz/50 g grated parmesan

2 large eggs

chopped parsley and melted butter to finish

Method:

1. Roast the butternut squash and scoop it out of its skin, having removed the seeds—which can be roasted with tamari as a snack—and purée with a mouli-de-legumes. You should get about ¹/2 lb/225 g. Spread it out on a tray and allow it to dry as much as possible.

2. In a heavy-bottomed pan put the semolina and stock and cook for 5–8 minutes until the mixture is a really stiff porridge, where the mixing spoon will virtually stand upright.

3. Add the dryish butternut purée, then butter, nutmeg, salt and pepper. Beat in the eggs and half the Parmesan. Pour this mixture into a buttered baking dish. Allow to cool and cut into fingers. Dot with butter, sprinkle with Parmesan and bake in a hot oven (190°C/gas mark 5) for 20 minutes. Garnish with finely chopped parsley.

Stuffed Crêpes and Galettes

SERVES 6

For crêpe and waffle batter:

6 oz/175 g plain flour

$^1/_2$ tsp salt

2 oz/50g melted butter

2 large eggs

8 fl oz/225 ml milk

2 fl oz/55 ml water

Method:

1. Sift flour and salt into a bowl.

2. Add melted butter.

3. Add eggs, milk and water. Beat vigorously to get rid of lumps. Let this mixture stand for at least half an hour to allow gluten to develop. Should be the consistency of thick cream.

For buckwheat galette mixture:

3 oz/75 g buckwheat flour

3 oz/75 g plain flour (necessary as buckwheat lacks gluten)

(Mix as in the recipe above.)

To cook pancakes:

Melt 1 oz/25 g butter in a frying pan and swish around so that the entire surface is covered. It should be hot but not smoking. Put a ladleful of the batter into the pan and let it run around so that the whole bottom is covered. Cook for $^1/_2$–1 minute, until it loosens from the sides and bottom. Tip and flip over to cook the other side until golden. Stack pancakes in a warm place.

Fillings (six portions each)—

Leek and Courgette filling

$^{1}/_{2}$ pt/275 ml thick béchamel sauce
(see recipe on page 114)

6 oz/175 g leeks, sliced and sautéd in 2 oz/50 g
butter

4 oz/110 g courgettes sliced into matchsticks

Mushroom and Shallot filling

2 chopped shallots

1 lb/400 g sliced mushrooms

1 oz (25 g) butter

1 tbsp olive oil

2 cloves garlic

$^{1}/_{2}$ tsp herbes de Provence

Sauté together, for 5 minutes, then add:

1 tbsp sherry

3 tbsp crème fraîche

whiz in a blender, but keep some texture.

Smoked Salmon filling

4 oz/110g smoked salmon pâté (see page 206)

2 tbsp crème fraîche

1 tbsp chopped parsley, chives and wild garlic,
mixed

Pumpkin, Chestnut and Porcini Croustade (Oat and Cheese Herb Topping)

SERVES 6

For the topping:

4 oz/100 g oat flakes

3 oz/75 g fresh breadcrumbs

1 tbsp finely chopped herbs (sage, rosemary, thyme, or Provencal dried herbs)

3 oz/75 g grated Emmental cheese (optional)

salt and pepper

1 tsp paprika

3 oz/75 g melted butter

For the filling:

1¹/₂ lb/500 g of peeled and sliced pumpkin (choose a variety with sweet, dense flesh, such as 'Hubbard', 'Crown Prince' or 'Hokkaido', not one of the watery, tasteless sorts

2 large onions, sliced finely

6 cloves of roasted garlic (it's good to roast several heads of garlic with oil, salt and rosemary when you have the oven going and then you have it to hand)

celeriac, small cubes (or 2 celery sticks)

2 oz/50 g dried porcini (wild mushrooms) washed carefully and soaked in boiling water for ¹/₂ hour

¹/₂ tsp cinnamon

¹/₂ tsp grated nutmeg

4 oz/100 g dried chestnuts (soaked in boiling water for 1 hour or so, then cooked separately with a little salt for ¹/₂ hour)

olive oil and butter for sautéing

Method:

To make topping:

Mix all the dry ingredients in a bowl, melt the butter and pour over dry ingredients. Work it through with fingertips.

To make filling:

1. Sauté the sliced onions in a mixture of butter and oil with a pinch of salt. Add garlic and sliced pumpkin, chestnuts, soaked porcini and celeriac.

2. Add 1 pt/20 fl oz stock and the strained porcini water (being very careful not to include grit!). You may need a little more stock later on. Bring to the boil in a heavy bottomed pot.

3. Turn down heat to minimum and allow to gently simmer for ³/₄ hour, or until vegetables are tender. The stock should be absorbed and the vegetables dense. Adjust seasoning. It should have just a hint of spice, for the accompanying red cabbage dish is quite spicy.

4. Fill an ovenproof dish with the pumpkin mixture, top with the oat topping mixture, dot with butter. Bake in the oven at 180°C/gas mark 4 until golden (about ¹/₂ hour).

Moroccan Couscous with Quinces

SERVES 8–10

Required: a large, heavy-bottomed casserole dish

2 quinces

4 large onions

4 cloves garlic

1 oz/25 g butter, for sautéing

4 tsp olive oil, for sautéing

4 carrots, roll-cut

1 lb/450g Hubbard or Butternut squash

4 sticks celery

4 leeks (separate the white parts from the green)

8 oz/225 g small green cabbage, sliced finely

1 lb/450 g almost—but not completely— cooked chick peas

1 tbsp *harrissa* (Moroccan spice for couscous)

$1/2$ tsp saffron threads soaked in $1/4$ cup boiling water

1 lb/450 g fresh, ripe de-skinned tomatoes, or a 400 g can of chopped tomatoes

1 handful chopped fresh coriander and flat-leafed parsley

1 lb/450 g courgettes, roughly chopped

1 tbsp chopped mint

1 lemon

salt and pepper

For couscous:

1lb/500 g whole couscous

2 tbsp olive oil

1 tbsp lightly roasted pine kernels

2 tbsp seedless raisins or apricots soaked for 10 minutes in boiling water

$1/2$ tsp sea salt

2 pts/1.2 l boiling stock

zest and juice of a lemon

Moroccan Couscous with Quinces cont.

Method:

1. Clean, peel and scrub vegetables

2. Slice the onions into half-moons and sauté in a large casserole in butter and olive oil. Add garlic and cook till translucent.

3. Add the other vegetables cut into largish pieces—except the courgettes, cabbage and green part of the leeks, which I cook separately with mint to keep the colour and vitality.

4. Stir in the *harrissa*, saffron and $^1/_2$ tsp salt. You can add more *harrissa* at the end if you want to make the dish spicier, or serve some separately diluted with 2 tbsp of the broth.

5. Add the tomatoes and top up with some stock just to cover the vegetables. Add chick peas.

6. Put the lid on and cook slowly for about $^3/_4$ hour on low heat until the vegetables are tender but haven't lost their form, and the flavours are developed.

Meanwhile, prepare the couscous grain:

In a bowl sprinkle the olive oil onto the grain. Rub through with fingertips.

Add lemon zest and juice, then the boiling stock. Allow to swell for 10 minutes before adding pine kernels and raisins, or apricots.

7. While the grain swells, lightly cook the three green vegetables with butter, salt and water and 1 tbsp chopped mint for 5 minutes approx. The couscous grain should ideally be finished off in the steam of the stew in a steamer or couscoussière to enhance the flavour.

8. Add the green vegetables to the stew. Sprinkle with fresh herbs and garnish with lemon slices.

Desserts

Blackberry and Apple Pie

SERVES 6

Required: a 10 inch/25 cm pie-dish

For the pastry:

10 oz/275 g unbleached flour

6 oz/175 g cold butter, chopped into small pieces

$^1/_2$ tsp salt

4 tbsp ice cold water

Make the shortcrust pastry (see pages 97–8) and allow to rest for one hour.

For the filling:

2 lb/900g Bramley cooking apples, peeled and sliced

6 oz/175 g blackberries

4 oz/110 g soft brown sugar

$^1/_4$ pt/150 ml water

juice of $^1/_2$ lemon

1 dsp arrowroot

Method:

Make a syrup with water, sugar and lemon juice. Poach the apple slices lightly for 5 minutes. Then add the blackberries for just long enough to start the juices oozing. Strain the fruit and cool. You should have about $^1/_4$ pt/150 ml juice. Adjust the sweetness of juice and thicken with 1 dsp arrowroot, mixed to a paste with 2 tbsp cold water, then bring to the boil. Cool.

Assembly:

1. Divide pastry in half. Use half to roll out and cover the plate, trimming the edges.

2. Pile on the cooled apples and blackberries, leaving an edge all round free. Then pour on top the cooled and thickened juices.

3. Paint the pastry edge with milk.

4. Roll out the second half of pastry and cut 3 small slits to allow steam to escape.

5. Place it over a rolling pin and gently ease over the lower half. Press edge down, trim off excess and crimp.

6. Brush with milk and sprinkle with caster sugar.

7. Make decorative leaves from trimmings and place on top, then glaze with milk and sugar.

8. Bake in hot oven (200°C/gas mark 6) for 20 minutes to set the pastry, then turn down to 180°C/gas mark 4 to finish cooking for a further $^1/_2$ hour, until golden brown.

9. Serve with crème fraîche.

French Apple Tart
with *Membrillo* (Quince Paste)

SERVES 6

Required: a 10 inch/25 cm, loose-bottomed flan case

Oven 200°C/gas mark 6

12 oz/350 g shortcrust pastry (see pages 97–8)

1½ lb/800 g Cox's eating apples

5 oz/150 g unrefined caster sugar

6 oz/175 g *membrillo* paste, sliced thinly (see recipe on page 212), or

½ jar of good quality apricot jam

¾ pt/425 ml single cream

4 eggs

a few drops of pure vanilla essence

½ tsp freshly grated nutmeg

Method:

1. Roll out the pastry and cover the flan case. Crimp the edges and prick the bottom. Let it rest in the refrigerator for 10 minutes.

2. Core your eating apples but do not peel. Cut in half and then slice fairly thinly and evenly. Sprinkle with a little caster sugar to prevent discolouring (lemon juice may curdle the cream, so I don't advise using it).

3. Beat eggs and sugar together. Then gradually add the cream and the vanilla essence.

4. Lay the slices of *membrillo* evenly on the bottom of the flan case. Then carefully arrange the apples in a 'wheel' on top, spiralling into the centre.

5. Pour on the cream and egg mixture. The spiral of apple slices should be visible through the custard. Sprinkle the top with nutmeg and place on a tray in the oven, 200°C/gas mark 6 for the first 15 minutes to set the pastry, then at 180°C/gas mark 4 for a further ½ hour until golden and the custard has set. Allow to cool a little. Serve with crème fraîche.

Poached Pears
in Spiced Red Wine

SERVES 6

Required: large, heavy saucepan

½ pt/275 ml red wine

½ pt/275 ml elderberry or blackcurrant juice

1 cinnamon quill

2 pieces crystallized ginger, sliced

1 lemon, sliced thinly

1 tangerine studded with cloves

3 oz/75 g Rapadura raw cane sugar

6 Conference pears, peeled but with stalks left on

Method:

To prepare the poaching liquid:

1. Put the first 7 ingredients in the saucepan. Bring to the boil and leave to simmer for 15 minutes, or until flavours are infused beautifully.

2. Carefully place the pears in this wine bath and bring to the boil, then turn the heat down to a simmer. Turn the pears gently from time to time so that they cook and colour uniformly a beautiful deep red (30 minutes cooking should leave them tender).

3. Remove the pears and boil the mixture until it has reduced to a syrup, or you can thicken the sauce (about ¾ pt/425 ml) with 1 dsp of arrowroot mixed with a little cold water and brought to the boil (whisking the while) and then left to cool.

4. Serve hot or cold, or at room temperature.

If you prefer not to use wine, just use all blackcurrant or elderberry cordial diluted.

Plum Compôte

1 lb/450 g plums, ripe but firm

^{1}/2 pt/275 ml water

4 oz/110 g soft brown sugar

a little greengage liqueur or kirsch (optional)

1 orange

1 tbsp plum jam or blackcurrant syrup

Method:

1. Scrub and then slice the orange very thinly.

2. Make a syrup by combining water, sugar, orange slices and jam.

3. Wash and halve the plums, removing the stones. Poach in the syrup until soft, but holding their shape. Add a dash of liqueur.

Date Tahini Parfait

SERVES 4–6

This is a simply delicious and quick-to-prepare dessert that would perfectly complement a Middle Eastern or Persian meal.

2 tbsp date syrup (available in wholefood stores)

1 tbsp light tahini

just over ^{1}/4 pt/250 ml whipping cream

16 oz/450 g Greek yoghourt

1 oz/25 g flaked almonds, roasted lightly in a dry frying pan

Method:

1. Combine the date syrup and tahini.

2. Whip the cream, add yoghourt, then just swirl a dollop of the date-tahini mixture on the top.

3. Decorate with roasted almond flakes.

Also lovely with sliced bananas mixed in.

Semolina, Apricot and Rose Water Pudding

SERVES 6

This dessert has a Persian influence—a hint of rose and layers of apricot 'leather' makes a milk pudding that is a treat and usually enjoyed by children.

Required: ovenproof dish with lid or foil to cover

Oven at 180°C/gas mark 4

4 oz/110 g yellow semolina

1¹/₂ pts/800 ml whole milk

1 tbsp honey

1 tsp date syrup

4 oz/110 g apricot 'leather' found in Middle Eastern stores. Or you may prefer to use reconstituted dried apricots, or 2 tbsp good apricot jam.

1 tsp rose water

grated peel of 1 large lemon

2 eggs, beaten

2 oz/50 g chopped unsalted pistachios

Method:

1. Bring the semolina and 1 pt/570 ml milk very gently to the boil and cook, stirring the while for about 5 minutes, allowing it to thicken. Gradually add the other ¹/₂ pt/275 ml of milk, until it is all absorbed.

2. Add honey and date syrup and test for sweetness (don't forget, though, that the apricots will be quite sweet).

3. Add lemon zest and rose water, half the pistachios and lastly the eggs. It should now have a thick, but still pouring, consistency.

4. Butter a fairly shallow ovenproof dish and pour a third of the semolina mixture into the bottom.

5. Cut squares of apricot leather (which melts during cooking), or jam or fruit, and dot over the semolina layer.

6. Cover with another third of the semolina mix and repeat the apricot layer.

7. Finish with the last layer of semolina. Dot with a few chopped pistachios.

8. Cover and bake in a medium oven for ³/₄ hour. But uncover for the last 10 minutes to allow the top to develop a few golden freckles.

A FUNGUS FORAY

My colourful Russian friend Laura grew up in Kazhakstan. Now with her mother and two children she has made her base in South Devon and has lost no time in exploring the countryside and developing an intuitive knowledge of wild herbs and fungi. One early October morning she invited a small group of us to go on a fungus foray in some local woods. Her amazingly keen eyes spotted edible mushrooms everywhere; her children were equally competent. There were mushrooms that looked like seaweed and, more easily recognized, there were boletus, chanterelles, some with pale lavender gills—all, she assured us with authority, perfectly delicious and edible. Within a couple of hours we had amassed an impressive haul of over a dozen varieties.

Now it began to drizzle and we found a sheltered picnic place with tables beneath some thick pine trees. Out from nowhere came the camping stove, a large, heavy frying pan, olive oil, salt, garlic and bread. The mushrooms were carefully wiped with kitchen paper and sliced into the hot oil with garlic. The fragrances of the forest, leaves, pine needles, cooking mushrooms and garlic were unforgettable. Then appeared chilled vodka, flavoured with lemon, garlic and rosemary, and tiny glasses. Fire water was slurped down—but only along with food! Once in a while it's a treat. We finished our meal with my plum and hazelnut brioche (see pages 240–1).

Winter

Winter
Praise wet snow
falling early.
Praise the shadow,
my neighbour's chimney
casts on the tile roof.

Denise Leverton

Crackling fires, indoors this time—
roasting chestnuts—mulled wine—
time to read that new book—
barley in scotch broth—bread-making—
plum pancakes—Mallorcan *sopas*—
rabbit and onion casserole—
red Camargue rice—red cabbage—
mincemeat—nutmeat pâté with
cranberry and orange sauce—
Seville oranges for marmalade making.

FESTIVALS

The first Sunday in Advent is the beginning of the Christian year. Advent begins on St Andrew's Day (30 November) or the Sunday nearest to it, and is the four-week period leading up to Christmas.

The Winter Solstice occurs on or about 21 December, which has the longest night of the year. Thereafter the sun continues to grow, overcoming the darkness and bringing increasing optimism. This is also the beginning of the Tamil new year, where rice and boiled milk is offered to the gods and then to the cows, which are decorated with garlands of fruits and flowers and have their horns painted, and then shared with the family.

Christmas Eve, on 24 December, is called Nochebuena in Spain. The main feast often takes place before the midnight mass or 'Cockerel mass' as it is called in Spain and Catalonia. In many churches the 'Sibylla', a haunting homily, is sung by a young boy dressed as a female sibyl or prophetess, in an ancient chant from the tenth century telling of the coming of the Messiah. Children hang up empty stockings for Santa Claus (St Nicholas) to fill with gifts.

Christmas Day, 25 December (since AD 440), celebrates the Nativity of Our Lord. The Virgin Queen of Heaven gives birth to the Light of the World. It was also the birthday of Mithra, Osiris, Tammuz, Attis and Dionysus and in Scandinavia it is the birthday of Freya. There is occasion for great feasting throughout the Twelve Days of Christmas. On Christmas morning in Mallorca the village people would carry their goose, suckling-pig or turkey in great roasting dishes to the baker who, after cooking the bread, would then with great skill cook these festive platters. And what a sight it was to see them all tucked into his great oven. And what a smell filled the entire street! In England the Christmas bird is stuffed with sage and onion and chestnuts. The dessert is a rich brandy-flamed fruit plum pudding, and minced pies are served with hot mulled wine. Festive crackers are pulled which contain gifts and mottoes.

New Year's Eve, 31 December, is the last day of the year (in Spanish Noche Vieja). In Spain there is a tradition of eating a grape for each of the twelve chimes of the clock, as the old year is ushered out. This is not as easy as it might sound. In Scotland there is 'first footing', where the first visitor to cross the threshold must bring a piece of coal to ensure warmth and fuel for the year, and of course lots of whisky and a black bun! (Recipe on page 238.)

Epiphany, on 6 January, is the Feast of the Three Kings, Caspar, Melchior and Balthazar, with their gifts of gold, frankincense and myrrh. This is the time in Spain when the children receive their gifts from the Three Kings. Special sweets are created with almonds and sugar. It is traditional to bake a cake for Epiphany within which is hidden a dried bean and a dried pea. The one who finds the bean is King for the night and the one who finds the pea is Queen. They rule over the party and wear crowns and can choose their favourite games.

Candlemas Day, on 2 Februrary, is called Groundhog Day in the USA. On this day, according to American popular tradition, the groundhog leaves his hole and his deep winter sleep to look for his shadow. If he sees it, he reckons on six more weeks of winter. If not, he stays above ground to enjoy an early spring.

If Candlemas Day be fine and clear,
Corn and fruit will then be dear.
If the wind's in the east on Candlemas Day
It's sure to stay to the second of May!

(Old English song)

Candlemas Day is when the candles to be used in the church during the coming year are blessed, a festival that is often celebrated in many Waldorf kindergartens. The children will have planted bulbs in the garden and in pots on Michaelmas Day (29 September). In late January they will begin to make hand-dipped candles. One year, on the morning of Candlemas, I was lucky enough to be invited to visit my local Waldorf kindergarten group. The tables were arranged in a circle with a sprinkling of flour at each child's place. On the centre table were bowls of candles and bunches of snowdrops also known as 'Candlemas Bells' or 'Mary's Tapers'. Jill, the teacher, had made a large batch of springy dough, which was divided between the children. They learnt how to make many things from their piece of dough such as snakes, which became snails, and while dividing the dough they sang counting songs. Each child was  given two apricots into which they inserted a whole almond, and then they made two rolls each from the dough and in the centre hid the apricot with its almond 'seed'. Then these were collected, allowed to rise and put in the oven. Next, the children were wrapped up warmly and went out into the garden where there was evidence of the sprouting and flowering of many bulbs. They each were given a spoon to make a little hole next to a bulb where a tiny candle was placed; when lit the candle would bring light and warmth into the cold winter soil. The children were totally engrossed in this activity and it was deeply touching. Then they huddled round their teacher who told them a Candlemas story and presently went back inside into the warm and beautiful room. After washing hands, we were given two rolls, one to eat and one to take home for Mummy and Daddy, together with delicate bunches of snowdrops and a candle wrapped in silver paper. A puppet show, about the seeds and bulbs being woken up, rounded off the morning's activities. As we went home we could see an occasional little light still burning in the dark soil.

SAMPLE MENU

Dolma (Stuffed Vine Leaves)
Hummus bi Tahina with Pitta Bread
Babaganousch (Aubergine Spread)
Green and Red Pepper Salad with Yoghourt
Lamb Koresh with Dumplings
Vegetarian Couscous with Quinces
Hallah Bread
Persian Olive Oil and Saffron Cake
Date and Walnut Sweetmeats

A Middle Eastern meal

My friend Haim, who is Israeli of Moroccan origins, loves cooking and was taught at his mother's knee. He responded well to my suggestion that we have a Peace Meal in the Camphill Community where he lives with his family. This meal was to contain elements and traditions of all these Middle Eastern cultures. Haim has done a lot of peace work and acknowledges how the sharing of each other's traditions and cuisines helps to further understanding and good will.

There was an amazing atmosphere is that large kitchen as breads were rolled out and plaited, garlic squashed, vegetables bubbled with *harissa* in couscous. I watched fascinated as Misha, Haim's, son picked out the jewel-like seeds of a pomegranate with the infinite grace of a child who has grown up doing this. A wonderful atmosphere was created around our candlelit table as we sampled the surprising combinations of flavours—from the tiny, cigar-shaped stuffed vine leaves to the Persian olive oil and saffron cake and walnut and date sweetmeats washed down with sweet fresh mint tea.

Soups

Beetroot Soup (Borscht) V

SERVES 6

$1^1/2$ lb/700 g raw beetroot (peeled)

8 oz/200 g carrots, sliced

8 oz/200 g onion, sliced

8 oz/200 g potatoes, sliced

3 sticks of celery or some celeriac

$1/4$ medium red cabbage

2 leeks (white part only)

4 cloves garlic

$1/2$ tsp cumin

$1/2$ tsp caraway seeds

salt and pepper to taste

1 tbsp tomato concentrate

1 bay leaf

3 pts/1.5 l good vegetable stock

1 oz/25 g each, oil and butter for sautéing

2 tbsp sour cream and chives for garnish

Method:

1. Slice all the vegetables finely but keep them separate.

2. Heat butter and oil in a heavy pot. Sauté onions and garlic first. This drives off excess sulphur. Add all the other vegetables, coating them with the oil by stirring over a low heat.

3. Add all other ingredients one by one, adding spices and some salt. Then add the stock and bring it to the boil.

4. Turn down the heat and let it simmer for approx. $3/4$ hour until the vegetables are all soft (the beetroot will take longest). Allow to rest for $1/2$ hour to let the flavours stabilize. Then blend in a food processor.

5. Adjust seasoning, heat to simmering point again and serve with a dollop of sour cream and chopped chives.

Scotch Broth

SERVES 6

A way to make a small lamb shank go a long way.

1 lamb shank roasted for 30–40 minutes with:

2 sprigs of rosemary

3 cloves of garlic

2 tbsp olive oil

zest of 1 lemon

salt and pepper

Having used half the meat from the roast, use the rest the next day for the Scotch Broth.

4 oz/110 g cooked lamb in small slices

2 oz/50 g pot barley soaked overnight

8 oz/225 g sliced onion

6 oz/175 g piece of swede

8 oz/225 g potato, cubed

2 carrots chopped small

2 leeks, thoroughly washed and sliced finely

3 sticks of celery, sliced

2 tbsp olive oil

2 tsp chopped rosemary

1 tsp chopped thyme

1 tsp chopped sage

3 pts/1.5 l stock

parsley to garnish

For stock:

lamb bone

2 bay leaves

1 carrot sliced

2 sticks celery

onion trimmings

3 pts/1.5 l water

salt and pepper

Method:

1. Start the stock with the lamb bone and other ingredients and boil for 1 hour.

2. Heat the olive oil in a large saucepan. Add onions and fry until browned. Add all the other vegetables and herbs and barley, except the leeks (which are only added 5 minutes before serving, to retain colour and freshness).

3. Add well-flavoured stock and simmer for a further hour until barley and vegetables are tender. Add leeks and then sprinkle on some finely chopped parsley.

Serve with crunchy bread rolls.

Mallorcan Broad Bean Stew (Fabada)

SERVES 6

You can spread the cooking of this stew over two days.

8 oz/225 g dried broad beans, washed and soaked overnight

3 tbsp olive oil

2 large onions, cut in half-moons

2 oz/50 g chopped streaky bacon

2 oz/50 g smoked chorizo sausage, sliced thinly

4 cloves garlic, finely chopped

2 bay leaves

2 carrots

2 sticks celery

1 large red pepper, chopped

1¹/₂ pts/750 ml good stock

¹/₂ pt/275 ml red table wine

4 ripe tomatoes, peeled, de-seeded and chopped or 1 can of tomatoes

1 tsp marjoram

Method:

1. Throw away the soaking water and put the beans in a heavy-bottomed casserole (the Mallorcans use an earthenware greixonera). Pour in the stock and the red wine (if you prefer not to use wine, then increase the amount of stock). Add 1 stick celery, chopped, half an onion, 1 carrot, chopped, and 2 bay leaves. Cook for up to 2 hours, until the beans soften.

2. At this stage you could cool the stew and leave overnight to let the flavours develop. The next day pick out the vegetables, which will have released their flavours, but be rather mushy and discoloured. The liquid should be fairly thick.

3. In a clean casserole (Le Creuset if possible) heat the 3 tbsp olive oil. Add the rest of the sliced onions and sauté until browned. Add the bacon and chorizo sausage, garlic, sliced raw carrot and celery, tomatoes, marjoram and the chopped red pepper. Cook for 5–8 minutes, then add the cooked broad beans. Bring gently to simmering and then place in the oven for 1 hour at 140°C/gas mark 3.

4. Adjust seasoning. This should be a thick, spicy, rib-sticking stew.

Serve with a crispy green salad and good country bread and olives.

> **V** For a vegetarian version just omit the bacon and chorizo.

Slightly Curried Smoked Haddock Soup

SERVES 6

2 oz/50 g butter

10 oz/280 g smoked haddock (undyed variety)

3/4 pt/425 ml whole milk

2 onions

1/2 lb/225 g potatoes

1/2 lb/225 g leeks, thoroughly washed

2 sticks celery

4 oz/110 g chopped celeriac (if available)

1 1/2 pt/725 ml stock

1/4 pt/142 ml single cream

2 pinches saffron threads

2 bay leaves

salt and pepper

1/4 tsp herbes de Provence

1 dsp medium hot Madras curry powder

1/2 tsp peppercorns

squeeze of lemon juice

1 tbsp chopped fresh parsley or coriander

Method:

1. Wash haddock and poach in the milk for 5–8 minutes (once boiling), with a pinch of saffron threads, 2 bay leaves, peppercorns and a few slices of onion. Allow to cool and infuse in the liquid. Remove the fish and de-skin and de-bone. Strain the liquid and reserve to add to the soup later. Taste for saltiness and adjust accordingly.

2. Chop onion finely, the celery in small slices on the diagonal, the celeriac, potatoes and leeks in small cubes. (Reserve the finely shredded green part to add at the end.)

3. Melt the butter and sauté the above vegetables with a little salt, the remaining pinch of saffron, the herbes de Provence and curry powder.

4. When all are coated and the aromas arising, pour in the 1 1/2 pts of good stock. Once boiling, allow to simmer on low heat for 30 minutes, or until the vegetables are tender.

5. Add cream and whiz half the soup in a blender, keeping the other half for texture—but you can purée it all if you prefer.

6. Now add the smoked haddock flakes and the finely chopped green leek tops. Cook for 5 minutes. Add a generous grinding of pepper, a tablespoon of chopped parsley or coriander and a squeeze of lemon.

Serve with crusty bread and a crisp green salad.

If you have some left-over long grain rice you could add 2 tbsp to give this soup more body and nutritional value.

Mallorcan Cabbage and Bread Stew (*Sopas*)

SERVES 6

This may sound disgusting but it is delicious, cheap, rib-sticking, cure-all peasant cookery at its best. In Mallorca you can buy the *sopas*—thin slices of dried bread, which you lay in the bottom of your soup plate and ladle the soup over it, controlling how thick or thin the final result is. Catalina, who demonstrated the dish for me, broke an egg into her soup plate, which cooked in the steaming hot broth. Here is my version.

3 tbsp olive oil

2 oz/50 g bacon lardons (pieces)

1 oz/25 g slices of chorizo, for the smoky flavour

1¹/₂ large onions cut into half-moons

3 cloves garlic, finely minced

2 carrots, cut smallish

2 leeks, sliced

¹/₂ lb/25 g skinned and chopped ripe tomatoes, or a 400 g can

¹/₂ small green cabbage, or

¹/₂ bunch chard, chopped

1 tsp salt and a few grindings of pepper

1 tsp smoked paprika

1 bay leaf

1pt/570 ml stock

4 oz/110 g very thin slices of dried bread, white or brown

Method:

1. In a heavy casserole, heat the olive oil and start to sauté onions and garlic till golden.

2. Add bacon and chorizo and continue to cook for further 5 mins. Add celery, carrots, leeks (keep the green parts to add at the end), tomatoes, stock and bay leaf. Cook for ¹/₂ hour.

3. Finely shred the cabbage and add to the soup. Cook for another 15 minutes. Adjust seasoning.

4. Pour onto the bread slices, either in a casserole or in individual soup dishes.

Serve with radishes and some crunchy fresh bread and olive oil.

> **V** Bacon and chorizo can be omitted, if you prefer, and you could also add some cooked white haricot beans to make it an even more robust meal.

Meat and Fish Main Dishes

Koulibiaka

SERVES 6

A rich and exciting dish from Russia designed in the kitchens of the Tsars. It is a complex, many-layered pie, involving some time and some knowledge of architectural principles, but it's worth the trouble for a festive occasion.

Required: a baking tray 16 x 12 inches/40 x 30 cm

Oven 220°C/gas mark 6 for 20 minutes, and 180°C/gas mark 4 for 45 minutes thereafter

1 lb/450 g puff pastry, made from 8 oz/225 g flour, the same weight of frozen butter and 4 tbsp ice-cold water (see method on page 98)

1^{1}/2 lb/700 g mixed fish (my fishmonger does a very good fish pie mix of salmon, cod and haddock, fresh and smoked, all skinned and de-boned)

6 oz /175 g long grain rice cooked in 1 pt/570 ml liquid, including mushroom soaking water

4 oz/110 g mushrooms (1 oz/25 g dried porcini or chanterelle, 3 oz/75 g fresh chestnut mushrooms)

4 oz/110 g butter

2 leeks, sliced finely

1 large onion, chopped finely

4 spring onions, sliced finely

2 chopped hard-boiled eggs

1 tbsp chopped capers

1 tbsp *smetana* or soured cream

2 cloves garlic

parsley

wineglass of white wine

beaten egg for glazing

^{1}/2 lemon

For poaching the fish:

^{1}/2 pt/275 ml milk

^{1}/4 tsp salt

freshly ground black pepper

2 bay leaves

continued overleaf …

Koulibiaka cont.

For roux:

2 oz/50 g butter

2 oz/50 g flour

For *blinichiki* (small pancakes):

4 oz/110 g plain flour, $^1/_4$ tsp salt, pinch of sugar all sifted together

$^1/_4$ pt/150 ml milk

$^1/_4$ pt/150 ml water

1 large egg

Method:

To make the *blinichiki*:

Beat all together, getting out all the lumps. It should be the consistency of thick cream. Leave for $^1/_2$ hour (or overnight) to develop the gluten.

To make the whole dish:

All elements of the pie filling must be cold before assembly.

To spread out the labour for this dish, you could make the pastry the day before and chill overnight. And soak the wild mushrooms in $^1/_2$ pt/275 ml boiling water overnight. Pancake batter, too, can wait overnight.

1. Wash rice carefully and strain the mushrooms. Keep the mushroom water in a measuring jug and top it up with stock to make 1 pt/570 ml. Sauté rice in 1 oz/25 g butter till all grains are coated, then add hot stock and bring to the boil in a heavy-bottomed casserole with a tightly fitting lid. Turn the heat down very low and allow to simmer for $^1/_2$ hour. Strain and cool.

2. Meanwhile hard-boil 2 eggs (8 minutes), cool and chop.

3. Melt 2 oz butter in a small frying pan, sauté the mushrooms, add 2 cloves chopped garlic and season with salt and pepper. You can add a splash of sherry and allow it to evaporate. Set aside to cool.

4. Place the fish, bay leaves and seasoning in a frying pan or sauté pan and pour on the warmed milk. Poach the fish briefly (5 minutes), allowing the juices to flavour the milk. Strain and cool. Keep the milk for the béchamel sauce.

5. Make the sauce. First make a roux by melting 2 oz/50 g butter, stirring in 2 oz/50 g plain flour and cooking together over low heat. Then add the fish-flavoured milk ($^1/_2$ pt/275 ml), whisking over a low flame. Add a wineglass of white wine and allow to thicken, then cool. Add 2 tbsp *smetana* or soured cream, the juice of $^1/_2$ lemon, and 1 tbsp chopped parsley.

6. Add the fish to this sauce.

7. Make the pancakes (you will need 6). This is where I cheat and use a non-stick frying pan. Heat a little butter, pour a ladleful of batter into the pan and swirl it around so that there is a thin patina. Cook until the underside is golden and the whole will move around freely. Flip over using a spatula or a flick of the wrist and cook another 2 minutes till golden brown. Stack them on a plate.

8. Sauté leeks, onions and spring onions in the remaining butter. Season and just sweat for 5 minutes. Cool. Grease a baking tray.

9. Roll out the pastry (which should be allowed 20 minutes to reach room temperature) into a 14 inch (35 cm) square approx. Leave a little for decoration.

10. To assemble, in the centre of the square put 1 pancake, a layer of rice, some leeks and mushrooms and half the fish mixture, add another pancake, a layer of leeks and mushrooms and the other half of the fish mixture, chopped egg, capers, another pancake, then repeat leek and mushroom layer, finishing off with a pancake.

11. Paint the edges of the pastry with beaten egg, then bring together in an envelope. Decorate with pastry in fish shapes.

12. Lift carefully with spatulas onto a baking tray and bake for 20 minutes at 220°C/gas mark 6, then $^1/_2$ hour at 180°C/gas mark 4.

I served this with sautéed slices of Hubbard squash, cooked in ginger and garlic, and a generous dish of tatziki (grated cucumber and sour cream), plus a green salad with wild rocket, and followed it by pears poached in spiced red wine.

Pheasant, Venison, Chestnut and Cranberry Casserole

SERVES 6–8

My collaborator Cathy, whose husband is a Dartmoor warden, gets given all sorts of game. This time it was a brace of pheasants and a large joint of venison. We cooked these together for a Sunday lunch with friends from the moors. A casserole like this is the epitome of wintertime, with red wine and cranberries thrown in for good measure! When I made it again I cut down the meat content to one pheasant.

Required: a large, heavy casserole dish

1 pheasant

1 lb/450 g venison shoulder, cubed (it is possible to buy it ready cubed)

$^1/_2$ lb/225 g dried chestnuts, or

1 lb/450 g fresh chestnuts, peeled

2 tbsp olive oil, for sautéing

2 oz (50 g) butter, for sautéing

1 large onion, sliced in half-moons

4 sticks celery

4 oz/110 g bacon, de-rinded and cut into small pieces

4 cloves garlic

4 oz/100 g cranberries

$^1/_2$ oz/10 g dried chanterelle or porcini mushrooms

12 baby onions, peeled

$^1/_2$ pt/275 ml red wine

1$^3/_4$ pts/1 l stock

For stock:

pheasant carcass

salt and pepper

$^1/_2$ onion

$^1/_2$ carrot

2 sticks celery

2 bay leaves

thyme, sage, rosemary

parsley stalks

2 pts/1.2 l water

1 tbsp blackcurrant jam or jelly

Method:

1. If using dried chestnuts, they need to be soaked in boiling water, preferably overnight, and then cooked in some stock until fairly tender.

2. Pour some boiling water on the cranberries (enough to cover), then soak the chanterelles separately (also in hot water).

3. Remove the breasts and as much of the flesh as you can from the pheasant and cube it evenly into bite-sized pieces (I had $^3/_4$ lb/350 g).

4. Put carcass into a large saucepan with 2 pts water and the other ingredients to create a good, richly-flavoured stock. Simmer for 1 hour, then strain.

5. Sauté the baby onions in 1 tbsp olive oil and 1 oz/25 g butter. Set aside.

6. In your heavy casserole put 1 tbsp olive oil and the remaining butter. Sauté the bacon and the large onion slices. Add venison and pheasant, celery, chopped garlic, salt and pepper and 1 tsp thyme leaves. Add stock and cooked chestnuts, chanterelles, cranberries and red wine. Bring to the boil and reduce heat to simmer for 1$^1/_2$ hours.

7. Strain off the juice and reduce until you have approx. 1 pt/570 ml of fairly thick sauce. (Or you can thicken it with a roux of 2 oz/50 g butter, 2 oz/50g flour.) Add 1 tbsp blackcurrant jam and the sautéed baby onions and return to the meat and vegetables.

Suggested accompaniments: *Pommes Dauphinoises* (see page 225), spiced red cabbage (see page 223), and carrots flavoured with rosemary.

It is wonderful reheated, too.

Rabbit with Onion, Wine and Chorizo

(Conejo con Cebolla)

SERVES 6

This dish is one of the classics of Mallorcan cookery. Rabbits are also very cheap and plentiful in England but many people do not seem to know what to do with them. Here is my version of the classic dish, with a cautionary word about wild rabbit—it may take a good long time to casserole!

Required: a heavy casserole dish

3 lb/1 kg rabbit jointed (I had a whole one and a haunch of another)

1 oz/25 g butter

2 tbsp olive oil

4 cloves garlic

1¹/₂ lb/700 g onions, sliced in half-moons

2 oz/50 g seasoned flour

2 oz/50 g streaky bacon, chopped

1 oz/25 g thin slices of chorizo (smoked paprika sausage)

2 tbsp brandy (optional)

¹/₂ pt/275 ml stock

¹/₂ pt/275 red wine

1 tbsp tomato purée

bouquet garni (bay, rosemary, sage and thyme)

1 tsp cinnamon

1 tsp mustard

salt and pepper

Method:

1. In a heavy casserole melt the butter with the oil, then add onions and fry until brown and slightly caramelized.

2. Meanwhile, check rabbit joints for any splinters of bone and remove, then dredge in seasoned flour.

3. Add to the onions with bacon and chorizo and sauté until slightly browned. Be careful not to burn. Add garlic.

4. Add bouquet garni, brandy, then wine and stock. Bring to the boil, taste and add some salt and pepper (but be aware that this gravy will condense during the long cooking, and so it will become saltier as the cooking progresses).

5. After two hours the rabbit should be tender and the sauce rich and flavoursome.

6. To finish add tomato purée, the mustard and cinnamon and perhaps a squeeze of lemon, if you think it is needed.

Served hot with a potato and celeriac mash and spiced red cabbage, this makes a nourishing, cheap and tasty winter meal. It's very good the next day, too—the flavours continue to develop.

Lancashire Hotpot

SERVES 6

This is another hearty traditional dish from my childhood, using a very cheap but incredibly sweet-flavoured cut of meat—best neck of lamb—and lots of vegetables. With a golden crusty lid of potatoes, it is one of those one-pot meals that satisfy and are also easy on the washing-up. I added a little optional red wine; you may leave it out if you wish, it is not traditional, but add more stock.

Required: deep ovenproof casserole dish

Oven 180°C/gas mark 4

1¹/₂ lb/700 g best end of lamb, cut into pieces

12 oz/350 g onion, sliced into half-moons

3 carrots, roll-cut

2 leeks, sliced thickly (keep green parts for later)

2 sticks celery, chopped

2 oz/50 g butter

2 oz/50 g flour

1 pt/570 ml stock

¹/₄ pt/150 ml red wine

1¹/₂ lb/700 g potatoes, peeled and sliced into rounds

2 tbsp vegetable oil

**1 tsp Worcester sauce or tamari to brown,
and for flavour**

2 bay leaves

1 tsp thyme

salt and pepper

Method:

1. Check lamb pieces for any splinters of bone.
   Lightly coat with flour and season.

2. Heat butter and oil in a heavy casserole and fry
   onions till golden brown. Add lamb and brown
   it, then add all the other vegetables and any
   residual flour. Cover with wine and stock and
   add herbs. Bring gently to simmering point.

3. Meanwhile in a large pan of boiling salted
   water blanch the potato slices, just to get the
   cooking process going. Then drain and allow
   to cool enough to handle.

4. If your stew is already in a Le Creuset casserole
   dish, just arrange the potatoes on top like
   slates on a roof. Otherwise, pour it into an
   ovenproof dish and arrange the potatoes.
   Finish with some grindings of pepper and dot
   with butter. Cook for $1^1/_2$ hours, then turn the
   oven up to 200°C/gas mark 6 for the last 15
   minutes to make the top golden. Or you can
   finish it off under the grill.

Serve with extra freshly cooked vegetables—
cabbage, green parts of leeks and more carrots.

Vegetarian Main Dishes

Beetroot and Fennel Risotto

SERVES 6

This is the most dramatically red and delicious quick supper—wonderful rich beetroot and al dente slices of Florence fennel. Cooks in half an hour.

8 oz/225 g Arborio rice

3 oz (75 g) butter

3 tbsp olive oil

1 pt/600 ml good hot vegetable stock

$^1/_4$ pt/150 ml white wine

4 sticks celery, sliced finely

large onion, sliced finely

1 Florence fennel, sliced

8 oz/225 g cooked beetroot

2 oz/50 g freshly grated Parmesan

chopped dill or fennel tops

Method:

1. In a heavy pot, warm the olive oil and 1 oz/25 g butter. Sauté the onion, celery and fennel until translucent.

2. Add rice, some salt and pepper and stir in the wine. Bring to the boil stirring, then gradually add stock gently stirring with the heat reduced, otherwise burning will occur. When rice and vegetables are tender (20-25 minutes), add the rest of the butter, then stir in the grated cooked beetroot. Check the seasoning. Add chopped dill and serve topped with freshly grated parmesan.

A salad of orange slices, chicory and watercress is a good accompaniment.

Two Vegetable Curries with Dhal

i. White and Green
ii. Red

SERVES 6

I often watched my Indian friend preparing curries. She would always make her own spice combinations, first roasting them and then grinding them in a pestle and mortar. The aroma filled the whole house. So I urge you to try at least once to make your own garam masala. Doing so allows us to stand in the timeless stream of ancient Indian practice, where it is thought nothing to spend the whole morning in preparing the meal for the extended family. All the actions are done with grace and purpose—making our often frenzied escapades in the kitchen appear somewhat sad. Of course, many of the prepared curry pastes and spice combinations are excellent and, stored in oil, tend to keep their flavours well.

For the garam masala:

1 dsp cardamom seeds (out of their husks)

1 tsp black peppercorns

1 tsp coriander seeds

1 tsp cumin

6 cloves

1 tsp nutmeg shavings

2 bay leaves

2 inch/5 cm piece of cinnamon bark

Dry roast the spices in a heavy frying pan on a low heat until the aroma starts to come off. (Don't let them go dark as they will taste bitter.) Let them cool a little, then either grind them in a pestle and mortar or whiz them in a coffee grinder.

For both the curries:

2 tbsp vegetable oil

2 oz/50 g butter or ghee

1 tsp mustard seed

$^1/_4$ tsp black onion seed

1 tbsp medium Madras curry powder

2 tbsp turmeric

1 tbsp *garam masala*

chilli ginger paste:
2 oz/50 g piece of fresh ginger root, 2 green chillies, 4 cloves garlic, 1 tsp sea salt, juice of 1 lemon, all whizzed together in a food processor

For the white and green curry:

1 lb/450 g potatoes

$^1/_2$ lb/225 g parsnips

3 sticks of celery

8 oz/450 g celeriac, cubed

large onion, sliced

400 ml can of coconut milk

4 leeks

For the red curry:

1 large onion, sliced

3 carrots, diced

4 assorted peppers

1 tbsp tomato purée

2 sticks of celery, chopped

400 ml can chopped tomatoes

handful chopped coriander for garnish

Method:

1. To make it easier, start off in a large casserole dish, melting butter and oil and frying all the onion, adding the mustard seed, *garam masala* (but reserving some for the last stage of the cooking), turmeric, the ginger-chilli paste and curry powder, and cook together for 5 minutes.

2. Then add white part of the leeks, potato, celeriac and celery, and cook for another 5 minutes, stirring frequently.

3. At this point divide the mixture into two saucepans. To one add the coconut milk and continue to cook for $^3/_4$ hour on a very low heat. Green slices of leek are added right at the end.

4. To the remaining half add chopped up peppers and carrots and tomatoes. Add a little stock to cover the vegetables and 1 tbsp of tomato purée, and continue to cook for $^3/_4$ hour until vegetables are tender and flavours developed. If you want a hotter curry you can always add a little cayenne.

Serve with steamed, spiced rice, lentil dhal (see below), cucumber and yoghourt with mint, Nan bread, coriander chutney, carrot chutney and lime pickles.

Curries are the one dish that seem to improve on reheating. So you can make this ahead and let it cool and reheat even the next day, but be very careful not to burn it (best done in the oven). Leftover curry, with the addition of some fresh peas, can be made into samosas or curry pasties.

Dhal

SERVES 6

8 oz/225 g red lentils, cleaned and soaked for 1 hour or so

$1^1/_2$ pts/800 ml water

$^1/_2$ tsp salt

1 bay leaf

3 tsp turmeric powder

2 large onions

3 oz/75 g melted butter

1. Cook lentils slowly with water and salt, bay leaf and 1 tsp of the turmeric for $^1/_2$ hour.

2. Slice the onion into rings and fry in the butter until brown and crispy. Sprinkle with 2 tsps turmeric and serve on top of the dish of dhal.

In my opinion, the dhal should provide an ocean of calm amidst all the fiery curry components, but of course you can make it spicier if you wish.

Leek and Mushroom Bake with Millet, Almond and Cheese Topping

SERVES 6

Required: an ovenproof dish

Oven 180°C/gas mark 4

For the topping:

4 oz/110 g grated Cheddar

6 oz/175 g millet, cooked in

1 pt/570 ml vegetable stock (hot)

3 oz/75 g roasted, chopped blanched almonds

2 oz/50 g butter for sautéing millet

1 tbsp chopped sage

1 tbsp chopped shallot

For the filling:

2 tbsp olive oil

8 oz/225 g mushrooms, finely sliced

1 lb/450 g leeks, thoroughly washed, finely sliced

^{1}/2 pt/275 ml vegetable stock

2 oz/50 g butter, for sautéing

2 tbsp olive oil, for sautéing

2 cloves of garlic, finely minced

2 fl oz/55 ml sherry

spring onions/parsley, chopped for garnish

béchamel sauce: 2 oz/50 g butter and 2 oz/50 g plain flour for the roux, ^{1}/2 pt/275 ml milk, ^{1}/2 pt/275 ml cooking juices and stock, 2 tbsp double cream, 2 bay leaves

Method:

1. Carefully wash the millet and leave to drain and dry in a sieve.

2. Melt 2 oz butter and sauté millet in a heavy pot until all grains are coated.

3. Pour on the hot stock and allow to come to the boil. Reduce heat until simmering and cover tightly. Leave to cook (approx. 30 minutes) until all liquid has been absorbed. Remove from the heat, fluff up the millet with a fork and leave to cool a little.

4. In a mixture of the butter and oil, sauté the leeks and then cover with ^{1}/2 pt stock. Cook for 5 minutes with a little salt. Drain and reserve juices.

5. Melt 2 oz/50 g butter in a sauté pan or frying pan, add chopped garlic, then mushrooms and ^{1}/3 tsp salt. Cook for 5 minutes. Add the sherry and a generous grinding of black pepper and cook for a further 5 minutes. Drain and reserve juices.

6. Place the leeks and mushrooms in an ovenproof dish.

7. Make a roux with butter and flour and add milk/stock (1 pt/570 m), stirring briskly so that no lumps remain. Add cream. The sauce should now be of a coating consistency. Adjust seasoning and pour half the sauce over the vegetables, keeping the rest to serve with the dish.

8. Mix the millet, almonds, cheese and chopped sage, keeping a little cheese to add on the top with the chopped shallot. Spread on top of the vegetable sauce mix.

9. Cover with foil and cook for 20 minutes at 180°C/gas mark 4. Remove foil and brown for another 15 minutes.

Chestnut and Walnut Pâté en Croute

SERVES 6

Originally based on a recipe from Anna Thomas's *Vegetarian Epicure*, this has 'morphed' over the years and is used as the main course for vegetarians at a festive Christmas dinner. It is a marvellous stuffing for turkey too. The pie is delicious cold in slices, revealing a seam of orange carrot-apricot mixture. Since it involves a fair amount of preparation I do a mix that will yield 3 lb/1.3 kg of nut stuffing, enough for two pies.

Required: 2 baking trays

Oven at 200°C/gas mark 6

For the pastry:

8 oz/225 g flour

4 oz/110 g cold butter

$^I/_2$ tsp salt

2 oz/50 g cream cheese

1 oz/25 g ground walnuts

3 tbsp ice cold water

For the nut filling:

1 oz/25 g butter, for sautéing

2 tbsp olive oil, for sautéing

2 onions (approx. 8 oz/225 g), finely chopped

3 cloves of garlic, finely minced

3 sticks of celery, finely chopped

1 tsp ground cardamom

$^I/_2$ tsp salt

2 tsp tamari

$^I/_2$ tsp ground ginger

1 pt/570 ml good stock

6 oz/175 g dried chestnuts (double, when reconstituted)

4 oz/110 g pecan nuts

4 oz/110 g good quality walnuts

4 oz/110 g cooked wild rice mix, or plain long grain rice

1 fl oz/25 ml sherry

$^I/_4$ pt/150 ml white wine

3 oz/75 g breadcrumbs, white or wholemeal

1 leek, finely chopped

1 tbsp cream cheese, to bind

3 medium eggs, beaten

4 oz/110 g cooked orange apricots

2 carrots, grated

zest of one orange, finely grated

Chestnut and Walnut Pâté en Croute cont.

Method:

The day before:

1. Make pastry (see pages 97-98) and refrigerate.

2. Soak chestnuts in 1 pt/570 ml boiling stock for approx. 2 hours, then cook gently till tender (may take an hour). Drain and remove brown bits of connective fibre, which is part of the shell and is bitter. Chop roughly. You should have about 12 oz/350 g.

3. Soak apricots in boiling water also for 2 hours, then cook gently until tender (approx. $^1/_2$ hour). Add grated carrots and cook for 5 minutes, then drain off any excess liquid.

On the day:

1. Take pastry out of fridge and let it soften a little. Chop and grind pecans and walnuts, leaving a few broken ones for texture.

2. In a heavy saucepan melt the butter with the oil and sauté the finely chopped onion and garlic until translucent. Add celery.

3. Add herbs and spices and salt and pepper. Continue to cook for further 5 minutes. Then add the tamari sauce, sherry and white wine (substitute stock if you don't want the wine). Cook a further 5–8 minutes until tender.

4. Add breadcrumbs and leave to soak up residual mixture.

5. Add finely chopped leeks (raw), the nut mixture, cooked rice, cream cheese and beaten eggs (keeping a little back to paint the outside). Adjust seasoning (it should be tasty, but the flavours will develop during cooking). The mixture should be stiff, sturdy, quite moist, but not wet which would melt the pastry. You should have now 3 lb/1.3 kg of mixture, which will make two 'pies' or one pie with the rest used as stuffing for the turkey (non-vegetarians could add 4 oz/110g sausage meat too for turkey stuffing).

To assemble:

1. Divide pastry and mixture into two halves. Preheat oven to 200°C/gas mark 6. On a *floured surface* roll out one half of the pastry in a rectangle approx. 12 x 14 in (30 x 35 cm).

2. Spoon half the nut mixture into the centre of the pastry in a smaller rectangle, allowing plenty of pastry all round to wrap over the mixture.

3. Spoon half of the carrot and apricot mixture in a layer and then cover this with the remaining nut pâté, creating a loaf shape.

4. Paint the edges to be sealed with beaten egg and fold the sides to meet on top. I usually take an extra strip of pastry and lay it over this join to strengthen it. Overall measurements now are approx. 7 in/18 cm long, 5 in/12 cm wide and 3 in/8 cm high.

5. Fold in the ends like a parcel and crimp. Make some decorative cut-out pastry shapes (holly leaves and berries, perhaps) to stick on the top. Paint the outside with beaten egg.

6. Put into a hot oven for 15–20 minutes to seal the pastry and then a further 30–35 minutes in a medium oven (180°C/gas mark 4) or until golden and firm.

Allow to cool a little and carefully transfer to a pretty serving platter and serve with a jewel-like cranberry and orange sauce or a wild mushroom sauce, plus all the vegetables. It is also wonderful cold.

Souffléd Polenta Pie

SERVES 6

Accompanied by Refried Beans with Rich Tomato Sauce (see pages 228 and 214).

10 oz/275 g yellow polenta

13/4 pts/1 l (approx.) hot water

4 large free range eggs, separated

1 red pepper, finely diced

1 green pepper, finely diced

1 large onion, finely diced

3 cloves of garlic, minced

1 tsp chopped sage

6 oz/180 g freshly grated Parmesan

1 dsp salt and pepper to taste

pine kernels to sprinkle on the top

1 oz/25 g butter, for sautéing

3 tbsp olive oil, for sautéing

oregano

Method:

1. Prepare the polenta (a kind of porridge) by gently sautéing the grains in a little of the butter and oil in a heavy-bottomed pot, until coated. Then pour on hot water with the sea salt and bring to the boil stirring briskly with a wooden spoon so that no lumps occur. Cook for 10–15 minutes, stirring from time to time so that it does not stick and burn. It should not be gritty by now and the grains should be cooked. Set aside to cool.

2. Sauté onions, garlic and peppers (in that order) with the chopped sage and a pinch of salt. Reserve a small quantity for garnish and add the rest to the polenta.

3. Add egg yolks and grated cheeses, reserving a little for the top. Mix well and adjust seasoning.

4. Whip egg whites until soft peaks arise. Then fold in gently to the rest of the mixture.

5 Pour into a buttered, oven proof dish. On the top, sprinkle with reserved cheese, peppers and onions and also some pine kernels, and oregano.

6. Put into an oven at 200°C/gas mark 6 for 20 minutes, or till golden on top. Then turn down heat to 180°C/gas mark 4 for a further 30 minutes, or until set.

Winter Desserts

Winter Fruit Salad

SERVES 6

$^1/4$ pt/150 ml elderberry or blackcurrant cordial

$^1/2$ pt/275 ml red wine or grape juice

splash of ginger wine

2 pieces of grated preserved ginger

2 inch/5 cm piece of cinnamon

1 tangerine, de-seeded and sliced

8 oz/225 g dried whole Hunza apricots, soaked in $^1/2$ pt/275 ml boiling water overnight

4 oz/110 g blackcurrants (can be frozen or bottled)

2 pears, cored, peeled and sliced

pomegranate seeds

Method:

1. Soak the Hunza apricots overnight.

2. Next day, place the first 6 ingredients in a medium-sized saucepan and boil steadily for about $^1/2$ hour, when the liquid will have reduced somewhat and has started to become syrupy.

3. Add blackcurrants, then pears and cook for about 5 minutes, long enough for pears to have taken up the wonderful deep purple of the juice and be tender but not too soft.

4. Add the Hunza apricots and cook for another couple of minutes. Serve warm or cold with crème fraîche or yoghourt and a scattering of jewel-like pomegranate seeds.

Hunza apricots can be bought in wholefood stores and are part of the Hunza people's diet, contributing to their legendary longevity. The apricots are so full of warmth and mellow sweetness, and the kernels inside are also delicious. The fruit can of course be eaten on their own, but they do need to be soaked and stewed a little.

Maple and Pecan Tart

SERVES 6

This is a wonderful combination of flavours with a hint of orange. Maple syrup—an American Indian tradition—involves the reduction of 40 litres of sap to make one litre of syrup. It is valued as the most sacred substance, rather like honey. So a little goes a long way.

Required: flan tin

Oven 200°C/gas mark 6

For sweet pastry:

6 oz/175 g unbleached flour

4 oz/110 g cold butter

1 oz/25 g icing sugar

$^1/2$ beaten egg

2–3 tbsp ice-cold water to mix

For the filling:

$4^1/2$ eggs (making 5 in total with the half-egg above)

1 pt/570 ml single cream

1 tsp vanilla essence

4 oz/125 g pecans (select 12 halves for decoration and chop up the remainder fairly small)

2 oz/50 g self-raising flour

$^1/4$ pt/150 ml maple syrup

grated zest of a large orange

Method:

To make pastry:

1. Sift the flour and icing sugar.

2. Rub in the butter with fingertips until like fine breadcrumbs.

3. Add the half beaten egg and cold water until the pastry will hold together, neither sticky nor so dry as to crack. Place in a polythene bag to rest for a minimum of half an hour.

4. After the pastry has rested, take out of the polythene bag and then, after 10 minutes, roll it out in a circle to cover the flan tin. With the trimmings roll out some very thin strips of pastry to strengthen the sides ('glue' them on with a little water). Press around this double rim to flatten, and by pinching the top you can flute the edges of the flan for a pretty finish.

5. Place in the fridge again to harden (15 minutes) and meanwhile heat the oven to 200°C/gas mark 6.

6. Take out of the fridge, prick the bottom with a fork and line with a circle of baking parchment or greaseproof paper. Fill with 'baking beans' to weigh it down, making sure the sides are well supported, otherwise they can shrink or collapse.

7. Bake in the hot oven for 10–15 minutes, or until the edges begin to turn golden. Remove from oven and take out baking beans and paper. Return to the oven for another 5–8 minutes, to set the bottom, but don't let it go brown.

8. Turn the oven down to 180°C/gas mark 4.

To make filling:

9. Beat the eggs until frothy and sift in the self-raising flour. Add maple syrup, cream, orange rind, vanilla and chopped pecans.

10. Pour into the pre-baked pastry shell. Float the 12 pecan halves evenly around the top.

11. Bake at 180°C/gas mark 4 for 1/2 hour, or until set and golden.

Serve warm with vanilla ice cream. Also wonderful cold.

Special Rice Pudding

SERVES 6

Required: buttered ovenproof dish

Oven at 180°C/gas mark 4

8 oz/225 g pudding rice or whole rice

1 1/2 pts/750 ml whole milk

1/2 pt/275 ml water

2 oz/50 g soft brown sugar

2 oz/50 g butter

1 tbsp maple syrup

pinch of salt

grated rind of 1 large lemon

6 oz/175 g grated eating apple

2 eggs, beaten

2 oz/50 g sultanas

2 oz/50 g roasted, chopped hazelnuts

1/4 pt/150 ml double cream

freshly grated nutmeg

Method:

1. In a heavy pot half-cook the rice using half milk, half water and a pinch of salt. Bring to the boil and simmer on low heat for 15–10 minutes. Transfer to a large bowl and allow to cool a little.

2. Add sugar, maple syrup, lemon rind, hazelnuts, apple and sultanas. Add the beaten eggs to the rest of the milk (1 pt/570 ml) and then add this to the rice mixture. Now add nutmeg.

3. Pour into a buttered ovenproof dish and dot with butter. Cover with foil and bake for 3/4 hour in a medium oven. Take off the foil for the last 15 minutes, to allow the top to brown. The pudding should be firm, but not dry. Serve with good double cream.

If you can get your children to eat a goodly portion of this, you know that they will have been truly nourished, for here you have the magic combination of grain, nuts and milk.

Spicy Apple, Date and Tangerine Pie

SERVES 6

Required: ovenproof pie plate, 9 inches (24 cm)

Oven 200°C/gas mark 6 to start

10 oz/275 g shortcrust pastry (see pages 97-98) at room temperature

2 lb/900 g apples (can be an assortment of eating and cooking. It's a good way to use up slightly withered apples)

6 oz/175 g light cane sugar

1 tsp grated nutmeg

1 tsp ground cinnamon

$^{1}/_{2}$ tsp ground ginger

4 tangerines (whole) de-seeded and puréed in a blender

about 8 stoned dates, chopped small

5 fl oz/130 ml ginger wine or apple concentrate

1 oz/25g butter

zest and juice of 1 lemon

pinch of sea salt

Method:

1. Peel, core and slice the apples, discarding any bruised parts. Squeeze the lemon juice over them to prevent discoloration.

2. Melt the butter in a saucepan, add the apples, pinch of sea salt, then all the other ingredients and stir gently. Allow to simmer for 5 minutes, to get all the flavours well distributed.

3. Allow to cool (if still hot it will melt the pastry). Any excess liquid you can drain off and serve separately, or thicken with a teaspoon of arrowroot dissolved in a tbsp of cold water and brought to the boil again. Add to fruit mix.

4. On a cool floured surface roll out half the pastry, not too thinly. Line the bottom of a greased ovenproof pie plate. Trim the edges and paint the rim with milk.

5. Pile on the filling, leaving a rim of pastry on which to fix the top.

6. Roll out the other half, flip it over your rolling pin and lay it on top of the apple. Seal and crimp the edges.

7. Make three small slits in the top to allow steam to escape. Brush the surface with milk and decorate with pastry leaves and roses. Sprinkle on a little caster sugar, which gives a nice frosted finish.

8. Put into oven at 200°C/gas mark 6 for 20 minutes, to harden the gluten in the pastry, then a further 20 minutes in a medium oven, 180°C/gas mark 4, or until golden and firm.

Serve alone or with crème anglaise or Greek yoghourt.

Spiced Pumpkin Pie

SERVES 6

When I lived in New York I made several attempts to like pumpkin pie but a watery sweet mouthful of cinnamon-flavoured cotton wool was my overriding experience. In recent years, however, I have felt that it could be improved upon, and become something lovely in autumn and winter. Do try this, but using the deeply flavoured Hubbard type of pumpkin.

Required: loose-bottomed flan tin

Oven 200°C/gas mark 6

For the pastry base:

10 oz/275 g 82% pastry flour, or 8 oz/225 g white flour sifted with 2 oz/50 g 100% flour

6 oz/175 g cold butter, cut small

2 oz/50 g icing sugar

3–4 tbsp ice-cold water

$^{1}/_{2}$ tsp sea salt

For the filling:

2 lb/900 g cooked and drained orange pumpkin flesh, preferably put through a food mouli, to have a nice smooth texture

Spiced Pumpkin Pie cont.

6 oz/175 g sugar (half unrefined caster, half Rapadura, unrefined molasses sugar)

4 large eggs

^{1}/2 pt/275 ml double cream

^{1}/2 tsp sea salt

1 tsp ground ginger

^{1}/2 tsp allspice

^{1}/2 tsp freshly grated nutmeg

1 tsp cinnamon

1 dsp marmalade

grated zest of an orange

Method:

1. Sift flour, salt and icing sugar into a large bowl.

2. Rub in the cold butter lightly, using fingertips, until mixture resembles fine breadcrumbs.

3. Add just enough cold water to hold the dough together—the more water you add the less crisp your pastry will be, so go carefully at this stage. Wrap the ball of pastry in cling film and allow to rest in the refrigerator.

4. Meanwhile make the filling. Combine the pumpkin purée thoroughly with the other ingredients.

5. Preheat oven to 200°C/gas mark 6.

6. Roll out pastry fairly thinly and line the flan tin, making sure that there are no air pockets round the edges. I often add a strengthening strip of thin pastry around the inside rim (use a pastry brush and some milk to make it stick). Crimp the edges and prick the bottom with a fork.

7. Pour the pumpkin mixture into your pie crust and bake for 10 minutes at 200°C/gas mark 6 to set pastry, then turn down to 180°C/gas mark 4 for 30 minutes. It may develop cracks in the top, but you can pipe some whipped cream on to hide them when it has cooled.

Date and Walnut Balls

SERVES 6

This North African sweetmeat can also be found in Iraq. Easy-to-make and very nutritious, it makes a perfect ending to a meal with a Middle Eastern twist.

12 oz/350 g pitted dates of a moist variety

8 oz/225 g good quality walnuts

grated zest and juice of 1 medium sized orange

Method:

1. If you cannot find softish dates, steep the ones you have in boiling water for 2 hours and pour off the excess liquid. You need to have a malleable paste.

2. Chop about a third of the walnuts fairly roughly and grind the rest (keep half the ground ones back for later).

3. Combine all the ingredients either by hand or in a food processor.

4. Oil your hands and take small pieces the size of a walnut and roll them in the finely ground walnuts. Leave somewhere uncovered at room temperature to dry out. Decorate the dish with flowers.

Bread and Breadmaking

In Homer's time the word for bread, *sitos*, was also the generic term for food, so not only was bread a nourishing food but it was considered to be 'the staff of life'. Up until quite recently the growing of grain, the maturing of wheat in the ear stacked in sheaves, the maturing of the grain, and the kneading, fermenting and rising of the dough—as well as the actual baking—had all been given time. These were breathing processes, incorporating pauses in the whole process. When breadmaking embraces such qualitative elements the outcome could truly be termed the staff of life.

However, in 1958 the Chorleywood Process (named after the Hertfordshire town where the British Bakers' Industrial Research Association is based) was born. A completely new step was taken with the invention of a speeded-up method of dough conditioning. Using huge machines a batch of dough weighing up to 600 lb is violently mixed for just five minutes. With the addition of a chemical oxidizing agent, the bread can be moulded, proved and baked in minutes, in place of the traditional several hours. About 85% of British bread is now made using this method, which is only possible because new cultivars of wheat were bred to contain increasing amounts of gluten. This increased gluten, which has the texture of chewing gum, allows modern bread to hold far more air, giving it lightness. But it lies behind much of the coeliac and gluten allergy problems that have become so prevalent.

Such denaturing of our staff of life has prompted the growth of many small artisan bakeries dedicated to restoring bread to its former status. Several of my friends have taken to making their own bread. When we lived on our farm in Mallorca, bread-making was an integral part of our lives—a rhythm that was sacred, morning and evening. Now I do bake, although not so regularly, but it is the regular rhythmic activity that gives one's baking reliable outcomes. My friend Kit Buckley, after a weekend in Cumbria, has become an accomplished baker and grinds her own biodynamic wheat.

I have included a few bread recipes and added the exciting story of Maria Thun and her rye-baking episode. Some of the people working with Steiner's ideas developed a bread known as Burkhardt bread, made with a combination of four grains: wheat, barley, oats and rye, with the addition of roasted walnuts or hazelnuts and aniseed (see page 200).

Basic Bread Recipe

Can be used for pizza bases, for focaccia breads and for the snail rolls at a harvest picnic. You can use half wholemeal flour or, indeed, all wholemeal if you want wholemeal rolls.

Makes two 10 inch pizzas or ten small rolls

Oven 200°C/gas mark 6

14 oz/400g strong unbleached bread flour

$^{I}/4$ pt/150 ml hand-warm water

1 oz/25 g fresh yeast (dried equivalent will do)

5 tbsp/75 ml olive oil

1 tsp salt

1 tsp honey

For focaccia:

1 tsp coarse salt for scattering

1 tsp rosemary leaves

1 tbsp reserved from the olive oil, for the top

Method:

1. Dissolve yeast with honey in the tepid water. Allow to stand 10 minutes.

2. Sift flour and salt into a large warmed bowl.

3. Add 4 tbsp olive oil and then the yeast mixture. Knead into a ball. Add a little more water if needed.

4. Turn out onto a floured surface and knead for about 10 minutes, or until it is smooth and elastic. Leave to rise in a warm place until dough has doubled in bulk.

5. Knock back the dough and knead again for a few minutes to get an even texture.

6. Preheat the oven.

7. For focaccia: roll into 2 equal discs and place on a baking sheet. Poke little dents into the dough with your fingers and sprinkle coarse salt, rosemary leaves and olive oil on top. Leave for 20 minutes to prove.

8. Bake in the oven for 20–25 minutes, or until golden brown. Cool on a cooling rack.

For bread rolls:

1. Divide into 12 and knead each one into a round shape. Leave for 20 minutes to rise. Brush with milk and sprinkle with sesame seeds or sunflower seeds. For snail rolls: divide into 8 portions. Roll into a snake shape, then spiral into a snail. Pinch out 2 little antlers. Brush with egg wash.

2. Bake in hot oven (200°C/gas mark 6) for 15–20 minutes.

Best eaten on the same day.

A Rye Bread Baking Surprise by Maria Thun

I was going to make bread. It was a Fruit day and the first stage of the coarsely ground rye with honey started to ferment reasonably fast. The rye dough has to rise five times to make a good bread; sometimes it takes almost two days before it can be baked. But on that day the dough was rising fast. After only a short time the second and the third times were ready. I had to go out to the fields. When I came back, the dough had risen up over the edge of the bowl, displacing the cloth, and was now all over the drawer and the cupboard door, and had even fallen on to the floor. It was very stormy outside.

I put the rest of the dough into baking tins. The oven did not get warm fast enough and the dough rose over the edge of the baking tins. What kind of bread was I going to get? What was left of the original dough gave me the idea of starting a new mixture and after only three hours I was baking the second batch of rye bread.

Both batches produced very wholesome and tasty bread according to family, workers and guests. What was the aspect of the planets that day? There were three trines: Mercury–Uranus, Jupiter–Uranus, Sun–Uranus. Mercury moved in front of the Sun and Jupiter behind the Sun. This aspect is very rare and therefore it is not a very practical recommendation for making bread.

In fairy-tales the dough rises during winds from the south. I will have to perform a new experiment if I want to prove that this is true. Rye dough needs a temperature of 28°C (82°F) to rise. Perhaps I should try it during Föhn weather. Once the dough rose so much that it blocked the door and prevented me from getting back into the kitchen. This was during a Mars occultation. Now it was nearly a Venus occultation, or perhaps the alignment of Mercury, Sun and Jupiter had the effect of an eclipse. Life is full of surprises.

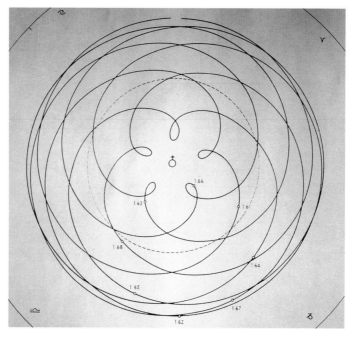

The orbital path of Venus

Naan Bread

Required: baking tray

Oven 200°C/gas mark 6

12 oz/350 g white flour

4 oz/110 g 85% flour

^{1}/2 tsp salt

1 level tsp baking powder

^{1}/2 oz/10 g yeast

1 tsp honey

2 oz/50 g melted butter

1 tbsp vegetable oil

^{1}/2 tsp cumin seeds

2 tbsp yoghourt

^{1}/4 pt/150 ml hand-warm milk (36°C)

Method:

1. Place the warmed milk, honey and yeast in a jug (a plastic measuring jug is good) and leave for 10 minutes to start frothing.

2. Sift the flours, salt and baking powder into a large bowl.

3. Add cumin seed, melted butter, oil, yoghourt and yeast mixture and work into a smooth dough.

4. Knead this for 10 minutes.

5. Cover the bowl with a damp cloth and leave to rise in a warm place for 1 hour, when it should have doubled in volume.

6. Punch the dough down and knead on a floured surface. Divide into 6–8 balls and roll out into the traditional tear-shaped form. Place on a baking tray to prove in a warm place for a further 30 minutes.

7. Paint with a little melted butter and spray with a fine mist of water. This helps the puffing up of the Nan in cooking.

8. Bake for 10–15 minutes, or until puffy and golden. Best results come from cooking them in a ceramic tandoor oven where they stick to the sides and cook, but few of us can claim access to a tandoor, which gives the authentic smoky, carbonized flavour.

Four-Grain Loaf

With roasted hazels, coriander, fennel and aniseed

This is a very tasty and nutritious loaf, one that can truly be said to represent the Staff of Life. The best results I have found come from using some unbleached white bread flour to lighten the loaf, but do experiment.

Makes two good-sized loaves

Required: 2 loaf tins, oiled or lined with baking parchment

Oven 190°C/gas mark 5

Total flour 1^1/2 lb/700 g:

10 oz/275 g unbleached white bread flour

6 oz/175 g rye flour

3 oz/75 g 100% wheat flour

3 oz/75 g barley flour

3 oz /75 g fine oat flour

1^1/2 tsp salt

2 tbsp olive oil

1 tsp honey

3/4 oz/22 g yeast

scant 1^1/2 pts/750 ml tepid (36°C) spring water

1 tsp fennel seeds, finely ground

1 tsp coriander seeds, finely ground

1 tsp aniseed or caraway, finely ground

3 oz/75 g roasted hazelnuts

For the ferment:

1oz/25g white flour

3/4 oz/22 g dried or fresh yeast

1 tsp honey (unpasteurized)

1 pt/570 ml tepid water

Mix flour and other ingredients in a jug. Leave in a warm place for 15 minutes to start to ferment.

Method:

1. Roast hazels and seeds separately for 5–10 minutes in oven at 200°C/gas mark 6.

2. Measure the flours into a large mixing bowl. Add salt and oil.

3. Add finely ground spices and hazel nuts.

4. Stir in the ferment, mix well, adding more water as needed. The dough should not be dry, yet not sticky.

5. Tip out onto a floured surface and knead for 5 minutes, or until dough is silky.

6. Return to the bowl, cover with a polythene bag, allowing room for dough to double in bulk. Leave in a warm place for 2–3 hours. Once during this time, just poke a finger in to release the gases.

7. Turn out again onto a floured surface and knead for another 5 minutes. Divide and shape into 2 loaves, pat into tins.

8. Leave, covered, for another $1/2$ hour to allow rising. Make some incisions on the tops. Paint the surface with milk.

9. Put in the pre-heated oven (190°C/gas mark 5) for $1/2$ hour, then turn down to 170°C/gas mark 3 for a further 35-45 mins. Turn out. When knocked the loaf should give a hollow sound.

Tsoureki

Earth (in the form of wheat flour), Air (the rising of the yeast), Water and Fire come together in this Greek Easter Bread.

Required: large baking tray (11 x 15 in/28 x 38 cm) lined with baking parchment

Oven 200°C/gas mark 6 for 15 minutes, and 180°C/gas mark 4 for further 20 minutes.

1½ lb/700 g strong plain flour

1 pt/570 ml whole milk

1 oz/25 g yeast (fresh or dried equivalent)

zest of 1 lemon and 1 orange, finely grated

1 tsp honey

2 tsp salt

6 oz/175 g soft brown sugar

3 large eggs

6 oz/175 g softened butter

4 pale or white hard-boiled eggs, either boiled with a few onion skins or in beetroot juice, which will give a yellow or red colour

Method:

1. Warm 3/4 pt/425 ml milk to tepid (hand-hot). Place in a jug with the 1 tsp honey and the yeast. Leave for 10 minutes until frothy.

2. In a large, warmed bowl sift flour and salt, add sugar. Make a well in the centre, into which pour the yeast mixture, the beaten eggs and add citrus zest.

3. Mix to a smooth silky dough. You have an extra 1/4 pt/150 ml milk if you need more liquid (but keep some to paint the loaf before baking). If the mixture is too sticky add a little more flour. So much depends on the size of the eggs and the absorbency of the flour. You need to be ready to adjust accordingly.

4. On a floured surface tip out the dough and knead it lightly. Then gradually incorporate the softened butter, folding it in bit by bit. This stage will be a little sticky, but eventually you should have a lovely soft and malleable dough. Return the dough to the bowl and cover with a damp tea-towel and leave in a warm place to rise for 2 hours. The dough will now have doubled in size, so knock it back and leave again until doubled in size (30 minutes).

5. Pre-heat the oven to 200°C/gas mark 6.

6. Knead again for a few minutes and divide into three sections, roll—using your hands—into three ropes of equal length. Plait the three strands and join neatly into a ring. Transfer to your baking tray. Insert the four hard-boiled eggs at equal distances (in their coloured shells), using one to cover the join, and allow to rise once more (approx. 20 minutes).

7. Paint the bread with milk and bake in a hot oven for 15 minutes to set the dough, then turn down (180°C/gas mark 4) for a further 20 minutes. It should be golden brown. Cool and serve with *paskha* or other Easter specialities.

Sweet Sunday Loaf

Malcolm works in the local Riverford Farm Shop and he has the most exotic pedigree. His mother is half Indian, half African, his father from Manchester, and he grew up with his family in Zambia. He is very creative and does a kind of 'fusion' cookery, which has threads of African, English and Indian. We got talking and exchanging recipes and here is one that I have 'morphed'. Malcolm calls it 'Sunday Loaf', but it's good on Monday, Tuesday and Wednesday . . . It has nice crunchy pumpkin seeds and is the kind of loaf that would give a good start to a healthy packed lunch. Children will love it!

Required: loaf tin lined with baking parchment

Oven 180°C/gas mark 4

6 oz/175 g 85% wheat flour and 2 tsp baking powder sifted together

4 oz/110 g softened butter

4 oz/110 g Rapadura raw cane sugar

4 oz/110 g grated carrot

3 eggs, beaten

2 bananas mashed

juice and zest of small orange

2 tsp freshly grated ginger

2oz/50 g sunflower seeds

2 oz/50 g pumpkin seeds

2 oz/50 g chopped dates

poppy seeds to decorate

Method:

1. Beat together the butter and sugar till fluffy.

2. Add beaten eggs a little at a time (add a little flour if the mixture begins to curdle).

3. Grate orange zest and add it to the mixture. Squeeze the juice and mash up the bananas in it.

4. Add the flour, folding in gently. Then add the bananas and all the other ingredients. Stir until well incorporated, but do not over-stir.

5. Turn into the prepared loaf tin, scatter some poppy seeds on top. Bake in pre-heated oven for 1 hour till golden and risen, and a skewer comes out clean when testing.

This will keep well. It is good toasted. In your child's lunchbox a slice will be very nutritious and delicious.

Honey Salt Bread

This bread is believed to originate with the Zarathustrans and uses the natural nectar yeasts contained in a good unpasteurized honey as leaven (which is how mead is made). It also works with the daily cycle of sunrise and sunset. You do really need to have your own grain mill and a place with a steady warm temperature, so this method could be difficult for many of us, but I have included it for interest.

1 lb/500 g coarsely milled rye flour

1 lb/500 g coarsely milled wheat flour

1 lb/500 g finely milled wheat flour

approx. 2 pts/1.2 l warm water, at about 40°C

1 tbsp salt

1 tbsp honey, unheated and untreated

1 level tsp each of anise, fennel or coriander seeds, according to taste

The 'tin' should be an unglazed clay vessel placed in warm water for about half an hour prior to baking. It is then brushed with oil or rubbed with butter and sprinkled with some groats or finely ground nuts.

Preparation:

Stage 1, evening

Mix together rye groats, 1 pt/500 ml water, half the honey and one third of salt, dissolved in some warm water. Keep warm and covered at room temperature until next morning.

Stage 2, morning (7 a.m.)

Mix together wheat groats, 1 pt/500 ml water, half the honey and one third of salt dissolved in warm water. Add to sponge from the previous evening and stir thoroughly. Keep warm and covered at about 28°C for about 3 hours.

Stage 3, morning (10 a.m.)

Add rest of salt and finely ground spices to flour and then add to the sponge to complete the dough. Knead well for at least 15 minutes, adding more warm water or fine flour to get a reasonably elastic dough. Place the loaf in the prepared baking form. Keep covered in a warm place for about 4 hours. After this time there should be evidence that the dough has risen 10–25% (or more on a good day).

Baking:

The temperature of a gas oven should be maintained at 120°C/gas mark 1 and checked regularly. An electric oven should be kept at 140–150°C. A bowl of water placed on the bottom shelf of the oven prevents the loaf from drying out.

Place the loaf in the unheated oven, which is then switched on. This allows the loaf to reach oven temperature slowly. Baking time is 6–7 hours. The oven is switched off and the bread allowed to stay in the warm oven until next morning. It is removed from the clay vessel and kept for 2 days before serving.

Kit's Biodynamic Bread

I went to have lunch with Kit on a sunny May day and the meal consisted of fresh asparagus turned in melted butter, home-grown green salad leaves, smoked trout pâté from the farm shop, some local Sharpham rustic cheese, some goat's cheese, and Kit's own wonderful freshly baked biodynamic bread. A couple of slices of this very special bread keeps you going for half a day. She has supplied the recipe, with kind permission from Andrew Whitley of Bread Matters Ltd.

Kit says:

Baking bread is a complete joy for me—I make a natural leaven bread from a starter begun on a wonderful bread-making course at the Village Bakery in Cumbria. My 'starter' is now in its second year: one of the great advantages of this method is it can last indefinitely if you treat it properly. This bread is 'slow' bread, where you learn to appreciate the gradual, active process of the naturally occurring yeasts and beneficial bacteria (which produce lactic and acetic acid), and the miracle achieved by flour and water, the kneading with one's hands and heat from the oven. Part of the pleasure of the whole process is milling my own flour in a beautiful wooden counter-top grain mill. I cannot be too enthusiastic about freshly milled flour (although of course it's fine if this isn't possible for you). The fresh flour is slightly warm from the action of the stones, and as I knead the dough there is a vital springy, spongy quality to it. The life forces of the sun-ripened grain are being rapidly released and transferred into the dough. There are various suppliers of grain for home bakers, but I get consistent, great results from the biodynamic wheat grown by Alan Brockman at Perry Court Farm in Kent.

It is a bit of a process making a starter leaven from scratch, but it is definitely worth persevering.

Making the original starter (the Imperial amounts are only approximate)

Day 1

2^{I}/2 oz/60 g unbleached white flour

3/4 oz/20 g wholemeal flour

3 fl oz/80 ml warm water (40°C). Total 5 oz/160 g

Mix to a sloppy paste, cover loosely with a polythene bag and leave in a fairly warm place (28°C is ideal). After one day refresh starter.

Day 2

5 oz/160g starter from Day 1

2^{I}/2 oz/60 g unbleached white flour

3/4 oz/20 g wholemeal flour

3 fl oz/80 ml warm water (40°C). Total 320 g

Mix thoroughly and cover as before. After one more day refresh again.

Day 3

11 oz/320 g starter from Day 2

1^{I}/4 oz/30 g unbleached white flour

^{I}/2 oz/10 g wholemeal flour

1 fl oz/20 ml warm water (40°C). Total 380 g

Mix thoroughly and cover as before. After one more day refresh again.

Day 4

13 oz/380 g starter from Day 3

1^{I}/4 oz/30 g unbleached white flour

^{I}/2 oz/10 g wholemeal flour

1 fl oz/20 ml warm water (40°C). Total 440 g

This is the starter. After another 24 hours you should have a leaven, which smells nicely acidic and is a bit bubbly. Use this to make the 'production leaven' and bread.

There are two stages for the actual breadmaking, which is all you have to do in future after having made the original starter.

Stage 1, making a production leaven

Scant ^{I}/4 pt/120 ml water

7 oz/200 g flour (75/25 wholemeal/white, or 100% wholemeal, or as you choose)

5 ^{I}/2 oz (160 g) starter (see above)

Mix to a dough in a bowl and leave covered with a polythene bag in a warm place (28°C) for approx. 4 hours or in a cool place (12°C or less) for 12–16 hours. Use this production leaven to make the dough.

Stage 2, making the dough for the bread

11 oz/300 g refreshed production leaven from Stage 1. (The remaining 180 g becomes the new starter and should be kept refrigerated)

13 oz/400 g flour (whatever percentage mix you prefer)

11 fl oz/300 ml water (35°C or luke-warm)

^{I}/2 oz/10 g salt (1 level tsp = 5 g)

Make a fairly soft dough and knead until smooth and elastic (about 5 minutes or so). You do not have to use a floured surface—a tiny spot of olive oil on the counter will stop it sticking. When sufficiently kneaded, quickly gather up the dough and place in a non-stick or prepared breadloaf tin. It may stick slightly to the hands, but this doesn't matter. If desired sprinkle sesame or poppy seeds on the top. Cover with a polythene bag and leave to prove in a warm place for up to 5 hours, until the dough has roughly doubled in size and has reached to the top of the tin. Bake in a fairly hot oven (220°C/gas mark 7) for the first 10 minutes and then reduce heat slightly for the rest of the cooking time (about 30–40 minutes).

Dips and Starters

Butter Bean with Lovage Pâté, with Garlic and Cream Topping

Beans:

1 lb/450g dried butter beans

3 pts/2 l approx. vegetable stock

2 shallots, finely chopped

1 stick celery, finely chopped

1 bay leaf

Pâté:

grated zest and juice of a large unwaxed lemon

$^{1}/_{2}$ yellow chilli, finely chopped

1 tbsp olive oil

1 tbsp tahini

2 handfuls chopped lovage

1 handful chopped wild garlic leaves, or 2 cloves of garlic

salt and pepper to taste

Garnish:

1 tbsp chopped wild garlic leaves

1 tbsp chopped lovage; 1 tbsp single cream, all liquidized together

$^{1}/_{2}$ yellow chilli

whole lovage leaves

Method:

1. Soak butter beans overnight, drain and rinse.

2. Cook beans in the stock with shallots, bay leaf and celery until tender (about 2 hours).

3. Strain off liquid and liquidize with the remaining pâté ingredients. Add more olive oil to create the required texture.

4. Arrange some whole lovage leaves in a shallow bowl before spooning the pâté on top.

5. Decorate with puréed chopped lovage and garlic and a swirl of cream.

Smoked Salmon Pâté

8 oz/225g good quality smoked salmon trimmings

4 pinches ($^{1}/_{2}$ tsp) cayenne

finely grated zest and juice of 1 lemon

2 oz/50 g softened butter

2 oz/50 g quark or marscapone (cream cheese)

4 spring onions, chopped

1 tbsp parsley, chopped

1 tsp capers, chopped

$^{1}/_{2}$ tsp green peppercorns, chopped

Whiz all ingredients together in a food processor. Pile into a pretty dish and sprinkle with paprika. Serve on hot toast or crackers.

Aduki Bean Pâté

8 oz/225g aduki beans

1 piece kombu (kelp)

1 dsp tamari (soy sauce)

1 tbsp cashew butter

$^1/_4$ tsp cayenne pepper

juice of $^1/_2$ lemon

10 finely chopped spring onions

1. Soak the aduki beans with the kombu overnight.

2. Cook until tender (45 minutes–1 hour)

3. Drain and blend about two thirds of the beans in a food processor or liquidizer, together with the remaining ingredients, reserving a third of the beans. This should give a thick paste.

4. Mix this with the reserved whole beans, for added texture.

5. Serve in an attractive bowl garnished with carrot or radish 'roses'.

Smoked Mackerel Pâté

8 oz/225 g smoked mackerel, de-skinned and boned, forked up

2 tbsp grated cucumber, lightly salted and squeezed out

$^1/_2$ tsp tamarind paste (this is a sour rhubarby, Indian paste and optional)

1 tbsp creamed horseradish

1 tbsp double cream

2 oz/50 g softened butter

4 spring onions

1 tbsp parsley

1 red pepper roasted (optional)

zest and juice of 1 lemon

salt and pepper

Combine all ingredients in a food processor till spreadable. Chill and serve on hot brown toast.

Blue Vinney and Roasted Walnut Pâté

This uses a local Devon cheese.

2 oz/50g roasted chopped walnuts (organic, others can be very bitter)

4 oz/110 g Blue Vinney cheese (Stilton will do, crumbled)

4 spring onions, finely chopped

1 tsp whole grain mustard

2 tbsp crème fraîche

1 tbsp port

Combine all ingredients in a food processor. Chill. Spread on crackers as an apéritif.

Walnut *Harrissa* Pâté

A rich and spicy cracker topping from Turkey.

4 oz/110 g walnuts roasted till golden (no more, or they become bitter)

2 spring onions, finely chopped

2 tbsp tahini

2 tbsp olive oil

1 tbsp tomato purée

2 tsp *harissa* paste

1 tbsp pomegranate syrup or lemon juice

2 tbsp chopped fresh coriander leaves

1 tbsp wholewheat breadcrumbs

1 tsp salt

1 tsp honey

1 tbsp Greek yoghourt

1. Grind the roasted walnuts to a rough paste.

2. Combine all ingredients in a blender and whiz till blended, but preserving some texture in the walnuts.

3. Serve with focaccia bread as a starter, or on oatmeal biscuits.

Guacamole

3 ripe avocados

3 cloves garlic, crushed

salt and pepper

small red onion, finely minced

juice of $^1/_2$ lemon

2 tbsp olive oil

1–2 tbsp fresh coriander, chopped

Method:

1. Peel and stone the avocados and mash with the lemon juice to prevent discoloration.

2. Add the garlic, onion and coriander, olive oil, salt and pepper. Chill and decorate with coriander leaves.

Babaghanouzh or Moutabal (Aubergine and Tahini Dip)

1 large aubergine or 2 of medium size

2 tbsp tahini (sesame paste)

grated zest and juice of a medium-sized lemon

2 cloves of garlic, crushed in a press

2 tbsp chopped flat-leaf parsley

1 tbsp chopped fresh mint

1 tbsp thick yoghourt

salt and pepper

Method:

1. Prick the aubergine in a few places with a pointed knife.

2. Grill on a griddle or under the grill until it is soft, but the skin is somewhat blackened. Allow to cool.

3. Soften the tahini with lemon juice, then add yoghourt, lemon peel and mashed aubergine flesh.

4. Season with salt and pepper and add garlic and chopped herbs. Serve with pitta bread.

Dolma from Greece and Turkey (Stuffed Vine Leaves)

These can be served hot or cold and make a wonderful starter, served with hummus, pitta bread and tatziki as part of a meze table—the beginning of a more informal meal where guests can mingle and chat.

MAKES 40

Required: a large shallow, heavy-bottomed sauté pan.

9 oz/250 g packet of vine leaves

8 oz/225 g long grain whole rice

400 g tin of chopped tomatoes or 1 lb/500 g fresh tomatoes, skinned and chopped

4 oz/110 g minced lamb (optional)

4 cloves of garlic, crushed

2 tbsp seedless raisins

2 lemons

4 tbsp good olive oil

1 pt/570 ml stock to cook rice

3 tbsp roasted pine kernels, dry roasted in a frying pan until golden (be careful not to burn them, as they then taste very bitter)

$^1/_2$ tsp sea salt

6 cardamom pods

small piece of cinnamon bark

1 level tsp ground cinnamon

$^1/_2$ tsp allspice

2 tbsp chopped fresh mint (or 1 tbsp dried mint)

1 tbsp chopped flat-leafed parsley

1 tsp sugar, or to taste

seasoning: salt and pepper to taste

Method:

1. Steep the vine leaves in boiling water for $^1/_2$ hour, then rinse and drain.

2. Meanwhile, sauté the rice in a heavy-bottomed pot in 1 tbsp of the olive oil. Add cardamoms, cinnamon bark and $^1/_2$ tsp salt, then the hot stock. Bring to the boil, then turn down the heat and allow to simmer with a heavy lid on for 15 minutes to allow the flavours to permeate.

3. Drain the rice, saving any liquid. Pick out the cardamom shells and cinnamon bark. Allow to cool.

4. To the rice, half-cooked by now, add the roasted pine kernels, the raisins, chopped mint, parsley, cinnamon, allspice, garlic and half the contents of the can of tomatoes (drained). This is when you add the raw minced lamb if you are using it. Add salt and pepper to taste and combine thoroughly.

5. Spread out the vine leaves, vein side up, and place a heaped teaspoonful near the stem in the centre of each one. Some may be larger, some smaller. Fold up the lower edge over the filling, then fold in the sides and roll up tightly, like a cigar.

6. Line your sauté pan with some lettuce or cabbage leaves to prevent the vine parcels from burning. Then lay them fairly closely packed together, tucking in slices of garlic and lemon between.

7. Add the rest of the tomatoes and juice to the remaining olive oil with a little sugar and a pinch of salt. Make up to $^1/_2$ pt/275 ml and pour over the vine leaves. Place a plate on top to keep them from unravelling and simmer gently for 1 hour, checking that they don't boil dry.

Serve hot or cold.

V Vegetarian option: omit lamb.

Preserves

Apple, Chilli and Coriander Tracklement

This goes well with cheeses and cold meats.

Yields about 4 lb/1.35 kg

Required: a sugar thermometer, a heavy saucepan and some sterilized glass jars.

1 pt/570 ml apple juice

2 chillies de-seeded and finely chopped

1 lemon and 1 lime, finely sliced

1^1/$_2$ lb/700 g apples, cored and chopped (can be a selection of apples, including crab-apples)

^{1}/$_2$ pt/275 ml water

^{1}/$_4$ pt/150 ml cider vinegar

1 tsp coriander seeds

a few sprigs of fresh rosemary (about 8)

1 lb/450 g brown demerara sugar for every pint/570 ml of juice

Method:

1. Put all ingredients (minus half the rosemary sprigs) into a saucepan and cook for ^{1}/$_2$ hour till apples are a mush and the flavours nicely combined. Strain off the solids but reserve till later.

2. Measure the liquid (I had 2 pts/1.2 l) and return to the saucepan. Add 1 lb/450 g Demerara sugar for each pint. Bring to a fast boil and continue to boil until jam/jelly setting point is reached on the sugar thermometer.

3. Add fruit pulp, perhaps some new red chillies (chopped), a few thin slices of lime and the remaining sprigs of rosemary. Bottle up and label.

A wonderful Christmas present!

Apricot, Sultana and Coriander Chutney

8 oz/200 g dried apricots

2 oz/50 g seedless sultanas

1 pt/20 fl oz apple juice, heated

1 red onion, finely chopped

2 oz Muscovado sugar

1 tsp coriander seeds

2 tbsp wine vinegar

salt and pepper to taste

Soak the dried apricots and sultanas in the hot apple juice for ^{1}/$_2$ hour. Add the other ingredients and bring to the boil, turn down the heat and simmer for another ^{1}/$_2$ hour or until the apricots are really tender and all the flavours combined beautifully. It should be thick by the end of the cooking.

Rhubarb, Date and Apricot Chutney

Cooking time is approx. 3 hours

Required: large, heavy-bottomed saucepan

1^{1}/$_{2}$ **lb/700 g rhubarb**

1 orange

3 eating apples

4 oz/110 g chopped dates

4 oz/110 g chopped apricots

4 oz/110 g sultanas

1 large onion

3 cloves garlic

salt and pepper

1 small chilli

3 pieces stem ginger

3 tsp turmeric

2 tsp ground ginger

2 tsp coriander seeds

approx 1 lb/450g unrefined granulated sugar

5 fl oz/150 ml wine vinegar

1 medium red pepper

Method:

1. Chop the rhubarb

2. Peel, core and chop the apples

3. Scrub the orange, slice it, removing the pips, then whiz it in a blender.

4. Peel and chop the onion and garlic.

5. Chop the chilli.

6. Put all ingredients except the red pepper into a large saucepan. Cover with cold water and bring to the boil.

7. Simmer till all ingredients are tender and rhubarb has disintegrated.

8. Strain off the liquid and measure remaining pulp.

9. For every pint/570 ml of pulp add 12 oz/350 g sugar.

10. Boil the sugar with the liquid and vinegar, then add this to the pulp and boil gently till thick. It should be thick enough to be able to see the bottom of the pan when stirred with a wooden spoon. (If you have an Aga or similar, you can cook and reduce the chutney in the oven.)

11. If using red pepper, de-seed and chop and add towards the end of cooking time.

12. Bottle in sterilized jars and keep for several weeks before using, to allow flavours to blend.

Membrillo (Quince Cheese)

5 lb/2 kg quinces

1 lemon, thinly sliced

¹/₂ pt/275 ml water

9 oz/250 g unbleached granulated sugar for every pound/450 g fruit pulp

Method:

1. Peel and core the quinces. You will need a sharp knife and strong muscles, as these are very dense fruit. (You can also bake them whole first and then skin and core them.)

2. Simmer the fruit for about ¹/₂ hour until tender and ready to be mushed. Put in a food processor. Weigh the resulting pulp (I had 4 lb).

3. Use 9 oz/250 g sugar warmed in the oven for each lb/500 g of pulp. Add to the pulp.

4. Boil gently (this can be quite volcanic!) until the fruit turns to a beautiful pink-amber translucency. Stir frequently, but keeping the lid on in between.

5. Test for setting on a cold plate.

6. Pour into a greased deep baking tray, which should be about 2 in/5 cm in depth. Leave to set. Cut into manageable portions, wrap in greaseproof paper or store in a tight-lidded container in the fridge.

Can be used in all manner of dishes.

Cathy's Coriander Chutney

(To go with curries.)

1 cup firmly packed fresh coriander leaves

1–2 fresh green chillies, seeded and chopped

1 small shallot, peeled and quartered

1 tbsp freshly grated or desiccated coconut

¹/₂ tsp sea salt

¹/₂ tsp sugar

1 tbsp white wine vinegar

1 tsp cumin seeds

Place all ingredients in a blender and blend until puréed.

PRESERVES | 213

Cathy's Simple Raspberry Jam

Produces a very fruity jam with a good colour and wonderful flavour that keeps well. The equal quantities of fruit and sugar make it easy to make with any quantity of raspberries. Be ready with a saucer in the freezer if you have no sugar thermometer, and sterilized jars kept on an ovenproof tray in a warm place. This quantity should make ten 1 lb/450 g jars.

6 lb/2.75 kg raspberries

6 lb/2.75 kg sugar, warmed in a bowl in the oven

Method:

1. Put raspberries in a preserving pan or large saucepan and heat very gently until they give up some of their juices.

2. Add sugar and stir until it is completely dissolved, still on low heat.

3. When you are sure all the sugar is dissolved bring to the boil and boil hard until setting point is reached. This should take about 10 minutes.

4. If you have no sugar thermometer, test for setting by dropping a little jam on a cold saucer. Prod the jam with a finger and if the skin wrinkles, the jam is at setting point. If it remains smooth, continue cooking for a few minutes and repeat the test.

5. Stir in a little knob of butter to help disperse any scum. Leave to cool for 10 minutes and then pour into warm jars using a ladle.

Cathy's Lemon Curd

Use the freshest eggs you can get. Our free-range Welsummer eggs have beautiful deep-colour yolks that make the lemon curd a gorgeous bright yellow. I prefer to use just the yolks, which I collect when making things that use only whites (e.g. macaroons).

The curd should not be kept too long, so you may wish to halve the amounts, keeping the proportions the same.

Makes 2³/4 lb/1.25 kg

1¹/2 pt/300 ml freshly squeezed lemon juice (5–9 lemons)

7¹/2 oz/215 g butter

1 lb 9 oz/700 g sugar

¹/2 pt/275 ml beaten fresh eggs (about 5–6 eggs)

Method:

1. Wash lemons and remove the zest using a fine grater or zester, taking care not to take the bitter white pith. Squeeze and measure juice.

2. Place butter in a bowl over a saucepan or in a double boiler (bain-marie). Add lemon juice, sugar and rind and leave till butter has melted. Lift bowl off the pan and leave it to cool slightly.

3. Lightly beat eggs in a large bowl, but do not whisk them. Gradually stir in butter mixture, then strain into a clean bowl and place over the saucepan of hot water, or into the double saucepan.

4. Stir continuously until mixture thickens slightly. The curd is ready when it will just coat the back of a wooden spoon. Do not overcook or it will curdle. The water in the pan should be kept just below simmering point and not allowed to boil.

5. Pot the lemon curd in clean jars, taking care to fill them absolutely to the top. Press a waxed disc down on the surface of the curd and leave to cool. Cover the pots when they are cool.

Sauces

Rich Tomato Sauce

1 large onion, finely chopped

4 garlic cloves, minced

1 large red pepper, finely chopped

1 large green pepper, finely chopped

3 sticks of celery, finely chopped

3 carrots, grated

2 tsp herbes de Provence

400 g can of chopped tomatoes (or $1^{1}/_{2}$ lb, 770 g skinned fresh tomatoes)

1 tsp Muscovado sugar

1 bay leaf

2 tbsp tomato purée

salt and pepper to taste

olive oil for sautéing

fresh basil

Method:

1. Sauté onions, garlic, herbs and all the remaining vegetables in a heavy cast-iron pot, adding them one by one and gently softening them.

2. Add the rest of the ingredients, apart from the basil, and stir. Bring to the boil, then turn down the heat and allow to simmer for approx. 3/4 hour until all the vegetables are completely cooked and the flavours blended. Add basil right at the end.

The carrot and celery help to alkalize the acidity of the peppers and tomatoes.

This sauce keeps well in the refrigerator and will be enough for two meals.

Cashew Nut Sauce

In reality, cashews are not a nut but a kind of legume. Their ivory waxiness when cooked makes them an ideal ingredient for a creamy, nutritious dairy-free sauce.

4 oz/110 g broken cashews

$^{1}/_{2}$ pt/275 ml well-flavoured stock

2 spring onions, finely sliced

zest and juice of 1 lemon

salt and pepper

Method:

Soak the cashews in the hot stock for $^{1}/_{2}$ hour and then simmer for 20 minutes, or until soft. Add the spring onions and zest and juice of lemon and blend. Adjust seasoning.

This can be served hot or cold.

Lemon Mayonnaise

Mayonnaise is reputed to have been created on the Balearic Island of Mahon. It is an emulsion of oil droplets suspended in a base of egg yolk, salt, lemon juice or vinegar, and mustard. I also use a little honey. These latter ingredients help to stabilize the mayonnaise. The emulsifying process* is most miraculous to watch, as the sauce at an early moment really starts to thicken – or to separate if you haven't got it right. (In Mallorca I was told on several occasions by local women friends that menstruating women always tend to curdle the aiolli or mayonnaise. See what you think.)

Using nothing but olive oil can make an unstable mayonnaise, so I use some refined oil and add the olive oil at the end. Though the vinegar or lemon juice disinfects the egg yolk to a certain extent, this is a perishable food so should be refrigerated and used fresh. All the ingredients work best at room temperature.

Required: a ceramic pudding bowl (2 pts/1.2 l), an electric hand-beater and an oil pourer that releases a thin stream of oil

2 egg yolks (medium)

level tsp honey

2 cloves garlic, crushed

zest and juice of one lemon

1 level tsp sea salt

ground black pepper

1 tsp Dijon mustard

10 fl oz/275 ml refined sunflower oil

4 fl oz/100 ml good olive oil to finish off

Method:

1. Put the first six ingredients in your bowl and whisk with the electric hand beater or a balloon whisk.

2. Very gradually, drop by drop to begin with, pour in the sunflower oil beating all the time. Carry on until you are sure that your sauce has emulsified, then you can pour steadily in a thin stream until all the oil has been incorporated. Finish off with the olive oil, to give a good flavour and a greenish-gold colour. Be careful at this stage, for as we have said, olive oil can be a little unstable. If the sauce curdles at an early stage you can begin again using a fresh egg yolk and then add the curdled version. It miraculously becomes emulsified too! You may do it in a blender, but to me this is sacrilegious.

For aiolli add more garlic. In Mallorca they add mashed potato too.

For sauce tartare, add 2 tbsp chopped capers, 1 tsp chopped gherkins, 1 tsp each chopped parsley and fresh tarragon.

Béchamel Sauce, see page 114.

The word 'emulsion' comes from the Latin for 'to milk out'. An emulsion is made from two liquids that don't dissolve in each other (here, oil and water). In a mayonnaise the lecithin in the egg molecules lowers the surface tension. In one molecule we find there are two different parts, one soluble in water and the other in fat. (Harold McGee in McGee on Cooking)

Vinaigrette

1 tsp runny honey

1 tsp Dijon mustard

large clove of garlic

level tsp salt

freshly ground pepper

2 tbsp balsamic vinegar

4 fl oz/100 ml good olive oil

Place all ingredients except the olive oil in a bowl and whisk. Then take the olive oil and pour gradually into the bowl whilst whisking. An emulsion should result.

Finish with juice of $^1/_2$ lemon and some scissored chives.

Tamari, Ginger and Green Onion Sauce

$1^1/_2$ pts/750 ml good vegetable stock (not too salty as the tamari is salty)

2 tsp finely grated fresh ginger root

1 tbsp tamari (soy sauce), more if necessary

$^1/_2$ bunch finely sliced green spring onions

$1^1/_2$ tbsp arrowroot mixed to a paste with a little cold water, no lumps

1. Heat stock until nearly boiling, add ginger and tamari

2. Carefully add the arrowroot mixture, stirring briskly. The sauce should thicken to a pouring consistency.

3. Add the shredded spring onions and serve.

I usually aim to have a salad as part of the meal. Fresh salads should be full of vitality and are more plentiful in summer, when they can form a central part of the meal. Root vegetables and the more mustardy leaves are there to stimulate digestion in winter. Remember that we have to 'cook' raw foods internally with our own body temperature, and this may be more challenging for elderly people and the very young.

Try to prepare salads as close as possible to the time of eating, remembering that as soon as a leaf or vegetable is cut or bruised it will start to oxidize, thereby losing its vitamins. So with, say, a grated carrot salad, have a dressing ready to pour on to keep that oxidation process in check. Never, however, dress leafy salads until the last possible moment.

Young Broad Bean, Carrot, Onion and Rice Salad

SERVES 6

8 oz/225 g whole brown rice (see pages 94-5) cooked in

1¹/4 pts/725 ml stock

1 tsp freshly grated ginger root

1 lb/450 g young broad beans, shelled

8 oz/225 g young carrots, cut into 'flowers' (see page 93)

1 mild red salad onion, sliced very thinly

¹/4 pt/150 ml lemon mayonnaise, seasoned

with 1 tsp curry powder (optional)

2 tbsp thick yoghourt

2 tbsp chopped mixed fresh herbs (dill, chives, parsley, mint)

salt and pepper

salad leaves to garnish the bowl

1 oz/25 g roasted pine kernels to garnish the top

Method:

1. Wash rice carefully and drain.

2. In a heavy pot place rice together with stock and bring to the boil. Turn heat down to minimum and let it simmer for 45 minutes, when all the stock should have been absorbed. Allow to cool.

3. Blanch the young broad beans in boiling water with ginger root and ¹/2 tsp salt. Add in the carrot 'flowers' and cook for 3–5 minutes. Strain, reserving liquid for the stockpot. Cool.

4. Mix mayonnaise with the yoghourt.

5. Put rice into a large bowl and mix in the mayonnaise and yoghourt, and all other ingredients, reserving just a little of each for decoration.

6. Line a flattish salad plate with crunchy leaves and spoon the rice salad in the middle. Sprinkle extra beans and onions, carrots and herbs on top, and finish with lightly roasted pine kernels.

Mixed Grain Salad

From Pauline Anderson's recipe. More interesting than rice.

SERVES 6

4 oz/110 g brown rice

2 oz/50 g pot barley

2 oz/50 g wheat berries

1 medium onion, chopped

1 large clove garlic

large pinch each, thyme and basil

a few bay leaves

1 pt/500 ml hot water or stock

2 oz/50 g butter

Also add:

2 oz/50 g pre-cooked corn

^{1}/2 green or red pepper, chopped

1 stick tender celery, chopped

2 oz/50 g raisins

a few stoned and halved olives

salt and pepper

1 tsp honey, dissolved in juice of ^{1}/2 lemon

Method:

1. In ovenware pan with lid, sauté onion and garlic in the 2 oz butter. Add grains and sauté for 5 minutes.

2. Add hot water or stock and bring to boil. Place in oven (if necessary, transfer to a lidded Pyrex casserole dish, preheated). Cook for ^{3}/4 hour at 180°C/gas mark 4–5 until all the water is absorbed and grain is soft and fluffy. Cool.

3. Add variety of vegetables, raisins, olives, salt and pepper and honey dissolved in lemon juice.

Serve with a surround of rocket and topped with roughly chopped parsley. This is a great accompaniment to a buffet meal of varied salads or as a nourishing filler in place of potatoes.

Turkish Barley Salad

SERVES 6

8 oz/200 g whole barley

double the volume of good vegetable stock

For the dressing:

^{1}/2 pt/275 ml Greek yoghourt

2 tbsp olive oil

finely grated zest and juice of 1 lemon

1 tbsp chopped mint

1 tbsp chopped flat leaf parsley

^{1}/2 tsp cumin

^{1}/2 tsp cayenne

small red onion, finely chopped

diced cucumber for garnish

Cooking the barley:

Soak the barley overnight or for a few hours, then pour away soaking water. Cook in the stock. Do not stir during cooking. The grain should be plump, having absorbed all the stock, and tender. Leave to cool to room temperature. (Note: many Middle Eastern dishes are served at room temperature.)

To make the dressing:

Whisk the olive oil into the yoghourt, then add all the rest of the ingredients. Adjust seasoning.

Garnish a bowl with crisp lettuce leaves and spoon in the barley salad. Sprinkle with parsley, chopped onion and a little paprika.

Carrot Relish

SERVES 6

8 oz/225 g finely grated carrots

1 tbsp melted butter or ghee

1 tsp mustard seeds

1 tsp freshly grated ginger

2 cloves garlic, puréed

zest and juice of 1 lime or lemon

1 tbsp olive oil

salt and pepper

Method:

1. In a saucepan melt the butter or ghee. Add carrots and sauté with garlic and ginger for a few minutes, just to take off the rawness.

2. Remove from heat and when cold stir in the oil and lime zest and juice. Serve in a pretty bowl.

Celeriac Remoulade

SERVES 6

1 peeled celeriac, approx. 1 lb/450 g in weight

1 pt/570 ml good vegetable stock (light coloured)

For the dressing:

^{1}/2 pt/275 ml home-made lemon mayonnaise (see page 215)

3 tbsp Greek style yoghourt

2 tbsp finely chopped parsley

Method:

1. Slice celeriac fairly thinly, then cut slices finely into matchsticks.

2. Bring the stock to a boil and drop in the celeriac matchsticks. Simmer for about 5 minutes. They should be al dente. Cool.

3. Mix the lemon mayonnaise with the yoghourt (which lightens it). Add two thirds of the parsley. Mix in the celeriac and spoon into a pretty bowl. Finish off with the rest of the parsley.

Avocado, Pear and Walnut Salad

(From Tim Coombs)

SERVES 4

2 avocados (just turning soft)

2 pears (ideally ripe, but still a bit crunchy)

16–20 walnut halves

lettuce, salad leaves or young spinach leaves

extra virgin olive oil

wine or cider vinegar

whole grain mustard

salt and pepper

Method:

1. Wash and prepare salad leaves. Cut pears in quarters and core them, cutting them in 1 cm thick slices. Peel and cut avocados the same as pears and chop coarsely the walnut halves.

2. Add a tsp whole grain mustard to ^{1}/2 tsp wine or cider vinegar and beat, adding salt and pepper and then 2–3 tbsp olive oil.

3. In a serving bowl or plate arrange the salad leaves and add avocado, walnut and pear and add dressing at point of serving. This salad can only be prepared at the last minute, as the avocado and pears will discolour if left for any time.

Variations could use different cheeses, particularly blue cheeses such as Roquefort, Gorgonzola or Dolcelatte. Adding cheese makes the salad a filling course in itself, or a good salad to serve with a simple soup. All the ingredients are available all year round, so this is a salad that can be made any time—the major variation being the type of salad leaves. Crunchy lettuce makes a good foil for a ripe avocado. Bitter radicchio rosso and endive are a good foil for the sweetness of the pears.

Beetroot, Orange, Chicory and Watercress Salad

with Orange and Yoghourt Vinaigrette

SERVES 6

Beetroot was singled out by Rudolf Steiner as an outstanding food to be included with enthusiasm in our diet. Beetroot stimulates metabolic processes, encouraging healthy elimination. It concentrates certain mustard oils in its roots and contains betacyanide. The addition of a tiny amount of horseradish to beetroot helps to stimulate our thought processes.

Required: a pretty salad platter

$1^1/2$ lb/700 g cooked beetroots (small young ones are the most delicious)

$^1/4$ mild red onion, finely shredded

2 chicory chicons

bunch of watercress (stems can go in the stockpot)

2 juicy oranges

chives for garnish

The dressing:

1 tsp Dijon mustard

1 tsp runny honey

2 garlic cloves

juice of 1 orange

1 tsp salt

pepper

5 tbsp olive oil

2 tbsp Greek yoghourt

$^1/2$ tsp grated horseradish (can be creamed variety)

Mix first 6 ingredients in a bowl. Gradually beat in olive oil, yoghourt and finally, horseradish. Should be thick and cohesive.

Method:

1. If the beetroots are raw, scrub their skins and boil them till tender (this can take at least 2 hours). You can include in the cooking water orange peel, $^1/2$ tsp salt, a bay leaf and $^1/2$ tsp sugar. You may need to top up the water. Drain and cool the beetroot.

2. Peel and slice beetroots thinly. Sprinkle with some of the dressing.

3. Segment the oranges, removing them carefully from their skin.

Decorate the plate with watercress sprigs and chicory leaves. Arrange slices of beetroot in the centre and orange segments on top. When ready to eat, spoon a little more of the dressing over the salad and sprinkle with chives and a little chopped red onion.

Mozzarella, Fennel, Chicory, Blood Orange and Black Olive Salad

SERVES 6

This dish is traditional in Sicily when the blood oranges have just come in. Their crimson juice is breathtaking on the white mozzarella studded with glistening black olives.

a mixture of salad leaves (crispy lettuce, lamb's lettuce, endive)

2 blood oranges peeled and segmented (save the peel to use it in marmalade)

1 small tender head of Florence fennel

1 small 'buffalo' mozzarella, sliced

1 red salad onion, sliced in thin rings

radishes, if available

small piece of cucumber, thinly sliced

2 oz/50 g black Provençal olives

vinaigrette (or plain lemon-flavoured olive oil)

Method:

1. Wash and spin salad greens and lay on a flat dish.

2. Slice fennel thinly and discard any fibrous parts (add to your stockpot!)

3. Slice onions, radishes, cucumber.

4. Arrange the salad on your platter and enjoy the wonderful colour contrasts. Trickle vinaigrette or olive oil over discreetly.

Leave the assembly till the nearest possible time of dining.

Vegetable Dishes

Le Puy Lentils with Spinach or Chard

SERVES 6

These tiny, slate-grey lentils grow in the rich volcanic soil of Le Puy. They are full of flavour and nutritious trace minerals. Served with a dish of whole rice and some carrot or beetroot salad they make a perfect warming wintry meal.

10 oz/275 g Le Puy lentils

$^1/_2$ lb/225 g spinach, washed and chopped, or chard (tough stems removed and used separately)

2 pts/1.2 l good stock

bouquet garni

2 onions, sliced

2 tbsp olive oil

tbsp tamari

$^1/_4$ pt/150 ml water

2 oz/25 g butter

salt and pepper

Method:

1. Pick over the lentils, wash and drain.

2. Cook in well-flavoured stock with bouquet garni, in a heavy pot. Bring to the boil and simmer for 1 hour with the lid on.

3. Sauté the onions in the oil till brown, add tamari. Add to the lentils.

4. Sauté the spinach or chard in the butter. Add $^1/_4$ pt boiling salted water and wilt the spinach. Do not overcook. Chard will take a little longer. Drain and add lentils with a little extra butter.

Colcannon (Cally)

SERVES 6

Colcannon is an Irish dish, a bit like bubble-and-squeak, made of potatoes and kale or cooked cabbage with onions, butter and cream. Traditionally it is eaten at Hallow'een.

It is also good with a few smoky sausages tucked in, if you like them.

> *Did you ever eat colcannon*
> *When 'twas made from thickened cream*
> *And the kale and praties blended*
> *Like the picture in a dream?*
> *Did you ever take a forkful*
> *And dip it in the lake*
> *Of the clover-flavoured butter*
> *That your mother used to make?*
>
> (Traditional)

This verse makes me realize how blessed Steiner school children are who learn to make butter as part of their science teaching.

3 lb/1.3 kg mealy potatoes

1 lb (450 g) lightly cooked kale, without the fibrous stems, or Savoy cabbage finely chopped

2 oz/50 g butter

$^1/_4$ pt/150 ml milk

$^1/_4$ pt/150 ml cream

salt and white pepper

bunch of spring onions, finely chopped

Method:

1. Peel and boil the potatoes in chunks in salted water until tender. Drain, keeping the liquid for the stockpot.

2. Heat milk and cream and add spring onions. Add to the potatoes and beat until fluffy.

3. Beat in the kale or cabbage. Dot with butter and serve.

This can be reheated.

Spiced Red Cabbage

SERVES 6

1 head of red cabbage (1$^1/_2$ lb/700 g approx.)

1 red onion sliced

1 small eating apple studded with about 10 cloves

1 heaped tsp ground cinnamon

1 tsp ground nutmeg

$^1/_2$ tsp cayenne (or to taste)

2 tbs muscovado sugar

1 tsp sea salt

$^1/_4$ pt/130 ml wine vinegar

a little vegetable stock

freshly ground pepper

Method:

1. Boil a kettle of water. Finely shred red cabbage, removing tough stalks and inner core. Pour boiling water onto shredded cabbage and let it steep for 10 minutes or so. This removes excess sulphur qualities or 'yin' as in the macrobiotic scheme. Drain.

2. Sauté red onion in a mixture of butter and olive oil (just enough to coat the bottom of the pan), add spices and sugar, steeped cabbage, salt, vinegar and clove-studded apple and some stock if necessary. The liquid should not cover the cabbage mixture but the mixture must not boil dry.

3. Bring to boil and reduce heat to simmering. Depending on the quality of the cabbage, the cooking should take about $^3/_4$ hour and should be a gorgeous colour of magenta, tender and subtly 'pickled'.

Lightly sautéd leeks would be a fine accompaniment to this meal. Their delicate flavour and colour will balance the deeply earthy rich and spicy main course. Red quinoa is a good grain to serve.

Baked Cream of Hubbard Squash

SERVES 6

Crema Calabacina—a delicious, smooth, golden accompaniment to a grain and crisp green salad

**Required: an ovenproof dish approx.
8 inches/20 cm across.**

1¹/₂ lb/700 g Hubbard squash (when cleaned and peeled), or Butternut squash

1 large onion, finely chopped

3 cloves garlic, minced

³/₄ pt/15 ml stock

1 oz/25 g butter, for sautéing

1 tbsp olive oil, for sautéing

3 eggs

4 fl oz/100 ml double cream

¹/₄ tsp grated nutmeg

salt and pepper

1 oz/25 g grated Parmesan to finish

Method:

1. Chop the squash into even-sized pieces

2. Cook this in the stock until tender (approx. 20 minutes)

3. Drain and reserve liquid for soups. Mash with potato masher.

4. Sauté onion and garlic in butter and oil. Season with a little sea salt and pepper.

5. Beat eggs and cream together.

6. Add squash and egg and cream mix and stir together until homogeneous. Add a little freshly grated nutmeg. Adjust seasoning.

7. Pour into buttered ovenproof dish and bake in a medium oven (180°C/gas mark 4) for ¹/₂ hour, or until golden. Sprinkle with a little Parmesan.

Stuffed and Roasted Onions

FOUR SERVINGS OF 2 EACH

Required: ovenproof dish

Oven at 190°C/gas mark 4–5

1 very large Spanish onion

1 pt/570 ml vegetable stock

3 tbsp olive oil

shavings of Parmesan or pecorina

toothpicks for fastening

For stuffing:

3 oz/75 g fresh light breadcrumbs

1 tbsp double cream

4 oz/110 g marscapone (cream cheese)

1 tbsp chopped chives or parsley

2 cloves garlic, minced

4 spring onions, finely chopped

salt and pepper

Method:

1. Peel the onion and cut a deep slit in one side, but not right through to middle.

2. Poach for 10 minutes in boiling stock. Drain, keeping the stock for a sauce. You should now be able carefully to peel off the various layers and lay them on a plate.

3. While the onion is poaching, combine all stuffing ingredients in a food processor/Robot Chef. You should get a firm consistency. Mould into small sausage shapes. Place one at the end of an onion leaf, roll up and secure with a tooth pick. Repeat with the rest of the onion layers.

4. Pack them all side by side in the baking dish and drizzle with olive oil and scatter shavings of Parmesan on top.

5. Roast until golden in a hottish oven (190°C/gas mark 5).

This could be a starter with a garnish and lovely bread, or part of a main meal.

Pommes Dauphinoise

SERVES 6

Required: ovenproof dish

Oven at 180°C/gas mark 4–5

1½ lb/700 g waxy potatoes (e.g. Desirée)

2 oz/50 g softened butter

3 cloves garlic

½ pt/275 ml single cream

½ pt/275 ml whole milk

½ tsp grated nutmeg

Method:

1. Have a large pan of boiling salted water ready. Peel and slice potatoes into scallops (a mandolin is very good for this).

2. Blanch the potatoes for 5 minutes in two batches, to get the cooking process going. Then drain and keep the water for the stockpot. Allow potatoes to cool a little.

3. Meanwhile in a saucepan heat up the cream and milk with a level tsp of salt and the crushed garlic (don't allow it to boil).

4. In your buttered ovenproof dish arrange a layer of sliced potatoes, dot them with butter and sprinkle some freshly ground pepper and nutmeg. Continue with the layers until the potato is finished, making the last layer the most beautifully arranged. Pour over the hot milk with cream and garlic, which should almost cover them. Cover with foil and bake for 1 hour.

5. Remove foil and return to the oven, with heat turned up to 200°C/gas mark 6, and bake for another 20 minutes or so until they are golden and tender—test with a skewer.

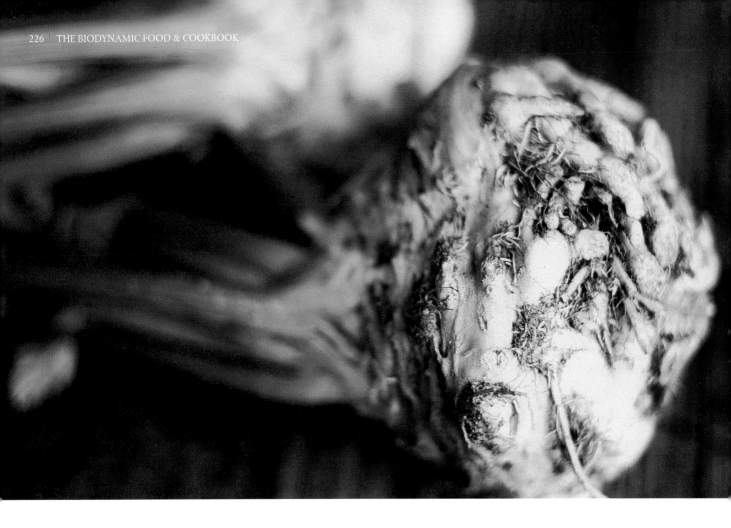

Celeriac, Apple Slices with Gruyère

SERVES 6

The gnarled, bulky roots of celeriac may be somewhat off-putting initially, if you are not familiar with them. But they are actually very versatile and quite delicious, with a deep, earthy, sweet flavour of celery. They contain a rich supply of calcium, magnesium and potassium, beneficial for the nervous and lymphatic systems.

Celeriac can be used in vegetable stews and casseroles, but be careful not to overdo the quantity, as like swedes and turnips, their flavour can overpower more delicate ones.

This recipe is from an idea given by a Dutch friend. It can be used as a starter on its own, or as a side dish. It has a clean and enlivening combination of flavours, is very simple to do, and looks interesting.

1 lb/450 g celeriac (when peeled), cut into rounds approx. $^1/_4$ inch thick

1 medium-sized tart apple, such as Bramley (approx. $^1/_2$ lb/225 g), peeled, cored and sliced (cover with acidulated water to prevent browning).

4 oz/110 g Gruyère cheese, grated

1 tsp chopped fresh rosemary

$^1/_2$ lemon

Method:

1. Poach the celeriac rounds in a good-flavoured stock with a squeeze of lemon juice for 5–8 minutes, or until al dente. Drain and keep the stock for sauces or soups.

2. Arrange in a buttered ovenproof dish. Drain apple slices and put on top of each slice of celeriac. Season lightly with pepper.

3. Finish off with grated Gruyère cheese and chopped rosemary.

4. Cook for 15–20 minutes in a hot oven (200°C/gas mark 6), or until the cheese bubbles and becomes golden.

Bouquet of Vegetables

SERVES 6

¹/2 lb/225 g broccoli florets

¹/2 lb/225 g carrots, thinly sliced

¹/2 lb/225 g Florence fennel, finely sliced

2 oz/50 g butter

1 tbsp olive oil

1 clove garlic

¹/4 pt/150 ml water

salt and pepper

Method:

1. Half an hour before eating, blanch broccoli florets in boiling salted water, keeping emerald green colour and al dente texture. Drain.

2. Fifteen minutes before eating. Melt butter and olive oil in a sauté pan, add garlic, then add the carrot slices and a sprinkling of salt and pepper and the water and steam for 5 minutes. Then add the fennel slices and continue for further 5–8 minutes. Test to see if vegetables are cooked and finally add the broccoli florets to reheat.

3. Drain and use the water for the sauce.

Serve hot with Cashew Nut Sauce (page 214), boiled kamut and wild garlic pesto.

Artichokes

Artichokes grow in the spring. They have a high mineral content and are extremely good for liver cleansing. There are many ways of using them, but the simplest and most delicious is to steam them until the outer leaves pull off easily. Serve with vinaigrette or melted lemon butter.

Curried Bombay Potatoes with Spinach

SERVES 6

I admit that this is a bit of a cheat, but why not now and again take a short cut—especially when it is the spicing of dishes by the masters of curry themselves? I found packets of Bombay Spice mix at my local farm shop and just added some of my own ingredients.

8 oz/225 g chopped onion

1 lb/450 g potatoes, cubed

1 lb/450 g spinach, chopped roughly

3 cloves garlic, finely chopped

2 tsp turmeric

1 packet Bombay Spice mix

2 oz/50 g butter or ghee

1 tbsp vegetable oil

2 tsp freshly grated ginger root

1 level tsp salt

¹/2 pt/275 ml stock

juice of a lemon

Method:

1. In a heavy saucepan sauté the onions and garlic together till golden.

2. Add cubed potatoes, Bombay Spice, turmeric, salt and ginger and continue to sauté and stir for 5 minutes on a fairly high heat. Then add the stock and cover with a lid. Cook gently for half an hour. Adjust seasoning. Add lemon juice

3. Meanwhile 'wilt' the spinach in a little boiling salted water, then drain and add to the potatoes just before serving.

Serve with Basmati rice, yoghourt and carrot raita.

Refried Beans

SERVES 6

With the souffled polenta pie, guacamole and sour cream and chives, this makes a really special meal.

1 lb/^{1}/$_2$ kg pinto or red kidney beans

piece of kombu (kelp)

piece of carrot

stick of celery

pinch of herbs

1 large onion

4 cloves of garlic

olive oil for sautéing

1 level tsp of cumin

1 dsp soy sauce

1 chilli (optional)

Method:

1. Soak the beans overnight with a piece of kombu. Next day throw away soaking water and cook beans in 3 pts/1.5 l of water with some herbs, celery and a piece of carrot. Add ^{1}/$_2$ tsp salt towards the end of the cooking time. Cook until soft (1 hour or more). If there is excess liquid pour some off, as this does not have to be too runny, more of a paste.

2. Slice the onion into fine rings and sauté in olive oil with the garlic cloves until soft. Add 1 level tsp of cumin and some soy sauce (about 1 dsp). You could add some chilli too.

3. Add the onion mixture to the beans and continue to cook, mashing the beans but leaving some whole for texture.

Serve with Rich Tomato Sauce. (see page 214).

Marinaded Roast Vegetables

SERVES 6

Selection of root vegetables (Hubbard squash, carrots, parsnips, red onions, potatoes, sweet potatoes)

For marinade:

5 tbsp good olive oil

1 tbsp tamari sauce

4 bay leaves

6 cloves of garlic, sliced lengthways

sprigs of rosemary or thyme

Method:

1. Scrub and cut into even-sized chunks squash, carrots, parsnips, onions (leave the skin on but halve the onions), sweet potatoes, potatoes.

2 Mix the ingredients for the marinade.

3. Marinade the vegetables for ^{1}/$_2$ hour.

4. Lay out vegetables in a roasting pan and bake in a moderate oven (180°C/gas mark 4) for 1^1/$_4$ hours until tender, turning from time to time.

Serve with green salad, ginger and tamari sauce, some steamed rice and roasted sunflower seeds.

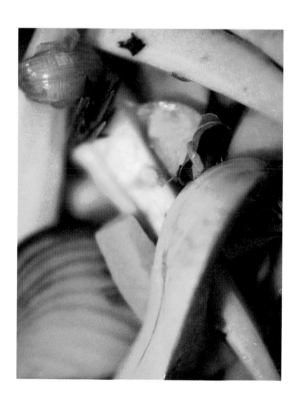

Chocolate, Orange and Chestnut Cake

SERVES 6

My daughter Lucy used to work at the Carved Angel restaurant in Dartmouth under Joyce Molyneux. I remember a delicious chestnut and chocolate cake she used to make. It was rich but nutritious. This is my version.

Required: two 9 inch/23 cm, loose-bottomed cake tins, buttered and lined with baking parchment

Oven 180°C/gas mark 4

6 large eggs

12 oz/350 g cooked chestnuts puréed or sieved. (Either fresh or dried chestnuts that have been rehydrated can be used. The total amount of cooked chestnut needed will be 15 oz/400 g, which includes the 3 oz/75 g in the filling.)

8 oz (225 g) caster sugar

6 oz (175 g) grated dark chocolate

grated zest of 1 large orange

For the filling, combine:

^{1}/2 pt/275 ml double cream, whipped

1 oz/25 g icing sugar

1 tbsp Grand Marnier

3 oz/75 g chestnut purée

For the icing:

6 oz/175 g dark chocolate

1 tbsp orange juice plus zest

2 oz/50 g unsalted butter

Method:

1. Separate the eggs one at a time, making sure there are no shell pieces left in.

2. Beat the yolks and caster sugar together until thick, pale and creamy.

3. Add the chestnut purée and grated chocolate (grating in a processor is best, as the warmth of the hand on a hand grater tends to melt the chocolate).

4. In a large bowl (copper is good, if you have one) beat the egg whites with a pinch of salt until stiff (here an electric hand whisk is helpful).

5. Fold the egg whites gently into the chestnut–chocolate mixture without losing too much air, but until the mixture is reasonably homogenized. The chocolate will stay in flecks.

6. Divide into two cake tins and bake for 30 minutes in moderate oven. Be careful when turning out on the serving plate as it will be it a little fragile (because it contains no gluten).

7. Sandwich the two cakes together with the filling.

8. Prepare icing by melting ingredients together over a double boiler. Pour evenly over the cake. Allow to cool and harden.

Honey and Apple Spice Cake

SERVES 6

This is nice done in a ring cake tin with a funnel.

8 oz/225 g softened butter

8 oz/225 g soft brown sugar

4 large eggs

4 oz/110 g roasted and chopped hazelnuts

2 oz/50 g sultanas

4 oz/110 g chopped apricots

3 pieces chopped crystallized ginger

1 tsp cinnamon and 1 tsp ground nutmeg, sifted together with 8 oz/225 g self-raising unbleached flour

2 Cox's eating apples (8 oz/225 g approx.), cored and chopped small

zest and juice of 1 orange

2 tbsp wildflower honey

Method:

1. Beat butter and sugar together till fluffy.

2. Add eggs gradually, beating in a little flour to prevent curdling.

3. Fold in the rest of the flour, then gently incorporate the rest of the ingredients.

4. Spoon the cake batter into the greased tin.

5. Bake in moderate oven (180°C/gas mark 4) for 3/4–1 hour, or until a metal skewer comes out clean.

6. Heat orange juice and honey together, but don't boil.

7. Pour onto the warm cake. Allow to cool. Take out of the tin and fill the centre with fresh blossoms.

This cake will keep well and children seem to love it.

Date and Apple Slices

SERVES 6

Required: baking tray 10 x 14 in/25 x 36 cm

Oven 180°C/gas mark 4

14 oz/400g oatflakes

6 oz/175 g melted butter

4 oz/110 g Rapadura raw cane sugar

8 oz/225 g stoned dates

4 oz/110 g sultanas

2 eating apples, cored and chopped

2 tbsp desiccated coconut

1 tsp roughly ground fennel seeds

1 organic seedless tangerine (or small orange), whisked in a blender with

1 tbsp maple syrup (or 1 oz/25 g extra sugar)

1/2 pt/275 ml boiling water

Method:

1. Steep the dates in the boiling water for 10 minutes.

2. Add sultanas and puréed tangerine and chopped apple. Cook, stirring gently, for further 5–10 minutes, or until water has evaporated and you have a soft, spreadable mixture.

3. In a large bowl mix oatflakes, Rapadura sugar and melted butter.

4. Grease a baking tray and spread half the oat mixture evenly.

5. Spread on the date mixture.

6. Cover with the rest of the oat mixture and sprinkle the coconut on top.

7. Press down firmly and bake in a medium oven, 180°C/gas mark 4 for 30 minutes or until golden. Allow to cool a little. Cut into slices and serve warm with crème anglaise or cold in the lunch-box.

Persian Olive Oil, Almond and Saffron Cake

SERVES 6

My neighbour, Valerie, arrived back from a visit to the pyramids of Egypt bearing me a large sachet of red-gold saffron and with it the story of its purchase in a Cairo souk. Upon enquiry of saffron and cardamom, Valerie was beckoned up a winding staircase that gave out to a room packed with every spice imaginable. At the end of the room, on a bare table, stood a pair of silver scales. The weighing of the saffron was a task requiring considerable focus, as the silver scales and weights quivered from side to side. Then the prices had to be discussed.

Now it is in my kitchen, this stamen of crocus with its slightly medicinal taste and its sun-gold vibrant colour. A homoeopathic amount of this spice gives this beautiful golden and pink cake its signature. It will keep well.

Required: a 9 inch/23 cm cake tin lined with parchment paper.

4 oz/110 g dried sour cherries or cranberries, soaked in boiling water, to just cover

4 oz/110 g ground almonds

4 oz/110 g roasted almonds, chopped

4 large eggs

7 oz/200 g unrefined caster sugar

9 fl oz/250 ml virgin olive oil

sifted together: 2 oz/50 g 100% wheat flour,

    4 oz/110 g unbleached white flour,

2 level tsp baking powder,

^{1}/2 tsp salt

^{1}/2 tsp saffron threads soaked in 2 tbsp warmed (not boiled) milk

grated zest and juice of 1 lemon

1 tangerine, deseeded and whizzed in the food processor

2 tbsp sesame seeds

2 tbsp wildflower honey

Method:

1. Whisk eggs and sugar together till thick and creamy (an electric hand whisk is very useful).

2. Gradually add small quantities of olive oil and flour, reserving about a third of the flour till later, but using all the oil.

3. Add lemon zest and juice and saffron infusion.

4. Then add the ground almonds, chopped almonds, drained cherries or cranberries (keeping the liquid separately in a small saucepan), and the tangerine.

5. Fold in the remaining flour.

6. Pour this batter into the cake tin, sprinkle on the sesame seeds and bake at 180°C/gas mark 4 for about 35 minutes. Do not open the oven door the first half-hour.

7. Whilst the cake is cooking add the honey to the reserved fruit soaking water (about 3 tbsp). Warm together and pour over the cake when it comes out of the oven.

Enjoy small slices with thick Greek yoghourt.

Mallorcan Almond Cake

SERVES 6

This cake makes me think of the exotic Moorish culture—with its taste for almonds and citrus—that created the exquisite palace of Alhambra in Granada. I imagine beautiful veiled women eating snips of this cake in a setting of tinkling fountains and jasmine-scented patios. It is very rich so you only need a little. Try it with a fruit compôte, fresh raspberries and/or crème fraîche. (It can also be eaten with home-made almond ice-cream. See page 145) As it contains no butter or flour it can be offered to those with dairy or gluten problems. It will keep well.

Required: a 9 inch (23 cm), loose-bottomed cake tin lined with baking parchment

Oven at 180°C gas mark 4

11 oz/300 g ground almonds

10 oz/275 g unrefined caster sugar

grated zest of 2 lemons

1 heaped tsp cinnamon

7 eggs, separated

a few drops of real almond essence

Method:

1. Beat egg yolks and sugar (an electric hand-beater is useful here) until thick and pale yellow.

2. Add lemon rind, cinnamon and a few drops of almond essence. Combine well.

3. Whip egg whites with a pinch of salt until soft peaks form, in a large metal bowl.

4. Gently combine the two mixtures together, sprinkling in the ground almonds little by little at the same time. (I find hands best for this; you don't want to knock the air out of the egg whites but you do need the mixture to be homogeneous.)

5. Spoon into the cake tin and cook for $^3/_4$ hour at 180°C/gas mark 4. Allow to cool gently; it will still be a little moist in the centre. Remember there is no flour in this, so it will be a little fragile to handle. Sprinkle with icing sugar when cool.

Hazelnut Sables (Biscuits)

SERVES 6

Required: baking tray, greased

7 oz/200 g butter, softened

5 oz/120 g unrefined caster sugar

3 oz/100 g roasted and finely chopped hazelnuts

8 oz/225 g unbleached self raising flour

1 egg

Method:

1. Combine all the ingredients in a food processor. Make into a sausage shape by wrapping in clingfilm.

2. Chill in the refrigerator until hard enough to slice.

3. Place slices on an oiled baking tray. Bake for 15 minutes at 200°C/gas mark 5.

4. Cool on a wire cooling rack.

Almond Macaroons

MAKES/10–12

This is a recipe to use up the egg whites left over from other recipes.

Required: baking tray, lined with parchment or rice paper.

8 oz/225 g ground almonds

6 oz/175 g unrefined caster sugar

$^1/_2$ tsp almond essence

2 egg whites

pinch of salt

a few flaked almonds

Method:

1. In a bowl whisk the egg whites with a pinch of salt and the almond essence until they form peaks. Gradually beat in the caster sugar.

2. Fold in the ground almonds. Spoon rounds onto the baking parchment (should produce 10–12 macaroons).

3. Scatter some flaked almonds on top and place in preheated oven (180°C/gas mark 4) for 15–20 minutes, or till golden and crisp on the outside and a little moist on the inside.

Pear Upside-down Cake

SERVES 6

Required: a 9 inch/23 cm, loose-bottomed cake tin, buttered and lined with parchment.

Oven 180°C/gas mark 4

3 Conference or Comice pears approx. 1 lb/450 g (firmish ones), marinaded in:

2 oz/50 g Rapadura raw cane sugar

2 oz/50 g melted butter

$1/2$ tsp ground cinnamon

zest and juice of 1 lemon

For the cake mixture:

6 oz/175 g softened butter

6 oz/175 g unrefined caster sugar

4 large eggs

4 oz/110 g self-raising flour

a few drops of almond essence

2 oz/50 g ground almonds

Method:

1. Warm together the Rapadura sugar, 2 oz butter and cinnamon. Add lemon zest and half the juice.

2. Peel, quarter and core the pears carefully, then cut them into 2–3 slices lengthways, depending on size. Toss in the Rapadura sugar mixture, then arrange as spokes in a wheel in the cake tin, thin ends pointing to the middle. Pour on the rest of the sugar-butter mixture, which will become fudgy by the end of the baking.

3. Beat together the soft butter and caster sugar until fluffy. (I use an electric hand-whisk.)

4. Add beaten eggs a little at a time, including a little of the flour to stop them curdling. Then gently fold in the rest of the flour, the ground almonds, a few drops of almond essence and the rest of the lemon juice. This is a fairly stiff batter.

5. Spoon large dollops of the mixture onto the pears and smooth it out.

6. Put in a medium oven for 35–40 minutes, or until risen and golden. Allow to cool in the tin before turning out the cake.

This is delicious warm with crème fraîche or yoghourt, but lovely cold too. And it keeps well.

Chocolate, Coffee and Almond Cake

SERVES 6

This recipe is derived from one that came with a Riverford Farm veggie box. It is very rich—you only need a little to satisfy your chocolate yearnings! It is also wheat free.

Required: a 9 inch/23 cm, loose-bottomed cake tin lined with parchment

Oven 180°C/gas mark 4

7 oz/200 g dark chocolate

5 oz/150 g unrefined caster sugar

4 oz/110 g unsalted butter

5 eggs, separated

4 oz/110 g ground almonds

1 tbsp cocoa powder, plus a little extra for finishing the cake

$1/2$ espresso cup/50 ml strong black coffee (if you crush a cardamom pod into the cafetière it balances the acidity)

1 tbsp crème fraîche or Greek yoghourt

pinch of salt

Method:

1. In a metal or ceramic bowl melt the chocolate in the coffee, over a pan of boiling water. Add the butter and stir occasionally until melted.

2. Meanwhile whip the egg yolks with the sugar until thick and pale golden (an electric hand-beater is good for this).

3. In a separate bowl sift the cocoa powder into the ground almonds.

4. Whip the egg whites with a pinch of salt until they form peaks.

5. Add the chocolate mixture, still runny but not too hot, to mixture of egg yolk and sugar. Stir in the almond and cocoa mix and 1 tbsp of crème fraiche. Then fold in the egg whites carefully.

6. Spoon into the prepared cake tin and cook for 40 minutes or till risen. It will still be a little sticky in the middle, but firm on the outside. *Please remember that as this cake does not have flour in it, it is slightly fragile so try not to handle until cooled.* Remove the parchment. Sieve some cocoa powder on top.

Serve with crème fraîche and a fruit salad. In winter, a bowl of stewed Hunza apricots make a lovely accompaniment.

Soul Cakes

SERVES 6

What would tempt back a soul? When I learned about the old tradition of going from house to house asking for 'soul cakes' on All Souls night, I set about thinking what those cakes might have been like. This is what I came to and how I came to it.

In Cornwall there is a traditional cake flavoured and coloured with saffron; in Dorset there is apple cake. Apple goes with Eve and Eve goes with Soul. Almonds are included because most of my sweet dishes have almonds in. Then, Cathy's prize-winning lemon curd (p. 213) lurks in the centre, hiding a piece of glacé cherry. Combining these elements produced a most tempting morsel for all souls.

Required: cookie pan—a tray for 12

Oven 190°C/gas mark 5

4 oz/110 g softened butter

4 oz/110 g unrefined caster sugar

2 good pinches of saffron, soaked in 2 tbsp boiling water

4 oz/110 g plain unbleached flour, sifted with

1 tsp baking powder

2 oz/50 g ground almonds

3 eggs

2 tbsp good quality lemon curd

1 medium sized apple, grated (2 oz/50 g approx.)

4 undyed glacé cherries, each cut in 3 pieces

a few flaked almonds or pine kernels to sprinkle on top

Method:

1. Cream butter and sugar together until fluffy

2. Beat the eggs with the saffron strands

3. Add this gradually to the butter and sugar mix, sprinkling in a little flour to prevent curdling

4. Fold in the rest of the flour and the ground almonds. Do not beat at this stage, as it will make the dough hard.

5. Make the lemony-apple centre by mixing lemon curd with freshly grated apple.

6. To assemble the little cakes, half fill buttered cookie pans with cake mixture (using about two-thirds of your mixture), then put in a scant teaspoon of lemon and apple mixture in the centre and press a small piece of cherry in the middle of this.

7. Put another spoonful of mixture on top and then sprinkle with some flaked almonds or pine kernels.

8. Bake at 190°C/gas mark 5 for 15–20 minutes, or until risen, golden and firm to touch.

Serve with hot elderberry cordial and the souls are sure to be placated!

Oatmeal Parkin

SERVES 6

Traditional, from Yorkshire. My mother used to make it for bonfire night. I don't think I've had any since my childhood, so it brought back many memories making this dark, gingery, chewy, treacly stuff to warm the innards and stick to the ribs. Bonfire smoke—fireworks—saltpetre and star-speckled skies. Do try it. It keeps very well and is a good way to get oats into the children.

Required: square 6 inch/15 cm baking tin, greased

Oven 140°C/gas mark 2

5 oz/150 g medium oatmeal

4 oz/110 g butter

4 oz/110 g molasses

4 oz/110 g Rapadura raw cane sugar

4 oz/110 g self-raising flour

2 pieces preserved ginger, chopped small

2 tsp ground ginger

1 tsp ground mixed spice

pinch salt

1 tbsp milk

1 egg (large)

Method:

1. Weigh a small saucepan on your scales and into it weigh the molasses. Add butter and sugar and heat gently until the butter has melted. Stir from time to time. It should not boil.

2. Sift salt, flour and spices into a mixing bowl, add oatmeal and chopped ginger. Then pour the warmed treacly mixture into the flours until all is thoroughly mixed through. Then add the beaten egg and milk, which will make a stiff pouring consistency.

3. Pour into the prepared cake tin and place in the centre of the cool oven and bake for 1¹/₂ hours or until the centre feels springy to the touch. Allow it to cool in the tin for half an hour before turning out and cutting into fingers. Enjoy!

Cheese and Herb Scones

MAKES 12 GOOD SIZED SCONES

Required: baking tray, greased

Oven at 200°C/gas mark 6

12 oz/350 g 82% flour, or white if you prefer

1 tbsp baking powder

6 oz/175 g grated Cheddar cheese

¹/₂ pt/275 ml approx. whole milk (or enough to mix to a soft dough)

3 oz/75 g butter

¹/₂ tsp cayenne

¹/₂ tsp sea salt

2 tsp herbes de Provence

Method:

1. Sift flour, baking powder, salt and cayenne into a large bowl.

2. Sprinkle in the herbs.

3. Rub in the butter.

4. Add two-thirds of the grated cheese.

5. Add the milk, to make a soft (not sticky) and 'rollable' dough. Add a little more flour if it is sticky.

6. Roll out onto a floured surface to 1 inch/2.5 cm thickness and cut out shapes with a pastry cutter.

7. Place on greased baking tray and sprinkle with the remaining cheese.

8. Bake at 200°C/gas mark 6 for 15–20 minutes, or till risen and golden. Cool on a wire rack.

Scones

MAKES 6 SCONES

For a Devon cream tea.

Required: baking tray, greased

Oven at 210°C/gas mark 6

8 oz/225 g unbleached self-raising flour, sifted together with a pinch of salt

1¹/2 oz/40 g caster sugar

1¹/2 oz/40 g cold butter

¹/4 pt/150 ml unpasteurized milk (soured milk is good, if you have it)

Method:

1. Preheat the oven to 210°C/gas mark 6. It is important to put the scones into a hot oven.

2. Sift flour and salt into a mixing bowl and add sugar.

3. Cut the cold butter into small pieces and rub into flour mixture until it is like fine breadcrumbs.

4. Stir in most of the milk, leaving a little for later, using a palette knife or wooden spoon. Gather the dough together. It should be soft but not sticky.

5. Place dough onto a floured surface. At this stage you can either pat it into a round or use a rolling pin and cut out 6 scones about ³/4–1 in/2–2 ¹/2 cm thick with a sharp cutter. If you have trimmings you can re-roll the dough, but *very gently*—overhandling or squeezing the dough will make the scones heavy.

6. Place scones on the baking tray and brush their tops with the remaining milk.

7. Bake for 15–20 minutes, or until well-risen and golden. Ovens vary, but try not to open the door during cooking.

8. Remove from tray and cool on a rack. They are best eaten shortly after coming out of the oven, certainly on the same day. But if there are leftovers, they may be gently warmed in the oven.

Serve with home-made strawberry or raspberry jam and clotted cream (if you are lucky enough to be in the right place, this will have been made in a local Devon farmhouse).

After splitting the scone across, you have the weighty decision to make: whether to put the cream on first and then the jam, or vice versa. You can find two distinct camps down here in the West Country. I leave the choice to you!

Jo's Scottish 'Black Bun'

SERVES 6

I have spent two occasions recently celebrating New Year in Norfolk with Brian and Jo Baxter, who have an organic smallholding near Swaffham. They have an extraordinarily hardworking but rich way of life and provide much of their own food and some of their own clothing. Jo, a champion spinner, spins and knits up the wool of the Shetland sheep and llamas that they keep.

On New Year's Eve Brian, who is a member of the MacMillan clan, dons full highland regalia and we have sped across snow-clad fields and country lanes to reach a pub where he pipes in the New Year. It is a moving occasion. Upon returning home Brian performs the 'first footing' where he carries a piece of coal across the threshold. (After 50 years of marriage they have enough coal stashed away to guard against improvident times!) Then we are served Jo's Black Bun—spicy poor man's Christmas cake, which contains no fat, and is interestingly done up in a pastry crust. It soaks up the New Year's celebratory dram of Highland whisky beautifully. So do give it a try!

Early on New Year's morning we woke up to a white landscape and the haunting sound of bagpipes stirring all to life as Brian played to the llamas, sheep, horses, pigs, chickens, geese and all creatures who inhabit their farm. Long may it last.

Required: rectangular cake tin 10 x 6 x 2^1/2 in (26 x 6 x 2^1/2 cm)

Oven at 190°C/gas mark 5

For the crust:

10 oz/275 g plain flour sifted with a pinch of salt

6 oz/175 g cold butter

4 tbsp cold water

Follow shortcrust pastry method (see pages 97-8) and let it rest in the fridge for ^{1}/2 hour

Black bun filling:

8 oz/225 g seedless Lexia raisins

8 oz/225 g currants

4 oz/110 g whole almonds, chopped

8 oz/225 g Muscovado sugar

10 oz/275 g self-raising flour

1 tsp baking powder

2 tsp ground cinnamon

1^1/2 tsp mixed spice

2 pieces crystallized stem ginger

2 oz/50g crystallized orange peel

2 eggs, beaten

scant ^{1}/2 pt/275 ml milk, enough to moisten the batter

2 fl oz/55 ml ginger cordial

Method:

1. Mix dried fruit, peel and spices and almonds together with the sugar and ginger cordial and leave a few hours or overnight.

2. Add flour, then milk and eggs, reserving a little to paint the crust. Stir well and make a wish!

3. Roll out two-thirds of the pastry and line the buttered cake tin. Fill it with cake mixture and then roll out the rest of the pastry for a lid, first brushing the edges with egg to seal. Place on top, making a few slashes to allow expansion, and decorate with pastry shapes. Paint with egg wash. Bake for 15 minutes at 190°C/gas mark 5, then 150°C/gas mark 3 for 2^1/2 hours.

Breakfast

Granola

SERVES 6

Crunchy breakfast cereal, made from oats, honey, malt and nuts. A bowl of this will keep you going energy-wise for a long time. Good also to take with you when travelling.

Required: roasting tins

Oven at 180°C/gas mark 4

2 lb/900 g pinhead oat flakes

4 oz/110 g sunflower seeds

4 oz/110 g sesame seeds

6 oz/175 g desiccated coconut

6 oz/175 g chopped almonds

4 oz/110 g chopped hazelnuts

$^{1}/_2$ pt/275 g sunflower oil

2 tbsp malt extract

1 level tsp sea salt

$^{1}/_2$ lb/225 g runny honey

6 oz/175 g sultanas

6 oz/175 g chopped dates

some figs or apricots (optional)

Method:

1. Mix the oats, seeds and nuts together in a large bowl.

2. Warm the oil, malt and honey mixture together in a saucepan until combined. Then pour it over the oats, seeds and nuts, and when the mix is cool enough use your hands to make sure all is coated.

4. Divide into 3–4 batches in roasting tins.

5. Roast in the oven (180°C/gas mark 4). When the edges start to turn golden you need to stir the mixture so that it all colours evenly, which will take frequent stirrings. It can burn easily if you don't keep an eye on the process.

6. When it is roasted tip into a large bowl and add dried fruit.

Granola stores well in a large glass lidded jar.

Bircher Muesli

MAKES 8 PORTIONS

This is one of the dishes created by Maximilian Bircher-Benner (1867–1939), who has had an impact on our feeding habits. In his time meat was regarded as the best suited and most valuable food for a human being; vegetables and fruits were considered food for the poor. Dr Bircher-Benner, however, insisted upon 'food of the sunlight' meals based on grains, nuts, seeds, fruits and honey as being of more support to human health. My Swiss friend Ursula tells me that muesli was a usual supper dish for her family.

Dr Bircher-Benner was also convinced that health care should be much more than just medical treatments. He founded a sanatorium in Zürich where his patients, as well as receiving healthy food, were encouraged to take a daily walk in addition to bathing and sunbathing.

Making your own muesli is easy and far cheaper than the bought variety—and you know what has gone into it!

Base:

8 oz/225 g oatflakes

4 oz/110 g roasted, chopped almonds and hazelnuts

2 oz/50 g seedless raisins

2 oz/50 g sunflower seeds

2 oz/50 g barley or millet flakes

Soak the dry ingredients (either overnight or less) in:

juice of 1 lemon

1/2 pt/275 ml apple or some other fruit juice

2 tbsp maple syrup or 1 tbsp honey

When you are ready to eat, add some grated apple, thick yoghourt and seasonal berries.

Plum, Hazelnut and Cinnamon Brioche

SERVES 6

This is a wonderful celebratory 'special' for a birthday or festival breakfast. The various stages will take 3-plus hours in all. If you want it for breakfast it can be cooked the day before and reheated in a medium oven.

Required: a loose-bottomed, 11 inch/28 cm flan tin, buttered

Oven 200°C/gas mark 6 to begin

Stage 1, for the ferment:

2 oz/50 g plain flour

2 fl oz/55 ml tepid water

1/2 oz/10 g yeast (dried or fresh)

1/2 oz/15 g soft brown sugar

Combine all these ingredients and keep, covered, in a warm place for 1 hour.

Stage 2, the dough

4 1/2 oz/125 g all of the ferment

7 oz/200 g plain flour

1 oz/25 g extra flour for kneading

1/2 tsp salt

2 medium eggs (save a little of the white for glazing)

1 oz/25 g softened butter

Knead all these together in a large bowl until you have a silky dough.

Stage 3

4 oz/110 g softened butter

In this stage you knead in the rest of the softened butter, just like the Greek Easter Bread (*Tsoureki*, page 202). It becomes sticky and you may need a tiny bit more flour, but resist the temptation to keep adding flour as the dough will become too tough. Now leave in the covered bowl in a warm place until it has risen to fill the bowl (2 hours).

Stage 4

Whilst the dough is rising you can prepare the topping:

3 oz/75 g roasted ground hazelnuts

3 oz/75 g soft brown sugar

1 tsp cinnamon

3/4 lb/350 g plums (Victorias are good), de-stoned and halved

Mix the first three ingredients together and divide into two halves. Dredge the plums in half the sugar, nut and cinnamon mix and leave, allowing the juices to begin to flow.

Stage 5

Knock down the dough and knead for another 5 minutes. Then roll out into a large circle. Sprinkle the other half of sugar, nut and cinnamon mix over the surface. Fold in half and roll out again into a circle that will fit the flan tin. Place it in the buttered tin and leave again for 1/2 hour to rise.

Stage 6

Now evenly distribute the plum halves and press into the dough. Paint the bare part of the dough with egg white and a little caster sugar.

Stage 7

Place in a hot oven (200°C/gas mark 6) for 10–15 minutes, to set the dough, which should by then be golden. Then turn the oven down to 180°C/gas mark 4 for a further 10 minutes to cook the brioche through.

Delicious warm, and can be reheated.

Yoghourt

SERVES 6

Yoghourt can be traced back 10,000 years and is such a nutritious and versatile food. It can be used with fruit, or in sauces and salad dressings, or just plain. People who find milk difficult to digest often find yoghourt much easier. It contains high quality proteins, minerals and vitamins, if you make it with a high quality milk such as green top biodynamic milk, and is a quarter of the price of commercial yoghourt. The special culture of bacteria is *Lactobacillus bulgaricus*.

You can make it in small or large quantities. I used to have a special lidded ceramic pot which held four pints/2 l. Wrapped in a blanket and left overnight in the airing cupboard the result usually lasted my family for a few days. Now I make yoghourt in a vacuum flask in small quantities—not so romantic, but reliable! Why don't you try it for yourself?

Required: wide-lidded vacuum flask or lidded container (pottery). Warm place with stable temperature, like an airing cupboard

For making 1 pt/500 ml thick and creamy yoghourt:

1 pt/570 ml organic or BD whole milk

^{1}/4 pt/150 ml double cream

1 tbsp live yoghourt (I use the Greek kind, but you can always keep some starter from a previous batch)

Method:

1. In a heavy-bottomed saucepan heat up the milk. (In the Balkans the tradition is to boil the milk and reduce it down to two-thirds the original amount, which increases the richness and sweetness.) Bring to the boil and let it simmer gently for about 30 minutes, stirring from time to time (a milk-saver—a small glass disc—is useful here). The milk reduces fairly quickly.

2. Add cream and leave to cool to about blood temperature (37°C). It is ready when you can put your finger in and count to 10. The temperature is crucial: too hot and it will kill the bacillus, too cool and it either won't activate or will take a very long time and produce acidity.

3. Stir in the live yoghourt starter and mix thoroughly. Warm your flask by rinsing out with hot water and pour milk and cream yoghourt mixture into it. Screw the lid on tightly. Leave overnight.

The next day you should unscrew your flask and reveal the butter-yellow topping of a thick stable curd. Magic! Store in a glass jar in the fridge.

Condiments

Gomashio

Gomashio is a condiment made of sea salt and ground roasted sesame seeds. As the oil of the sesame seeds coats the salt crystals, it makes them more digestible. So this is a better way to have salt on the table.

A suribachi is a Japanese ridged bowl with a wooden pestle that is specially used for gomashio making, but you can use a pestle and mortar or grind the mixture in an electric spice grinder. The handmade mix is best.

1 level tbsp sea salt

6 tbsp washed and drained whole white sesame seeds

Method:

1. Roast the salt in a heavy skillet over medium heat, stirring constantly.

2. When the salt has finished releasing a chlorine odour put it into the suribachi or pestle.

3. Toast the sesame seeds in the skillet until a golden brown and releasing their distinctive aroma. Add to the salt and grind in the suribachi till about 70% of the seeds are crushed. Store in an airtight jar.

Raspberry Vinegar

Required: a large glass stoppered jar or Kilner jar.

1 lb/450 g fresh raspberries

1 pt/570 ml white wine vinegar

$^1/_4$ lb/110 g unrefined caster sugar

Method:

Bruise the raspberries with a wooden spoon. Cover with the vinegar and leave for 2–3 days, stirring each day. Strain through a muslin or jelly-bag. To this liquid add sugar and heat to simmering point for 5 minutes. Do not boil, or you will lose the wonderful bright red colour. Cool and bottle.

Use in salad dressings. A dash in lemonade is also excellent and gives it an extra zing.

Drinks

Elderflower Champagne

The elder tree loves to grow wild and is found abundantly in chalkpits, woods, hedgerows and in gardens when it is allowed. Soon after the appearance of the elder's leaves the flower-buds form, and by the end of May or early June the trees are laden with the flat heads of tiny white flowers: five cream petals, five yellow stamens and star-shaped green sepals on the back of each tiny flower. This exquisite symmetry gives a clue to its ruling planet, Venus.

Elders were used medicinally by the ancient Britons, Celts and Romans, who thought that the Elder Mother could cure all the ills of mankind. In the mid-eighteenth century diarist John Evelyn said of the elder:

> If the medicinal properties of the leaves, bark and berries were thoroughly known, I cannot tell of what our countryman could ail, for which he might not fetch a remedy from every hedge.

Elderflowers are sudorific, diuretic, febrifuge (good against fevers), and anodyne in that they allay pain and have a cooling effect. Infusions of elderflowers are used to relieve bronchial catarrh and head-colds. They are also delicious to eat and make drinks from. The flowers should be picked when fully open, preferably on the day of the full moon. They should be dry and full of pollen, which helps the fermenting process in our Elderflower Champagne.

The flowers are delicious freshly picked, dipped into a pancake batter as beignets with a light sprinkling of fine sugar. Add some to a gooseberry fool or into a wine or fruit posset. But only use them fresh as they bruise easily and thus lose their healing vitality. By late summer the berries, borne on heavy flat heads, have turned from green to purple-black—the birds love them. With the berries we can make elderberry wine and cordials, full of condensed sunshine and meteoric iron.

Legends have it that witches would often turn themselves into elder trees. In one story, an invading Danish king, with his men on his way to do battle for the crown of England, encountered an Elder Witch who turned them into stones. This is the legend behind the famous Rollright Stones in Oxfordshire. (See *Tree Wisdom* by Jacqueline Memory Paterson, which is the definitive guidebook to the myth, folklore and healing power of trees.)

Elderflower Champagne is very easy to make and deliciously refreshing.

Required: largish plastic tub or bucket (2 gallon size)

7 dry, fully open elderflower heads (harvested in the morning)

2 lemons

1^1/2 lb/700 g unrefined caster sugar

2 tbsp white wine vinegar

1 gallon/4.5 l spring water

Method:

1. Boil 1 pt/570 ml of the water and dissolve the sugar in it. Cool.

2. Slice the lemons thinly and place in the bottom of the tub.

3. Add elderflowers, dissolved sugar solution, white wine vinegar and the rest of the water.

4. Cover and leave for 24 hours.

5. Strain into clean, dry, strong bottles (Grolsch beer bottles are good). Fermentation causes the 'sparkle' but weak bottles have been known to explode.

6. Drink chilled from two weeks onwards.

Refreshing Silk Road Yoghourt Drink

^{1}/2 pt/275 ml plain live yoghourt

^{1}/2 tsp sea salt

1 tbsp fresh mint, chopped

a few grindings of black pepper

^{1}/2 pt/275 ml chilled sparkling mineral water

Cider Apple Vinegar and Honey

3 tbsp organic cider apple vinegar

^{1}/2 pt/275 ml very hot water

1 generous tsp of good quality honey

Mix together and start the day with this drink. It can be sipped throughout the morning. A wonderful cleanser and can dispel cravings for coffee—it does for me, anyhow!

The Bombe

Wayne Schroeder has been chef at Schumacher College for the past three years. When his helpers are looking a little wilted he gives them this drink. The work then gets done friskily!

1 pt/570 ml fresh apple juice

1 pt/570 ml fresh orange juice

2 oz/50g sprouted alfalfa

2 oz/50 g pre-soaked linseeds (soaked overnight)

^{1}/2 tsp cayenne

^{1}/2 tsp freshly grated ginger root

handful of parsley

^{1}/2 handful of mint

^{1}/2 handful of coriander

2 ripe bananas

Blend and serve immediately.

Rosehip Syrup

2 lb/1 kg rosehips

5 pts/3 l spring water

1¹/₂ lb/700 g unrefined granulated sugar

Method:

1. Choose ripe rosehips from the hedgerows, chop them and add to a saucepan of boiling water (3 pts/2 l).

2. Bring to the boil. Remove from the heat and allow to infuse for 20 minutes.

3. Ladle this mixture through a scalded jelly bag, allowing the juice to drip through.

4. Return the pulp from the jelly bag to the remaining litre of boiling water and repeat the process.

5. Pour the strained juice into a clean saucepan and simmer it until reduced to 2 pts/1 l.

6. Add sugar and dissolve, stirring. Then boil for 5–10 minutes. Allow to cool a little and add to the first juice.

7. Pour into warm sterilized bottles and cork or use screwtops.

Apart from being an excellent source of vitamin C, there are many uses for this wonderful vermilion syrup, full of sunshine—pour on ice cream, and use in sauces and desserts (e.g. fruit salads). There is also rosehip and almond soup (Swedish nypsasoppa).

Barley Water (Traditional)

3 tbsp whole barley

4 pts/2.25 l water

2 lemons, thinly sliced

honey or Rapadura raw cane sugar to sweeten

1. Wash barley in warm water. Put into saucepan with water and lemon slices

2. Simmer covered for 3 hours. It may be necessary to top up the water during simmering.

3. Strain and cool. Sweeten according to taste.

One cupful before breakfast and half a cup on going to bed strengthens weak kidneys.

Resources

THE BIODYNAMIC 'DEMETER' LABEL

The following text is reproduced from the Demeter website:

'When the Label Says Demeter, Demeter is What You Get: Demeter is the brand for products from Biodynamic Agriculture. Only strictly controlled and contractually bound partners are permitted to use the Brand. A comprehensive verification process insures strict compliance with the International Demeter Production and Processing Standards, as well as applicable organic regulations in the various countries; without a gap, through every step, from agricultural production to processing and final product packaging. Yet, the holistic Demeter requirements exceed government mandated regulations. Not only do they exclude the use of synthetic fertilisers and chemical plant protection agents in agricultural crop production, or artificial additives during processing, but also require very specific measures to strengthen the life processes in soil and foodstuffs. Demeter farmers and processors actively contribute toward the shaping of a future worth living for, creating healthy foods of distinctive tastes, truly "Foods with Character".'

See the Demeter website for links to biodynamic organizations around the world:

www.demeter.net   **info@demeter.net**

Here are the main contacts in the chief English-speaking countries:

UNITED KINGDOM

The Biodynamic Agricultural Association (BDAA)
Painswick Inn Project
Gloucester Street, Stroud
Glos. GL5 1QG
Tel./Fax: 01453 759501
Email: BDAA Office
www.biodynamic.org.uk

Biodynamic Organic Agriculture Training
Emerson College
Forest Row
East Sussex RH18 5JX
Tel.: 01342 822238
Fax: 01342 826055
Email: info@emerson.org.uk
www.emerson.org.uk

The Botton Land Training
Botton Village
Danby
Whitby
North Yorkshire YO21 2NJ
Tel: 01287 661301
Fax: 01287 660888
Email: botton@camphill.org.uk
www.camphill.org.uk/botton.htm

IRELAND

Biodynamic Agricultural Association
Watergarden, Thomastown
Co. Kilkenny
Tel.: 056 77 54 214
Email: bdaai@indigo.ie
www.demeter.ie

USA

Biodynamic Farming and Gardening Association, Inc.
25844 Butler Road
Junction City
OR 97448
Tel. 888 516-7797 or 541 998-0105
Fax: 541 998-0106
Email: biodynamic@aol.com
www.biodynamics.com

For **CANADA**:
www.biodynamics.com/canada.html

NEW ZEALAND

Bio Dynamic Farming and Gardening Association
P.O. Box 39045
Wellington Mail Centre
Tel.: 0 4 589 5366
Fax: 0 4 589 5365
Email: demeter@biodynamic.org.nz
www.biodynamic.org.nz

Biodynamic Agriculture Course
Taruna College
PO Box 8103, Havelock North 4230,
Hawke's Bay
New Zealand
www.taruna.ac.nz

AUSTRALIA

Biodynamic Association
PO Box 54
Bellingen
NSW 2454
Tel.: 02 6655 0566
Fax: 02 6655 0565
www.biodynamics.net.au
bdoffice@biodynamics.net.au

Here are some notes about the development of biodynamics around the world by my friend Tadeu Caldas:

It is a fact that a lot of the recent commercial developments in the field of organic agriculture are adaptations of market-oriented farming, having as a sole purpose the profit-seeking production and sale of commodities consumed far away from its origins, a heritage of colonial structures. But what happens when a holistic, value-laden system is applied to these structures? Inevitably, wide ranging changes takes place, starting from the resulting quality of the produce and continuing into the impact over the local environment, internal social and labour dynamics and the re-enacting of cultural expressions of reciprocity with nature's bounty.

Although overtaken by the flood of organics, biodynamics is firmly at the roots of the worldwide organic movement, and the philosophical caretaker and steward of its core values. In a world of reductionism, simplification and cultural standardization, biodynamics stubbornly holds on to its holistic, cultural, ecological and therapeutic perspective to land use and agriculture. It is within its movement that we can find the oldest 'organic' farms and the most vigourous and youngest movements in lands where individual freedom has been curtailed for some time, such as in the former communist countries.

Having worked with thousands of farmers in the poorest and most isolated regions of the planet, I find biodynamics the closest worldview to traditional rural cultures worldwide, and a good basis for a fruitful dialogue, enabling processes of change and renewal of local values and knowledge about nature. Yet, Demeter certified produce is still scarce, but with more understanding of its quality we shall manage to create the necessary market environment to generate a healthy demand and increase supply at affordable prices. That is my wish as this excellent book becomes available to the public.

Statistics: Around 300,000 acres (not including over one million acres of extensive biodynamic management in Australia) and 4,000 farmers, 422 processors and 200 distributors in approximately 40 countries worldwide.

Ecological zones: Temperate and sub-arctic to Mediterranean, subtropical, tropical, equatorial, desert and semiarid, high mountains climates such as Alpine, Himalayan and Andean.

Cultural zones: Christians, Buddhists, Hindus, Muslims, Confucianists, Judaism, etc.

Socio economic: industrialized and developing countries.

Largest areas: Germany has over 130,000 acres or about half the certified areas, although Australia has over one million acres managed biodynamically. Other countries with total holdings above 5,000 acres: in Europe Great Britain, France, Netherlands, Italy, Switzerland, Brazil, New Zealand, Egypt and India.

Europe

Germany has had a string of award-winning biodynamic farms, including the oldest in the world, and consequently a very mature market and a wide range of fresh and processed products as well as cosmetics and medicinal, garments, drinks. i.e. first Demeter certified beer.

Traditional presence in Netherlands, Luxembourg, Denmark, Switzerland. France first certified wines and champagne. Britain and Irish farms have a strong links with therapeutic communities.

Scandinavia (Sweden, Norway, Finland).

Mediterranean region: Spain, Italy. Strong presence in Sicily with citrus and fruits, small groups in Portugal and Greece.

East Europe: strong underground movement during the communist regime, some very early and now restarting with vigour in Slovenia, Hungary, Ukraine, Poland, Russia (all the way to Siberia), Bulgaria, Croatia.

Near and Middle East

Israel: citrus, Kibbutz Harduf. Turkey: dried fruits, nuts.

Asia

India first certified tea plantations in Darjeeling, but also cotton, coffee, tropical fruits, spices, pulses, cereals.

Sri Lanka, tea.

Japan, Korea, Thailand: small groups starting focus rice, vegetables.

China, beginnings with silk, grains, pulses, tea, Chinese herbs and vegetables.

Pakistan beginning with cotton, dried fruits.

Oceania

Australia: wool, cereals.

New Zealand: fruits.

Africa

South Africa: oldest organic farm was Demeter certified; grains, fruits.

Egypt: award winning Sekem project was the first certified cotton and garments project, but also aromatic and medicinal herbs, herbal teas and vegetables.

Morocco: citrus, vegetables, 5 star hotel.

Tunisia: dates.

North America

US and Canada: Demeter wines have made a big impact in the US.

Mexico: oldest organic coffee plantation is Demeter certified.

South America

Brazil: oldest organic farm was Demeter certified; sugar, orange, cocoa, rice, tropical fruits, vegetables, herbs.

Argentina: wine, grains.

Chile: wine and temperate fruits.

Ecuador: banana, palm oil, cut flowers.

Peru: vegetables for local markets.

Initiatives in Colombia and Venezuela.

Central America & Caribbean

Costa Rica: spices and vanilla.

Dominican Republic: bananas and cocoa.

Bibliography

Books referred to in the text:

Bober, P P: *Art and Culture and Cuisine*, University of Chicago Press, 2001

D'Adamo, P J & Whitney, C: *Eat Right for Your Type*, Penguin, 2003

Davy, J: *Hope, Evolution and Change*, Hawthorn Press, 1985

Hauschka, R: *Nutrition*, Sophia Books, 2003

Humphrys, J: *The Great Food Gamble*, Coronet Books, 2002

Kolisko, E & L: *The Agriculture of Tomorrow*, Kolisko Archive Publications, 1978

Korten, D: *When Corporations Rule the World*, Earthscan Publications, 1995

Lang, T & Millstone, E: *The Atlas of Food*, Earthscan Publications, 2002

McGee, H: *McGee on Cooking*, Hodder & Stoughton Ltd, 2004

Memory Paterson, J: *Tree Wisdom*, HarperCollins, 1996

Pfeiffer, E., *Sensitive Crystallization Processes*, Anthroposophic Press, 1975

Pitchford, P: *Healing with Wholefoods*, North Atlantic Books, 2002

Pliny the Elder, *Natural History*, Penguin, 1991

Roden, C: *The Book of Jewish Food*, Penguin Books Ltd, 1999

Schmidt, G: *Dynamics of Nutrition*, Bio-dynamic Literature, 1980

Simontaachi, C: *Crazymakers*, Jeremy P Tarcher, 2001

Steiner, R: *Agriculture Course*, Rudolf Steiner Press, 2004

Steiner, R: *Bees*, Anthroposophic Press, 1988

Steiner, R: *Nutrition and Stimulants*, Biodynamic Farming and Gardening Assoc., 1991

Swimme, B & Berry, T: *The Universe Story*, HarperCollins, 1994

Symons, M: *History of Cooks and Cooking*, Prospect Books, 2001

Further reading:

Carey, D & Large J: *Festivals, Family and Food*, Hawthorn Press, 1982

Cook, W E: *Foodwise*, Clairview Books, 2003

Philbrick, J & Philbrick, H: *Gardening for Health and Nutrition*, Anthroposophic Press, 1995

Schilthuis, W: *Biodynamic Agriculture*, Floris Books, 2003

Steiner, R: *Agriculture, An Introductory Reader*, Sophia Books, 2003

Steiner, R: *Festivals and their Meaning*, Rudolf Steiner Press, 1996

Thun, M: *Gardening for Life*, Hawthorn Press, 1999

Waldin, M: *Biodynamic Wines*, Mitchell Beazley, 2004

Wright, H: *Biodynamic Gardening*, Mitchell Beazley, 2003

Photo Credits

All photos are by Kate Mount, apart the following: page 42, Dr Ursula Balzer-Graf; page 10 left and bottom, Wendy Cook; author picture, back cover Tim Cuff; page 10 right, Oliver Edwards; pages 2, 11, 21, 54, 59, 60, 89 left and right, 90, 101, 103, 104, 105, 112, 113, 115, 116 left, 140, 141, 146, 148, 151, 174, 176, 201, 224, 246, Selby McCreery; pages 19, 67, 196, 197, 199, Diulio Martins; pages 23, 51 middle and right, 52 top, 64, 71, 78, 79, 81, 82, 83, 84, 85, 87, 132, 133, 137, 142, 178, 180, 222, Jaume Moranta; pages 37, 42, NASA; page 39, Ingrid Schauberger; pages 27, 32 top, 34 middle, 38 top, 43, 49 middle, 51 left, 161, Hans Steenbergen; page 31, Still Pictures; page 231, Mary Topper; pages 13 middle and right, 36, 40, 48, 49 top and bottom, 50, 172, 198, June Woodger; and pages 63, 99, 123, public domain images.

Index of recipes

Emerson College

Full-time and part-time training in Biodynamic Organic Agriculture

Other courses

Steiner Waldorf Teacher Training (part-time and full-time)
Foundation Studies, Visual Arts and Sculpture
Orientation Gap Year, Spirit of English
Creative Writing, Storytelling

We also have a programme of weekend courses running October to June
and a programme of longer summer courses
Please call for a brochure or visit our website for more information

Emerson College, Forest Row, E Sussex, RH18 5JX, UK
Tel: + 44 (0)1342 822238 www.emerson.org.uk mail@emerson.org.uk